About Island Press

Island Press is the only nonprofit organization in the United States whose principal purpose is the publication of books on environmental issues and natural resource management. We provide solutions-oriented information to professionals, public officials, business and community leaders, and concerned citizens who are shaping responses to environmental problems.

Since 1984, Island Press has been the leading provider of timely and practical books that take a multidisciplinary approach to critical environmental concerns. Our growing list of titles reflects our commitment to bringing the best of an expanding body of literature to the environmental community throughout North America and the world.

Support for Island Press is provided by the Agua Fund, The Geraldine R. Dodge Foundation, Doris Duke Charitable Foundation, The Ford Foundation, The William and Flora Hewlett Foundation, The Joyce Foundation, Kendeda Sustainability Fund of the Tides Foundation, The Forrest & Frances Lattner Foundation, The Henry Luce Foundation, The John D. and Catherine T. MacArthur Foundation, The Marisla Foundation, The Andrew W. Mellon Foundation, Gordon and Betty Moore Foundation, The Curtis and Edith Munson Foundation, Oak Foundation, The Overbrook Foundation, The David and Lucile Packard Foundation, Wallace Global Fund, The Winslow Foundation, and other generous donors.

The opinions expressed in this book are those of the author and do not necessarily reflect the views of these foundations.

The Green Building Revolution

The Green Building Revolution

Jerry Yudelson
Foreword by S. Richard Fedrizzi, CEO
U.S. Green Building Council

 ISLANDPRESS

Washington • Covelo • London

The Green Building Revolution
© 2008 Jerry Yudelson

All rights reserved under International and Pan-American Copyright Conventions. No part of this book may be reproduced in any form or by any means without permission in writing from the publisher: Island Press, 1718 Connecticut Ave. NW, Suite 300, Washington, DC 20009.

ISLAND PRESS is a trademark of the Center for Resource Economics.

Library of Congress Cataloging-in-Publication Data

Yudelson, Jerry.
  The green building revolution / Jerry Yudelson ; Foreword by S. Richard Fedrizzi.
      p. cm.
  Includes bibliographical references and index.
  ISBN 978-1-59726-178-4 (hardcover : alk. paper) — ISBN 978-1-59726-179-1 (pbk. : alk. paper)
  1. Sustainable buildings—Design and construction. 2. Green movement. I. Title.
  TH880.Y634 2008
    720'.47—dc22   2007026207

Printed on recycled, acid-free paper ✹

Manufactured in the United States of America
10 9 8 7 6 5 4 3 2

Search terms: Green building, environmental building, U.S. Green Building Council, US-GBC, Energy Star, carbon emissions, revolution, LEED, indoor air quality, rating systems, commercial building, risk management, productivity, health benefits, public relations, marketing, new construction, core and shell, commercial interiors, existing buildings, property management, Greg Kats, Davis Langdon, World Green Building Council, Canada, China, India, Australia, Spain, socially responsible property investing, industrial buildings, private development, public development, campus sustainability, green schools, National Association of Home Builders, mixed-use development, retail design, hospitality design, green healthcare, workplace design, building operations, neighborhood development, local government, real estate finance.

Contents

List of Tables

Foreword

A revolution is going on all over this land, and it's about time! It is transforming the marketplace for buildings, homes, and communities, and it is part of a larger sustainability revolution that will transform just about everything we know, do, and experience over the next few decades. This revolution is about green building, and its aim is nothing less than to fundamentally change the built environment by creating energy-efficient, healthy, productive buildings that reduce or minimize the significant impacts of buildings on urban life and on the local, regional, and global environments.

In 1993 the U.S. Green Building Council (USGBC) was founded to drive this change, and in 2000 we launched the LEED® (Leadership in Energy and Environmental Design) Green Building Rating System™ to provide a common definition and way to measure green buildings. A point-based system, LEED rates buildings according to key environmental attributes such as site impacts, energy and water use, materials and resource conservation, and indoor environmental quality.

To our delight and somewhat to our surprise, by 2006 LEED had taken the country by storm. As of early 2007, 18 states and 59 cities, along with some of the biggest and most prestigious names in the building industry—including the developer of the "Ground Zero" World Trade Center site, Larry Silverstein—had all made serious commitments to using the LEED rating system for their projects (the first new building built and occupied at "Ground Zero," Seven World Trade Center, was LEED Gold-certified). In 2006 the U.S. General Services Administration, the country's biggest landlord, along with 10 other federal agencies, endorsed LEED as its rating tool of choice. This is not surprising, because LEED provides a rigorous road map to building green. Projected resource savings from the first 200 LEED-certified projects show that well-designed, fully documented and third party–verified projects get results: an average of 30 percent water-use reduction and 30 to 55 percent energy savings, depending on the level of certification.

A version of this foreword was presented at the Plenary Session of the Greenbuild conference in Denver, Colorado, in November 2006.

U.S. Energy Consumption Projections

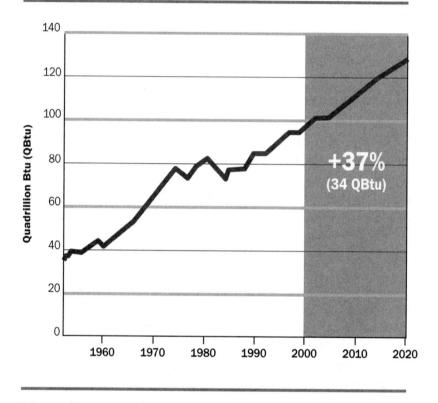

U.S. energy consumption projections to the year 2020. Courtesy of Architecture 2030, used with permission.

Through the USGBC, business professionals, policymakers, developers, designers, scientists, and citizens are joining together to conquer some of the most intractable problems of our time. Two of these are front and center, and they are interconnected in a very important way. These are the health of our cities and the impact of climate change.

We build green buildings because they matter. But nowhere do they matter more than in this epic battle we've just begun with ourselves over carbon dioxide emissions, which are driving global climate change.[1]

The greatest sources of those emissions are the very things that have helped us prosper—the cars we drive and the electricity we generate to run our buildings. These emissions are also the primary cause of the climate changes that have begun to significantly affect our quality of life. By now we know these changes by heart: melting ice caps are causing rising sea levels; monumental storms such as Hurricane Katrina have altered forever the lives of people we know and care about. The shifting temperature and weather patterns are poised to stress our economic and social fabric in unprecedented and alarming ways. Figure 0.1 shows the projected increase in primary energy use—and carbon emissions—by 2030 if we do not act now.

We are fortunate because we have the resources and the know-how required to achieve immediate and measurable results in our efforts to reverse global warming. Green buildings reduce carbon emissions by about 40 percent compared to conventional buildings.

Recognizing the need for urgent action, in 2006 the USGBC signed the Wingspread Principles, which lay out an assertive response to global climate change. These principles are an outgrowth of a national leadership summit on energy and climate change, and are part of an initiative to review and update the 140 recommendations developed in 1999 by President Bill Clinton's Council on Sustainable Development. The Wingspread Principles aim to create a road map for moving beyond words to action.

The principles respond to two questions:

- What is our nation's responsibility as the largest producer of the greenhouse gas emissions that cause global warming?
- Can the many individuals and groups concerned about climate change be heard better if we begin to speak with one voice?

The answers are intended to guide the nation in taking comprehensive, immediate action to address the threat of climate change.

The USGBC is working closely with other groups such as the American Institute of Architects, Architecture 2030, and the American Society of Heating, Refrigeration and Air-Conditioning Engineers to develop tools, professional training, and new evaluation software to help design and construction professionals create more energy-efficient and "climate responsive" buildings. The possibilities are exhilarating and endless. But perhaps most importantly, we'll finally begin to act on the knowledge we've acquired, that better health, improved productivity, and a slowing and then a reversal of climate change are the absolute immediate results of building green.

In 2006, the USGBC's board proposed that, beginning in 2007, all new commercial LEED-certified projects be required to reduce carbon emissions

S. Richard Fedrizzi, president, CEO, and founding chairman of the U.S. Green Building Council. Courtesy of USGBC.

by 50 percent compared to current levels. By resetting the benchmark for our green building rating system, we hope to persuade everyone to take action against further buildup of the atmospheric carbon dioxide concentrations that drive climate change.

The USGBC challenges every architect, every contractor, every builder, every interior designer, every facilities manager, every student on a college campus, every CEO and CFO in corporate America, every commercial real estate broker, every building owner, every governor, every mayor, every city council member and every county commissioner, every consultant, every corporate real estate director—*everyone*—to commit to learning how they can do more to limit emissions from every new building that is constructed.

Those architects, engineers, and builders who have begun to make green design their standard need to challenge their colleagues and hold them accountable. Design for the sake of design alone is no longer an option. Design for higher performance is our pathway to a better future.

To drive ourselves and others to achieve higher-performance outcomes, the USGBC has set two audacious goals for green builders everywhere:

- 100,000 LEED-certified buildings by the end of 2010
- 1 million LEED-certified homes by the end of 2010

For those of us in the green building movement, outcomes will always matter more than good intentions. By convening the best minds, building consensus for direction, and inspiring action, we can realize our vision of a planet powered by renewable energy, populated by sustainable communities housed in green buildings and driven by clean, green innovation.

The Green Building Revolution will guide you to a deeper understanding of the problems we face and the numerous solutions now emerging from the creative work of architects, designers, engineers, contractors, building owners and facility managers, insurance and financial organizations, and manufacturers of every type across the country, and even around the world. I hope that you will take something valuable from this book and put it into immediate and measurable action in your home, your office, your school or college, and your community.

S. Richard Fedrizzi, president, CEO, and founding chairman,

U.S. Green Building Council

Washington, D.C.

March 2007

Preface

From San Diego to Boston, Seattle to Savannah, Montreal to Miami, Tucson to Toronto, Vancouver, B.C., to Washington, D.C., New York to Monterrey, Mexico, builders and developers, public agencies at all levels, and major corporations are all discovering the extraordinary benefits of green building. Between 2000 and the end of 2006, the number of green buildings has grown from a handful to more than 5,000 projects actively seeking certification of one kind or another.[1] This is the fastest-growing phenomenon to hit the building industry since the Internet.

By 2010 this revolutionary wave will inundate the worlds of architecture, finance, engineering, construction, development, and building ownership. The green building revolution responds to the great environmental crises of the early 21st century—global warming, species extinction, droughts, and severe floods and hurricanes (or typhoons), all of which are affecting our world in unprecedented ways. If we had to date this revolution, two milestones stand out: the events of September 11, 2001, which highlighted the vulnerability of an advanced economy to terrorism; and Hurricane Katrina in late August 2005, which all but destroyed a major American city, New Orleans, in a drama of natural forces and human suffering that played out on TV before an anguished public for weeks on end.

If global warming is the poster child for the problem set described above, green buildings are part of the solution toolkit. Progressive companies, government agencies, and nonprofits across the United States, and indeed around the world, are using them to create value and maintain competitive advantage. This book chronicles that revolution.

In *The Green Building Revolution*, you will learn of the abundant evidence supporting the economic and policy case for green buildings. I wrote this book for the intelligent layperson who is perhaps not actively engaged in architecture, development, construction, or building engineering, but who wants a quick introduction to the rationale for green building and an overview of how it is being implemented throughout the United States.

I also designed the book to be useful for public officials; for those dealing with green building or sustainability requirements from within or outside a company, organization, or agency; for those whose livelihood depends on financing, building, or marketing commercial and residential developments; and for senior executives in universities, government agencies, and large corporations who need to understand what all the fuss is about.

The book addresses several key questions: How large is the green building movement today? How is it affecting commercial, primary and secondary school, higher education, hospital, and government buildings? What are the economic benefits and costs of green buildings? And what can you do to further the green building revolution?

For the past ten years I have been involved in building design and construction, and I've been active in the green building movement since 1999. Knowing how long it has taken me to become conversant with the world of green building and the larger issues it addresses, I wanted this book to accelerate public understanding of the importance of the green building revolution in addressing the climate-change, energy, and environmental challenges of our times. According to NASA climate scientist James Hansen, the continuation of "business as usual" in business, transportation, and industry will likely result in the destruction of 50 percent of all species on the planet by 2100 unless we take firm, irrevocable actions to reduce the continuing increase in carbon dioxide generation from human activities by 2016.[2] Time is short, and we need action.

I hope this book will help you to play a role in this great undertaking. I welcome your feedback at my personal e-mail address, jerry@greenbuildconsult.com, or via my web site, www.greenbuildconsult.com.

I want to thank all the people who contributed to the case studies and interviews in this book and to all those leading the green building revolution in their companies, organizations, agencies, cities, and states. We interviewed and obtained valuable information from the following: John Boecker, Penny Bonda, Jim Broughton, Laura Case, Richard Cook, Peter Erickson, Huston Eubank, Rebecca Flora, Jim Goldman, Robin Guenther, Holley Henderson, Don Horn, Kevin Hydes, Ken Langer, Mary Ann Lazarus, Jerry Lea, Gail Lindsey, Thomas Mueller, Kathleen O'Brien, David Payne, Russell Perry, Sonja Persram, Elizabeth Powers, Aurelio Ramírez Zarzosa, Anne Schopf, Paul Shahriari, Leith Sharp, Kim Shinn, Lynn Simon, Matthew St. Clair, Judy Walton, Dennis Wilde, Rod Wille, and Kath Williams.

Especially I want to thank my research associate Gretel Hakanson, who provided invaluable assistance in pulling together the case studies, interviews, photos, and graphics in this book. Thanks to Lynn Parker of Parker Designs, Beaverton, Oregon, for the graphic images created specially for this book. And a very special thanks to Rick Fedrizzi, CEO of the U.S. Green Building Council for generously writing the foreword.

I also want to thank all the green building professionals who furnished project photos, project information, and insights. A special thanks to the reviewers, Sue Barnett, Anthony Bernheim, Russell Perry, and Paul Shahriari, who helped hone the message of this book. Thanks also to my editor at Island Press, Heather Boyer, for her understanding, excellent feedback on drafts of the manuscript, and generous encouragement for this project.

And a very special thanks and appreciation to my partner in everything, Jessica Yudelson, and our ever-tolerant Scottie, Madhu. They put up with me working at the computer many a day (and night).

Jerry Yudelson, PE, MS, MBA, LEED AP

Tucson, Arizona

April 2007

chapter 1
Green Buildings Today

The green building revolution is sweeping across not only the United States but most of the world. It's a revolution inspired by an awakened understanding of how buildings use resources, affect people, and harm the environment. This revolution is further fueled by the knowledge that the world has little time to respond to the growing dangers of climate change, especially global warming, and that buildings play a huge role in causing carbon dioxide emissions that drive global climate change. According to Architecture 2030, our commercial and residential buildings generate, directly or indirectly, nearly half the carbon emissions of the entire United States.[1]

How important is the green building revolution? A 2007 study by McKinsey, an international consulting firm, showed that changes in building design and construction could offset up to 6 billion tons of carbon emissions annually "through measures with a zero or negative net life-cycle cost." This amount constitutes about one-fourth of the abatement required to keep atmospheric carbon emissions below 450 parts per million in 2030. In other words, green building saves carbon emissions and money at the same time, through effective insulation, glazing, water heating, air-conditioning, lighting, and other energy-efficiency measures.[2] This is a win-win scenario on which both climate-change activists and hardheaded businesspeople can agree.

The green building revolution is part of a paradigm shift toward sustainability, a growing realization that current ways of living, made possible largely because of cheap and abundant fossil fuels, are not sustainable in the long term. Green building revolutionaries work in all industries, in all income groups, in all social strata, and in all guises. They may be aging baby boomers or high school students taking an early interest in building and design. In my own experience, the present decade (and particularly the second half of it)—a fresh new decade of a fresh new century—marks the first time in a generation that the American public has been worried, very worried about the state of the world and the provenance of energy to fuel the myriad activities of a global postindustrial economy.

With these thoughts in mind, let's see what we can learn about green buildings as a solution to the many global issues associated with climate change, human health, and the quality of the environment.

The Origins of the Revolution

The revolution can be traced to many causes over the past several decades, just as the seeds of the American Revolution were planted fifteen years or more before the country erupted into open rebellion. In the 1980s, the Montreal Protocol limited the use of chlorinated fluorocarbons, which were found to be harmful to the ozone layer that is so vital for human life. In 1987 the United Nations' World Commission on Environment and Development, aka the Brundtland Commission, was the first to define sustainability, calling it the ability of the present generation of people to meet their needs without compromising the ability of future generations to meet theirs—echoing the American Indian seventh-generation rule: Each generation is responsible for making decisions that ensure the survival of the seventh generation. In the late 1980s, a group of farsighted architects formed the Committee on the Environment within the American Institute of Architects and began the process of steering the profession toward sustainable design.

Two major events occurred in the early 1990s that influenced the creation of the U.S. Green Building Council (USGBC).[3] In the United States, the 20th anniversary of the original Earth Day took place in 1990; in Brazil, the U.N. Conference on Environment and Development, popularly known as the Earth Summit, was held in Rio de Janeiro in 1992. Both of these events precipitated the formation of the USGBC in 1993.

The USGBC is a consensus-based group consisting solely of other organizations: companies, government agencies, universities, primary and secondary schools, nonprofits, environmental groups, and trade associations. Its membership growth has been rapid, as shown in Figure 1.1. From a base of about 150 companies in 1998, the USGBC has grown 50-fold, to 7,500 companies, as of early 2007. This rapid growth is emblematic of Victor Hugo's mid-19th-century remark that "one withstands the invasion of armies; one

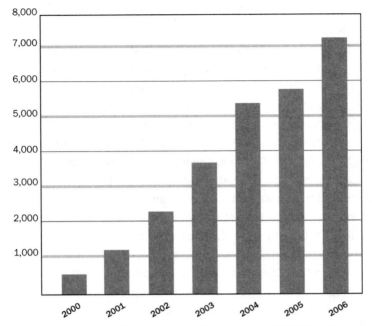

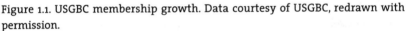

Figure 1.1. USGBC membership growth. Data courtesy of USGBC, redrawn with permission.

does not withstand the invasion of ideas," often paraphrased as "nothing can stop an idea whose time has come."

The late 1990s saw the establishment of the Kyoto Protocol, an amendment to the U.N. Framework Convention on Climate Change that represented the first attempt to regulate greenhouse gas emissions on a global scale. More than 170 countries, which together produce more than 55 percent of global greenhouse gas emissions (but not including the U.S.), have so far signed and ratified the protocol.[4]

In 2000, the USGBC unveiled the Leadership in Energy and Environmental Design (LEED) Green Building Rating System for public use. LEED was the first rating system in the United States to hold commercial projects up to scrutiny for the full range of their effects on energy and water use, municipal infrastructure, transportation energy use, resource conservation, land use, and indoor environmental quality. Prior to LEED, most evaluation systems, such as the Environmental Protection Agency's Energy Star® program, had focused exclusively on energy use.

Over the ensuing seven years, LEED has become the de facto U.S. rating system for commercial, institutional, and high-rise residential buildings. In the process, LEED has defined what it means for a building to be sustainable and how architects, engineers, builders, owners, and developers should approach creating green buildings. This is a remarkable achievement for a nonprofit organization, especially one conceived by three guys in a bar.

Projects register to use the LEED rating system; when finished, they submit documentation to receive a certification at one of four levels: basic (Certified), Silver, Gold, or Platinum. The initial LEED system covered only new construction and major renovations of commercial and institutional developments and then, with some modification, became usable for residential developments above three stories. This original system is now generally referred to as LEED for New Construction (LEED-NC), to clearly indicate its primary focus.

Since 2000, the USGBC has unveiled five additional LEED rating systems. They apply to commercial interiors (tenant improvements), existing buildings (operations and maintenance activities), core and shell buildings (for developers), homes (for single-family and low-rise residential), and neighborhood development (for urban districts and higher-density mixed-use developments).

Figure 1.2 shows the rapid growth of LEED-NC registered and certified projects since 2000.[5] By year-end 2006, cumulative LEED-NC registrations exceeded 2005 totals by 50 percent, growing to nearly 4,000, while the number of LEED-NC certified projects increased over that same period by nearly 70 percent, to 513, as shown in Table 1.1. In an industry (construction and development) that typically grows about 5 percent (or less) per year, this rapid growth is an earthshaking phenomenon. You can also see the large numbers of projects in the other major rating systems.

For 2007, I predict that more than 1,500 U.S. new projects will register to use the LEED system, representing about 150 million square feet of new construction, or about 8 to 10 percent of the total U.S. commercial and institutional building market. Based on the current rate of growth, I anticipate that 300 to 400 of those projects will receive LEED certification in 2007, representing about one per day. By year-end 2008, I conservatively predict that more than 1,500 LEED-certified projects will exist throughout the United States and Canada.

Table 1.1

LEED Projects (2006 year-end)

	Certifications	Certified area (million sq. ft.)	Registrations	Registered area (million sq. ft.)
LEED-NC	513	53	3895	477
LEED-EB	37	12	244	72
LEED-CI	92	3	462	23
LEED-CS	27	6	325	68

LEED-NC: LEED for New Construction & Major Renovations (new commercial construction, institutional, and high-rise residential).

LEED-EB: LEED for Existing Buildings (for the operation and maintenance of existing buildings).

LEED-CI: LEED for Commercial Interiors (for tenant improvements).

LEED-CS: LEED for Core & Shell (goes hand in hand with LEED-CI, for building owners and developers to certify the core and shell of their structure)

Source: U.S. Green Building Council, unpublished data furnished to the author, May 2007.

As Rick Fedrizzi wrote in the foreword, the USGBC has even more dramatic goals for the LEED rating system: by the end of 2010, the council hopes to see 100,000 LEED-certified commercial and institutional projects and one million LEED-certified homes in the United States. If achieved, this would represent a 200-fold increase in certified commercial buildings and a 100-fold increase in certified homes (estimating that about 10,000 homes were certified green in 2006).

In the residential sector, there has long been a focus on energy efficiency through the Energy Star home-certification program, which is aimed at cutting energy use 15 percent below a 2004 baseline. In 2006 this program certified 174,000 homes, about 12 percent of all new homes built.[6] Other industry-based certification programs produced thousands of additional green homes in 2006.

The USGBC estimates that through its member organizations, its programs are affecting hundreds of thousands of people each year. One indication of this is the growth in attendance at workshops that show building industry professionals how to work with the LEED system. By the end of 2006, nearly 45,000 people had taken an all-day LEED training workshop. At the same time, nearly 35,000 people had passed a national exam to become

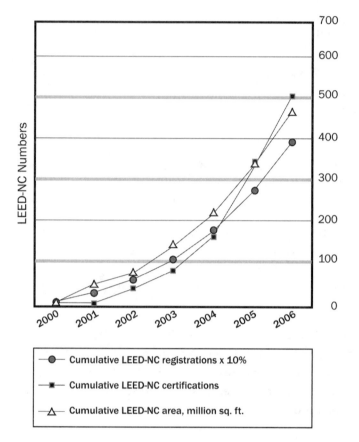

Figure 1.2. LEED-NC project growth, 2000–2006. Data courtesy of USGBC, redrawn with permission.

LEED Accredited Professionals, or LEED APs.[7] These numbers indicate LEED's tremendous reach within the commercial building sector; they also show how the USGBC is building the capacity for people to take part in the green building revolution. The USGBC's goal is that each green building project use at least one LEED AP to guide it through the LEED certification process.

But the green building revolution is not just about the USGBC and the LEED process. It is a broader movement by the building industry to become more responsible: toward the occupants of its buildings; toward community infrastructure, energy and water, and other natural resources and materials; and toward the global environment.

The Present Market for Green Buildings

Kathleen O'Brien runs a small green-building consulting firm in Seattle. Speaking of her experience, she says, "Now that more compelling information about climate change is available, people who were on the fence are deciding that green building is definitely the right thing to do. They are starting to see the connection between global environmental impacts and possible costs to their operations. In additional to potential immediate operational savings, marketing savings, design savings, for example, they are also thinking about long-term protection from volatile energy pricing, energy security, and things like that."

The market for green buildings includes commercial, institutional, and residential buildings as well as public, educational, nonprofit, and corporate owners. Green buildings are found in locations all over the United States and Canada, from the Arctic Circle to the tip of Florida, from the rocky coast of Nova Scotia to the tropical beaches of Hawaii. They comprise a vast array of building types, including offices, police stations, baseball stadiums, museums, libraries, animal shelters, and industrial buildings. Green building projects involve new and historic buildings; urban infill, brownfield restoration, and suburban "greenfield" sites; and all sizes of projects, ranging from a few thousand to more than one million square feet.

LEED-registered public-sector and nonprofit green buildings in the U.S. are approaching 10 percent of the total annual new construction value of such buildings, while commercial green buildings are approaching 5 percent of the total annual new construction.[8] While these numbers may seem small, they indicate solid acceptance by the early-adopter market and provide a basis for predicting a rapidly growing market share of green buildings in each component of the building industry: commercial, primary and secondary school, higher education, government, health care, retail, and hospitality.

The Policy Case for Green Buildings

Until the USGBC formed and began to talk about the need for market transformation, few people were aware of the tremendous impact of buildings on the environment. According to the USGBC, buildings directly account for

12 percent of all freshwater use, 30 percent of all raw materials, 30 percent of all greenhouse gas emissions (the indirect effects of materials and transportation account for another 18 percent), 45 to 65 percent of waste outputs to landfills, 31 percent of all mercury in solid waste, and 70 percent of all electricity consumption.[9] On the other hand, we know that green buildings offer a 30 percent energy savings, a 30 to 50 percent water savings, a 35 percent reduction in carbon emissions, and a 50 to 90 percent reduction in construction waste and waste generation from building operations.[10] Buildings are long-lived: the typical life of a nonresidential building is 75 years, while a public school building might last 60 years.[11] Since energy costs may increase dramatically over the lifetime of a building, total lifetime energy costs can often exceed the cost of the building itself.

From the perspective of governments, these impacts are too large to ignore. In addition, governments take a longer-term perspective than most businesses. Government agencies are perpetual owners of most of their buildings. The federal General Services Administration is the largest landlord in the country. Designing to a higher standard creates public benefits well into the future.

Universities are another type of building owner with a long-term perspective. Early in 2007, I facilitated a green building "eco-charrette" for a new science building at Westminster College in Salt Lake City. I noted that the university had been founded 20 years before Utah became a state, giving it a longer-term perspective than even the government. And in Europe, universities are among the oldest continually operated buildings. So it makes sense for universities to design great buildings. The world's largest LEED Platinum-certified building is the Oregon Health & Science University's Center for Health and Healing in Portland, Oregon, a 400,000-square-foot building completed in 2006. This project was built for a net cost increase of only about 1 percent, net of all utility and government incentives. Many organizations are finding out how they can design the highest-performing green buildings on conventional budgets, through a process known as integrated design, covered in more detail in Chapter 4.

Government Leadership and Private Initiative

At the beginning of the present decade, government leadership was vital for the growth of green buildings, with government and nonprofit buildings

Figure 1.3. Designed by GBD Architects and Interface Engineering for Gerding Edlen Development, the Oregon Health & Science University's Center for Health and Healing in Portland, Oregon, is the world's largest LEED Platinum-certified building. Courtesy of Gerding Edlen Development.

making up more than 70 percent of all LEED project registrations and more than 60 percent of the value of all green buildings. By mandating LEED standards for their own buildings, government set an example for the private sector. In 2001 the Seattle City Council became the first governmental body in the nation to issue a LEED-related mandate, requiring LEED Silver certification for all new public buildings over 5,000 square feet. In 2004, the city of Vancouver, British Columbia, mandated LEED Gold certification for all new public buildings above a certain size. And in 2004, California governor Arnold Schwarzenegger signed Executive Order S-20-04, requiring the LEED Silver certification for all new state buildings, while also mandating a 15 percent reduction in electricity use in state buildings within ten years.[12]

These examples energized the private sector to follow suit. By 2005 the momentum had shifted, with nearly half of all LEED registrations and new green building certifications coming from nongovernmental sources. Corporate goals of pursuing sustainability in all its dimensions have played a part in this growth, as has a growing awareness of the business-case benefits of green buildings, described in detail in Chapter 3. Large corporations such as Toyota, with worldwide operations and a strong mission statement

Figure 1.4. The south campus of the Toyota Motor Sales USA headquarters in Torrance, California, is a LEED Gold-certified project. Courtesy of Turner Construction Company and Toyota Motor Sales.

in favor of corporate social responsibility, have emerged as leaders in this revolution. Figure 1.4 shows the 624,000-square-foot south campus of Toyota Motor Sales, USA, located on 40 acres in Torrance, California. Designed by LPA Architects and built by Turner Construction Company, the project is LEED Gold-certified. Housing more than 2,500 employees, the project has an estimated energy savings of 42 percent compared to a comparable conventional building, worth about $400,000 annually to the company. Potable water demand was reduced by 80 percent compared with a similar building. The project also has one of the largest photovoltaic solar arrays in California, providing about 536 kilowatts of power and 20 percent of the building's electricity.[13]

Drivers for Green Buildings

In Chapter 5, I examine trends favoring a robust future for the green building revolution. But what has driven it thus far? Events beyond the scope of architects' and owners' individual project decisions have played a major role, especially the following:

- Average crude oil prices surged above $40 per barrel in October 2004 and above $50 in July 2005, and threatened to stay above $50 for a long time. In November 2005, the U.S. Energy Information Administration's long-term forecast estimated that oil in 2025 would cost $54 per barrel in 2005 dollars, up 65 percent from its year-earlier estimate of $33 per barrel.[14] These developments changed the mind-set of many building owners and developers, from complacency about energy prices to deep concern over long-term trends.
- Increasing oil prices, heightened prospects of uncertain supplies because of geopolitical factors, and mounting evidence of human-induced global warming combined to help change the psychology of the public for the first time in a generation, increasing interest in energy conservation in building.
- Congress passed the Energy Policy Act of 2005, which dramatically increased incentives for solar and wind power, and provided strong support for energy conservation in new and existing buildings. Although these incentives are scheduled to expire at the end of 2008, most observers expect them to be extended well into the future.[15]
- New state laws were passed to support green buildings, including a 2005 Nevada law reducing property taxes on green buildings, a 2005 Washington state law mandating LEED Silver certification for all new state buildings, and a Nevada law mandating LEED certification for all new state facilities.[16]
- Local governments in cities as small as Frisco, Texas, and as large as Seattle, Boston, Chicago, San Francisco, and New York have begun adopting policies and programs promoting private-sector green buildings.
- Inside many design firms, architects and engineers have begun working through their professional organizations and with the U.S. Green Building Council to make dramatic changes in the ways in which buildings are conceived, produced, and operated. In 2005 the board of directors of the American Institute of Architects issued its most ambitious policy statement yet in support of sustainable

design, stating that all new buildings be designed to reduce current consumption levels by 50 percent by 2010.[17]

This is an exciting time to be a green building revolutionary. As we take this journey together, you'll discover how the revolution is seeping into all aspects of the building design, construction, development, and operations industry, and you'll undoubtedly find many opportunities to participate through your home, work, school, religious, and civic activities. After all, what's a revolution without revolutionaries?

Chapter 2
What Is a Green Building?

Let's get more specific about the term "green building." A green building is a high-performance property that considers and reduces its impact on the environment and human health. A green building is designed to use less energy and water and to reduce the life-cycle environmental impacts of the materials used. This is achieved through better siting, design, material selection, construction, operation, maintenance, removal, and possible reuse.

In 2007, a commercial green building is generally considered to be one certified by the LEED Green Building Rating System of the U.S. Green Building Council. The rating system is a publicly available document; though it is owned by the USGBC, an extensive committee structure is charged with keeping it current and improving it over time. More than 98 percent of certified green buildings come from the LEED system.[1] In September 2006, the U.S. General Services Administration (GSA) reported to Congress that it would use only LEED for assessing its own projects.[2]

In the commercial and institutional arena, if a building is not rated and certified by an independent third party with an open process for creating and maintaining a rating system, it can't really be called a green building. If building owners and designers say they are following LEED but not bothering to apply for certification of the final building, you should rightly wonder if they will really achieve the results they claim. If they say they are doing "sustainable design," you have a right to ask, "Against what standard are you measuring your design, and how are you going to prove it?"

The LEED Rating Systems

In this brief discussion, I'll acquaint you with four of the major LEED rating systems and how they are used. These four, which account for the vast majority of LEED projects, are as follows:

- LEED for New Construction, or LEED-NC
- LEED for Core and Shell (speculative buildings), or LEED-CS
- LEED for Commercial Interiors (tenant improvements and remodels), or LEED-CI
- LEED for Existing Buildings (upgrades, operations and maintenance), or LEED-EB

I cover the other two systems, LEED for Homes and LEED for Neighborhood Development, in Chapters 10 and 11, respectively, as they are still in pilot (evaluation) stages. (For more details, peruse Appendix 2 or download the rating systems from the USGBC web site.)

The essence of LEED, and its particular genius, is that it is a point-based rating system that allows vastly different green buildings to be compared in the aggregate. Since Americans are competitive and obsessed with keeping score, the LEED system is particularly well suited to our culture.

LEED is also an amalgamation of best practices from a wide variety of disciplines including architecture, engineering, interior design, landscape architecture, and construction. It is a mixture of performance standards (e.g., a project achieves a 20 percent energy reduction compared to a conventional building) and prescriptive standards (e.g., a project uses paints with less than fifty grams per liter of volatile organic compounds), but it is weighted toward the performance side. In other words, LEED holds that best practices are better shown by results (outcomes) than by efforts alone (inputs).

Each LEED rating system has a different number of total points, so scores can be compared only within each system; however, the method for rewarding achievement is identical, so a LEED Gold certification for new construction represents, in some way, the same level of achievement (and difficulty) as a LEED Gold certification for commercial interiors (tenant improvements).

LEED certifications are awarded as follows:

- Certified: The project scored more than 40 percent of the basic, or core, points in the system.
- Silver: The project scored more than 50 percent of the core points.
- Gold: The project scored more than 60 percent of the core points.
- Platinum: The project scored more than 80 percent of the core points.

The LEED rating is a form of "eco-label" that describes the environmental attributes of a project. Prior to the advent of LEED, there was no labeling of buildings other than for their energy use, via the Energy Star program. While useful, Energy Star gives an incomplete picture of a building's overall environmental impact.

Figure 2.1 shows how a building eco-label might appear based on the six major categories of the LEED rating system. Ironically, until this system was created, a $20 million building had less labeling than a $2 box of animal crackers, in terms of its benefits and its basic ingredients. Owners of commercial and institutional buildings often had little knowledge of what was in the building they had just built or bought. The construction process is often messy, involving many substitutions and changes, and money is seldom left over to prepare a final set of drawings and specifications that document what actually ended up in the building. Thus, to understand a building's ingredients and its expected performance (including operating costs for energy and water usage), an eco-label such as the LEED rating is especially valuable both to building owners and to occupants (who might be more concerned about how healthy the building is than about how much water it saves). The commissioning tests and reports required in LEED also give a building owner confidence that the building will operate as designed.

In addition to securing a certain number of points, the four major LEED rating systems have prerequisites that every project must meet, no matter what level of certification it seeks. For example, one prerequisite is that a building either must be entirely nonsmoking or must have a very strict method for containing environmental tobacco smoke and exhausting it from the building without contaminating the breathing air for nonsmokers. In apartments and condominiums, it's often impossible to ban smoking, so more technical methods must be used to contain and eliminate secondhand smoke.

LEED is a self-assessed, third party–verified rating system. Applicants estimate the points for which their project qualifies and submit their documentation to the USGBC, which assigns an independent reviewer to the project. The reviewer either agrees and awards the points claimed, disagrees and disallows the points, or asks for further information or clarification. With the LEED system, there is a one-step appeal process.

This system is not dissimilar to the federal tax system, in which we estimate our tax liability and send our estimate to the Internal Revenue Service,

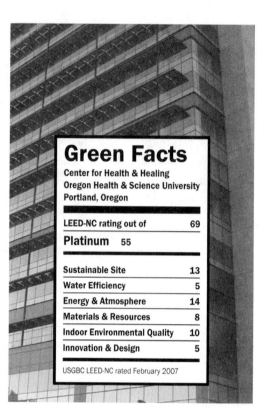

Green Facts

Center for Health & Healing
Oregon Health & Science University
Portland, Oregon

LEED-NC rating out of	69
Platinum 55	

Sustainable Site	13
Water Efficiency	5
Energy & Atmosphere	14
Materials & Resources	8
Indoor Environmental Quality	10
Innovation & Design	5

USGBC LEED-NC rated February 2007

Figure 2.1. A suggested
eco-label for a building.

which either accepts our calculations, asks for more information, or disallows them and invites us to an unfriendly meeting called a tax audit. And at the IRS, there is also an appeal process. The LEED system also features private and public credit interpretation rulings, in which the USGBC makes interpretations either for one project at a time or for more general situations. The public rulings are published for everyone to use as a precedent.

LEED for New Construction

The most widely known and used LEED system is LEED for New Construction (LEED-NC), which covers all new buildings (except core and shell developments), major renovations, and housing of four stories and above. Table 2.1 shows the six major categories in the LEED-NC rating system: sustainable sites, water conservation, energy efficiency and atmospheric protection, materials and resource conservation, indoor environmental quality,

Table 2.1
Key Factors in Rating a Green Building under LEED-NC

Green Building Category	Some Issues Addressed in the Category
1. Sustainable sites	Develop only on appropriate sites, provide for non-auto access, preserve open space, manage stormwater, reduce urban heat island effect, and reduce light pollution of the night sky.
2. Water conservation	Reduce use of potable water for irrigation and for building water use and sewage conveyance.
3. Energy efficiency and atmosphere protection	Reduce building energy use, use less harmful chemicals for refrigerants, generate renewable energy on-site, provide for ongoing energy savings, and purchase green power for project use.
4. Materials and resource conservation	Provide for recycling, reuse existing buildings, reduce construction waste generation, use salvaged and recycled-content materials, source materials regionally, and use rapidly renewable (agricultural) materials and certified wood products.
5. Indoor environmental quality	Improve indoor air quality; increase outside air ventilation; manage air quality during construction; use only nontoxic finishes, carpets, and composite wood products; reduce exposure to toxic chemicals during building operations; provide for individual comfort control; maintain thermal comfort standards; and provide daylighting and views to the outdoors.
6. Encourage innovation and integrated design	Provide for exemplary performance above LEED standards and encourage other innovations; use accredited professionals on the design team.

and a sixth category that yields up to five bonus points for innovation and integrated design.

Through the end of 2006, about 77 percent of LEED projects were registered and/or certified under the LEED-NC rating system[3] (see Table 2.2). LEED-NC is also used for projects on campuses, in which common systems (parking, transportation, and utilities) often supply a number of buildings.

Figure 2.2 shows an example of a LEED-certified building on a campus, the Whitehead Biomedical Research Laboratory at Emory University in Atlanta—the largest LEED-certified facility in the Southeast. An early example of a green building, it inspired that campus to make a commitment to ten more green buildings over the past several years. Greening the project started when it was 90 percent designed and workers were already pouring concrete for the third-floor slab, according to Laura Case, the project manager. "Facilities and administrators took the business case to the board of trustees and got buy-in from them. We had to get acceptance to put in a heat wheel [an energy recovery device], which increased the price of the project, but the payback was about four years. It saved a considerable amount of money because as a lab building, it uses 100% outside air with up to 12 air changes per hour that has to be heated or cooled."[4] Completed in 2001, the eight-story Whitehead building in 2002 became the first LEED-certified laboratory in the United States and one of the first LEED-certified higher education projects as well.

The Whitehead building received a Silver rating under the LEED-NC system. It has an estimated operational energy savings of 22 percent compared to a conventional building of comparable size, shape, and compass orientation, owing to a number of innovative features.[5] Standard biology and chemistry laboratories, for instance, blow lots of conditioned outside air through the building and up the fume hoods in a one-pass, wasteful system. By installing an "energy recovery wheel" that allowed the outgoing air to give up some of its coolness or warmth to the incoming air, the college saved considerable energy. By recovering water from the air-conditioning condensate and pumping it to the cooling towers for use as makeup water, the project also saved 2.5 million gallons of water per year. The building harvests rainwater for irrigation purposes and provides daylight to about 90 percent of the regularly occupied spaces, a rarity in lab buildings.

The cost of achieving the LEED Silver rating was about 1.5 percent of construction, or $990,000, almost half of which was attributable to the energy recovery wheel. With an estimated $167,000 in annual energy savings, payback for the entire green building investment will take less than six years. The project also demonstrated exemplary performance in the use of recycled materials, which made up 78 percent of the value of all building materials. In addition, over 40 percent of all materials came from local sources within 500 miles. Because of this project's success, Emory now aims to achieve at minimum a LEED Silver rating for all new buildings.

A LEED-NC rating is typically awarded after a building is completed and occupied, since it requires a final checkout process known as building commissioning. Under the current version of LEED-NC 2.2, certain design-phase credits can be assessed at the end of design and prior to construction, but no

Figure 2.2. Emory University's Whitehead Biomedical Research Laboratory is the first LEED-certified laboratory in the United States. Courtesy of Emory Creative Group.

final certification is made until all credits are reviewed after final completion of the project.

LEED for Core and Shell Buildings

The LEED for Core and Shell (LEED-CS) rating system is typically employed by speculative developers who control less than 50 percent of a building's final improvements. They may complete 40 percent of the space for a lead tenant, for example, and then rent the rest of the building to general tenants who will take much smaller spaces. LEED-CS allows a developer to pre-certify a design, then use the LEED rating to attract tenants and, in some cases, financing. Once the building is finished, the developer submits documentation to secure a final LEED rating.

The benefit of the LEED-CS system stems from the fact that a developer cannot wait until a building is finished to begin marketing a LEED rating to prospective tenants. By allowing a precertification using a system very similar to LEED-NC, the USGBC assists the developer and encourages more green buildings. Not only that, LEED-CS awards a point for creating tenant guidelines that encourage each tenant to use the LEED for Commercial Interiors (LEED-CI) rating system when building out their interior spaces. If that happens, the result is similar to a LEED for New Construction building, so everyone is happy. Because a developer doesn't control the final build-out, the LEED-CS rating system has four fewer total points than LEED-NC.

A good example of a LEED-CS Gold-certified project is 1180 Peachtree at Symphony Center, a 41-story high-rise tower in Atlanta, completed in 2006 by Houston-based Hines and shown in Figure 2.3. Certified in October 2005, it was the first such speculative development project in the country to achieve that level of performance. The office tower contains several green features, including a unique water-management system that uses captured and stored storm water and condensate from the building's mechanical system and provides 100 percent of the project's irrigation water, circumventing the need for city water for irrigation.

The 670,000-square-foot building was sold by Hines in September 2006, although the firm continues to manage and lease the property.[6] Both Hines's LEED Silver-certified One South Dearborn in Chicago and the Atlanta project were sold after completion of construction and leasing activity. Jerry Lea, senior vice president of Hines, comments on the benefits of the rating system: "Both buildings got the highest sales price (dollars per square foot) for buildings ever sold in those two markets. Is it because they were green? I can't say that's why. Is it because they are almost fully leased with good-quality tenants? That's probably a good part of it, and those tenants are in the buildings partially because they are green. I think there is some correlation that green buildings help you lease the space, and that helps sell them."[7] Lea says that LEED-CS gives Hines "third-party verification that we're building very good buildings, and better buildings than our competition."[8]

LEED for Commercial Interiors

LEED for Commercial Interiors (LEED-CI) is designed mainly for situations in which the base building systems are not changed and in which a tenant takes up only a few floors in a much larger building. In this situation, the ability to affect energy and water use, for example, or open space, landscaping, or stormwater management is either much smaller or nonexistent. Thus, other green building measures have to be incorporated into the evaluation system. These measures include choices that tenants can make about lighting design, energy-using equipment, lighting control systems,

Figure 2.3. The 41-story 1180 Peachtree building in Atlanta, built by Hines and sold for a record price, is a LEED-CS Gold project. Courtesy of Hines.

sub-metering, furniture and furnishings, paints, carpet and composite wood products, and length of tenancy.

A good example of a LEED-CI project is the 12,000-square-foot remodel of the Seattle office of the international architecture firm Perkins+Will. The project received the first LEED-CI Platinum rating in Washington State and the third in the entire United States, out of the 92 projects that have been certified under LEED-CI. According to Amanda Sturgeon, an architect and sustainable design leader in the office, "A common issue that prevents tenant improvement projects from obtaining LEED-CI Platinum is the limitations of the existing space and building. The Perkins+Will space was no different, full of enclosed offices around the perimeter, a low suspended ceiling, windows that did not open, and an energy-intensive HVAC [heating, ventilation, and air-conditioning] system, so the likelihood of getting LEED Platinum seemed slim."[9]

Using a simple design concept, the design team disconnected the building's HVAC system, installed new operable windows, and relied solely on natural ventilation. The existing ceiling was removed to reveal the original 12-foot ceilings and heavy timbers. To provide for winter heating, a new perimeter heating system was installed.

Natural ventilation is an ideal strategy for the maritime Pacific Northwest's mild climate. The project team added external shades to the west side of the space to reduce heat gain from the summer afternoon sun. Other sustainable strategies included sub-metering of tenant electrical use, installing lighting that was 46 percent more efficient, purchasing 78 percent of the materials from local and regional sources, and using only sustainably-harvested wood products. The project is estimated to reduce typical energy use by 50 percent and water use by 40 percent (it uses water-free urinals, among other tactics), and it recycled 98 percent of its construction waste.[10]

LEED for Existing Buildings

LEED for Existing Buildings (LEED-EB) was originally designed to be a method for assuring ongoing accountability of LEED-NC buildings over time. It has instead become a stand-alone rating system for building owners who want to benchmark their operations against a nationally recognized standard. By early 2007, five projects had received a LEED-EB Platinum rating, all in California. Two were occupied by state agencies, and three in San Jose were owned and occupied by Adobe Systems, a large software maker. LEED-EB addresses many issues not dealt with in new construction, including upgrades, operations and maintenance practices, environmentally preferable purchasing policies, green housekeeping, continuous monitoring of energy use, retrofitting water fixtures to cut use, and re-lamping.

One early LEED-EB Gold-certified project paved the way for others in California: a unit of the California State University system known as Moss Landing Marine Laboratories. Building services engineer Barry Giles took on the task of helping to beta-test the LEED-EB system. Located on the shores of Monterey Bay, the 60,000-square-foot building was only two years old, yet it proved to be a good candidate for an operations upgrade.

Figure 2.4. The architectural firm Perkins+Will's remodel of their Seattle office received a LEED-CI Platinum rating. Courtesy of Perkins+Will.

Giles talks about his experiences in promoting and managing the project:

I initially put the idea out to the directors because I realized that Moss Landing had a holistic vision. So in this project, we looked to integrate the entire site. We did some very innovative things across our 21 acres, and we're expanding those ideas into the surroundings as well. Anecdotally, I can tell you there is a big payback to everything that's done within the LEED-EB process. We have great sun shading; clerestory windows provide fantastic daylighting; the views to the ocean and to outside windows are about 80 percent of the whole building.

Inside the group at Moss Landing, the reaction has been great; it's just another arrow in our quiver. [The project] demonstrates that we don't just think about ourselves, we think about the surroundings, our neighbors, and the area in which we live. Our footprint on the land is very shallow compared to others in the state.[11]

The project included stormwater runoff reduction, natural landscaping, a 20 percent reduction in water use, a 20 percent reduction in energy use, recommissioning and preventive maintenance, 50 percent occupant recycling, daylighting 65 percent of the building area, seven different green housekeeping measures, protection of a local endangered species on the sand dunes through extensive site restoration, and sustainability education.

Typical Green Building Measures

While there's no such thing as a "typical" green building, there are measures that are used in many green buildings. Understanding these measures will help you work with green builders, whether you are a building owner, developer, facility manager, government official, business or nonprofit executive, or just an interested stakeholder in a green building program.

Table 2.2 shows typical measures used in green buildings, based on an analysis of the first 200 LEED-NC certified projects (there are now more than 500). Used in less than a third of projects are some measures you might associate with typical green buildings, such as the following:

- solar photovoltaic systems
- high-efficiency ventilation and underfloor air distribution systems
- operable windows and greater control over thermal comfort by occupants
- native plants to restore sites
- certified wood products
- rapidly renewable materials such as cork and bamboo flooring

Most of these systems and approaches aren't common because projects do not have the opportunity to use them (e.g., sites in dense urban areas may be hard to restore), supply-chain difficulties are involved, or the initial cost is substantial.

Other ways exist to use green products in LEED systems, however, in particular by using furniture and furnishings made from salvaged or reclaimed materials, such as partitions; high-recycled-content materials, such as recycled plastics; agricultural products, such as wheatboard and strawboard, cotton, or wool; and 100 percent certified wood that comes from sustainably managed forests and contains no added urea-formaldehyde resin from composite wood products.

Table 2.2

Key Measures Used in LEED-NC Certified Projects

Highly likely to be used (67% or more of projects)

Low-VOC-content paints, coatings, adhesives, sealants

Low-VOC-emitting carpeting

10% or more recycled-content materials

Views to the outdoors from 90% or more of spaces

Two innovation points such as public education, extra water conservation, or higher
levels of construction waste recycling

Somewhat likely to be used (33% to 67%)

Two-week building flushout prior to occupancy (except in the humid Southeast and
South)

Carbon-dioxide monitoring to improve outside air ventilation

Bioswales, detention/retention ponds, and other stormwater control measures

Green roofs or Energy Star reflective roofs

Construction-period indoor air quality best management practices

Permanent temperature and humidity monitoring system

Daylighting for at least 75% of spaces

Cutoff light fixtures and lower outdoor ambient lighting levels to control light trespass from site

Water-conserving fixtures and waterfree urinals (30% or more reduction in 54% of
projects)

At least a 35% energy use reduction over conventional buildings

Additional building commissioning, with peer review of design documents

Purchased green power for at least two years

No added urea-formaldehyde in composite wood or agrifiber products

---

Source: Author's analysis of USGBC certified project data, using LEED-NC project scorecards.

Other Green Building Rating Systems

Other rating systems besides LEED exist, particularly for the residential market, as described in Chapter 10. (LEED-NC addresses only multi-unit residential projects four stories and above.) The other rating system in use for commercial and institutional buildings is Green Globes™, a program of the
nonprofit Green Building Initiative™. The Green Globes system is web-
based and supposedly easier for teams to use, but it currently has less than
2 percent of the market.[12] It has its adherents, however, mostly because its
certification process is said to be less costly than LEED. Because the system
is a self-assessment, critics contend that it lacks the rigor and therefore the

credibility of an independent third-party rating system.

Green Globes has been approved for use in meeting green building requirements in six states: Arkansas, Connecticut, Hawaii, Maryland, Pennsylvania, and Wisconsin. Like the USGBC, the Green Building Initiative is an accredited U.S. standards-developing organization. A 2006 study by the University of Minnesota compared the credits offered by the two systems and found that 80 percent of the available points in Green Globes are addressed in LEED-NC version 2.2 (the current standard) and that 85 percent of the points in LEED-NC version 2.2 are addressed in Green Globes.[13] In essence, the standards are virtually identical, but LEED has market dominance and will likely keep it in the years ahead.

A 2006 report to Congress by the U.S. General Services Administration concluded that LEED was the preferred system for the government's use, compared with Green Globes and three other non-U.S. rating systems: the Japanese CASBEE (Comprehensive Assessment for Building Environmental Efficiency) system, the European GB Tool, and the British BREEAM (Building Research Establishment Environmental Assessment Method).[14] The GSA report, prepared by the Department of Energy's Pacific Northwest National Laboratory, compares these five systems for rating the greenness of a building design and construction project. Although the researchers found that each of the rating systems had merits, they concluded that the LEED rating system "continues to be the most appropriate and credible sustainable building rating system available for evaluation of GSA projects."[15]

GSA cited five important reasons for its conclusions about the LEED system. First, LEED applies to all GSA project types, including new and existing buildings and interiors covered by USGBC standards. Second, it "tracks the quantifiable aspects of sustainable design and building performance," a major focus of federal programs under the impetus of the Government Performance and Results Act and a general requirement for performance measurement. Third, trained professionals verify LEED. Fourth, it has a "well-defined system for incorporating updates" (the USGBC is currently preparing a LEED version 3.0). And fifth, LEED is "the most widely used rating system in the U.S. market."[16]

Chapter 3
The Business Case for Green Buildings

The business case for commercial green buildings in 2007 is simply stated: if your next project is not a green building, one that's certified by a national third-party rating system, it will be functionally outdated the day it's completed and very likely to underperform the market as time passes.[1] That bold statement has been echoed by a well-known real-estate expert, who bluntly claimed that trillions of dollars of commercial property around the world would soon drop in value because green buildings are going mainstream and would render those properties obsolete.[2] In a meeting in Sydney, Australia, in February 2007, the head of Australia's Property Council, representing the entire development industry, claimed that no large developer in that country would ever start another project that wasn't going to be at least LEED Silver (Australia 4 Green Stars) certified.[3]

Within two years, the business case for green buildings is going to be part of "business as usual." Jerry Lea of Houston-based Hines, a strong proponent and developer of Energy Star and LEED buildings, says, "I think sustainable is here to stay. I think the definition of 'Class A' buildings very soon will include sustainable design and probably LEED certification."[4] Richard Cook, a prominent architect in New York City, says, "In five years, it will be clear that buildings not reaching the highest standard of sustainability will become obsolete."[5]

Incentives and Barriers to Green Development

Still, there are barriers to the widespread adoption of green building techniques, technologies, and systems, some related to real-life experience and the rest to the perception in the building industry that green buildings still add extra cost. This is surprising because senior executives representing architectural and engineering firms, consultants, developers, building owners, corporate owner-occupants, and educational institutions have held positive attitudes about the benefits and costs of green construction for some time, according to the 2005 Green Building Market Barometer, a survey conducted by Turner Construction Company.[6]

When asked to compare green buildings with traditional construction, the respondents agreed that green construction yields greater benefits in terms of the following:

- occupants' health and well-being (88 percent)
- building value (84 percent)
- worker productivity (78 percent)
- return on investment (68 percent)

Fifty-seven percent of the 665 executives surveyed said their companies were involved with green buildings; 83 percent said their green building workload had increased since 2002; and 87 percent said they expected green building activity to continue. Thirty-four percent of those not currently working with green construction said their organization would be likely to do so over the next three years.

Given these positive views, it is surprising that the top obstacles cited in the Turner survey are perceived higher costs (68 percent) and lack of awareness regarding the benefits of green construction (64 percent). Other factors discouraging green construction are the perceived complexity and cost of LEED documentation (54 percent), short-term budget horizons (51 percent) and the perceived long wait for payback (50 percent), the difficulty of quantifying the benefits (47 percent), and the more complex construction involved (30 percent).

Overcoming Barriers to Green Buildings

Over the next three years, everyone in the green building industry will be focused on lowering the key barrier of cost. Architects, engineers, builders, and developers will be working hard to bring the costs of green buildings into line with benefits in five specific ways:

1. They'll work aggressively to lower the costs of building green by accumulating their own project experience and strengthening their focus on integrated design approaches that might lower some costs (such as HVAC) while increasing others (such as building envelope insulation and better glazing), but with a net positive cost-reduction impact.
2. To offset the perceived risks of trying something new, they'll develop communication and marketing strategies that make good use of available research demonstrating the benefits of green buildings. We'll see some of that research later.
3. They'll find ways to finance green building improvements that reduce or eliminate the first-cost penalty that often frightens away prospective buyers, using incentive payments from utility "public purpose" programs, and local, state, and federal governments to maximize leverage. There are also a growing number of third-party financing sources for energy-efficiency and renewable-energy investments in large building projects that can defray or offset added initial costs.
4. They'll study and try to duplicate the successful project results for institutional owners, who represent nearly half of the current market for LEED-registered buildings. This means documenting the full range of green building benefits so that building owners with a long-term ownership perspective can be motivated to find the additional funds to build high-performance buildings.
5. They'll use good project management and cost management software to show the benefits of various green building measures in real time. Decisions about green building measures are often made quickly, during project meetings that can last all day. Having good information about costs, benefits, and return on investment can be critical to keeping good green measures under consideration, instead of losing them to strictly financial considerations.

Paul Shahriari is the developer of the leading software for green-project cost management, Ecologic 3.[7] He developed this product because, in advising dozens of green building projects, he found that cost was the only consideration ever placed on the table. He says,

We've created web-based collaborative software that allows a team to attribute certain cost savings or premiums associated with each LEED credit.

They can also attach a cost impact profile to each LEED credit. The tool combines the soft costs of design, consulting, and engineering and the hard-cost component (construction) and presents a life-cycle benefit structure.

It shows you when the project will break even and then—the powerful thing—it shows when that green building will start generating additional income in terms of reduced operating costs, electricity, water, O&M, maintenance, etc. It shows that green buildings are the only kind of buildings that can produce more revenue for clients, as opposed to traditional buildings that cost the owner money to operate. So far, for every project that's in the system right now, the average payback period is less than five years for certified projects.

Some of the return-on-investment calculations of individual credits have over 1,000 percent return on investment by doing something environmentally friendly and green. Our philosophy is that we want to harness economic value from the environmental performance of a project. We show people that there is money to be had by greening their project. The most important thing I discovered is that prior to having an economic framework with which to discuss LEED, I had a lot of projects that never went forward. I've never had a client who's seen the output from the software decide not to build a green project.[8]

Chapter 4 shows the many ways in which design and construction decisions influence the costs of green buildings.

Benefits That Build a Business Case

The business case for green development is based on a framework of benefits: economic, productivity, risk management, health, public relations and marketing, recruitment and retention, and funding.[9] Table 3.1 presents an outline useful for understanding the wide-ranging benefits of green buildings, each of which are examined in detail below.

Economic Benefits
Reduced operating costs. With the real price of oil likely to stay above $50 per barrel for the next twenty years,[10] natural gas prices at record levels, and peak-period (typically summer air-conditioning times) electricity prices ris-

Table 3.1
Business Case Benefits of Green Buildings

1. Savings on energy and water, typically 30% to 50%, along with reduced "carbon footprint" from energy savings
2. Maintenance cost reductions from commissioning and other measures to improve and assure proper systems integration and performance
3. Increased value from higher Net Operating Income and better public relations
4. Tax benefits for specific green building investments
5. More competitive real estate holdings for private-sector owners, over the long run
6. Productivity improvements, typically 3% to 5%
7. Health benefits, reduced absenteeism, typically 5% or more
8. Risk management benefits, including faster lease-up and sales and lower employee exposure to odors or the effects of irritating or toxic chemicals in building materials
9. Marketing benefits, especially for developers and consumer-products companies
10. Public relations benefits, especially for developers and public agencies
11. Easier recruitment and retention of key employees, higher morale
12. Fund-raising incentives for colleges and nonprofits
13. Increased availability of debt and equity funding for developers
14. Demonstration of commitment to sustainability and environmental stewardship; shared values with key stakeholders

ing steadily in many metropolitan areas, energy-efficient buildings make good business sense. Even in "triple-net" leases (the most common type), in which tenants pay all operating costs, landlords want to offer tenants the most economical space for their money. For a small additional investment in capital cost, green buildings will save on energy operating costs for years to come.

Many green buildings are designed to use 25 to 40 percent less energy than current codes require; some buildings achieve even higher efficiency levels. Translated to an operating cost of $1.60 to $2.50 per square foot for electricity (the most common energy source for building), this energy savings could reduce utility operating costs by 40 cents to $1 per square foot per year. Often these savings are achieved for an added investment of just $1 to $3 per square foot. With building costs reaching $150 to $300 per square foot, many developers and building owners are seeing that it's a wise business decision to invest 1 to 2 percent of capital cost to secure long-term savings, particularly with a payback of less than three years. In an 80,000-square-foot building, the owner's savings translates into $32,000 to $80,000 per year, year after year.

Reduced maintenance costs. More than 120 studies have documented that energy-saving buildings that are properly commissioned at 50 cents to $1 per square foot of initial cost (equal to one year of savings) show additional operational savings of 10 to 15 percent in energy costs. They also tend to be much easier to operate and maintain.[11]

By conducting comprehensive functional testing of all energy-using systems before occupancy, it is often possible to have a smoother-running building for years because potential problems are fixed in advance. A recent review of these studies by Lawrence Berkeley National Laboratory showed that the payback from building commissioning in terms of energy savings alone was about four years, while the payback fell to about one year when other benefits were considered, such as fewer callbacks to address thermal comfort problems.

Increased building value. Increased annual energy savings also create higher building values. Imagine a building that saves $37,500 per year in energy costs versus a comparable building built to code (this savings might result from saving only 50 cents per square foot per year for a 75,000-square-foot building). At capitalization rates of 6 percent, typical today in commercial real estate, green building standards would add $625,000 ($8.33 per square foot) to the value of the building. For a small up-front investment, an owner can reap benefits that typically offer a payback of three years or less and a rate of return exceeding 20 percent.

Tax benefits. Many states have begun to offer tax benefits for green buildings. Some, such as Oregon and New York, offer state tax credits, while others, like Nevada, offer property and sales tax abatements. The federal government offers tax credits as well.

Oregon's credit varies based on building size and LEED certification level. At the Platinum level, a 100,000-square-foot building can expect to receive a net-present-value tax credit of about $2 per square foot.[12] This credit can be transferred from public or nonprofit entities to private companies, such as contractors or benefactors, making it even more beneficial than one that applies only to private owners.[13]

New York's tax credit allows builders who meet energy goals and use environmentally preferable materials to claim up to $3.75 per square foot for interior work and $7.50 per square foot for exterior work against their state tax bill. To qualify for the credit, a building must be certified by a licensed architect or engineer, and must meet specific requirements for energy use, materials selection, indoor air quality, waste disposal, and water use. In new buildings, this means energy use cannot exceed 65 percent of use permitted under the New York State energy code; in rehabilitated buildings, energy use cannot exceed 75 percent.[14]

The Nevada legislature passed a law in 2005 offering a property tax abatement of up to 50 percent, for up to ten years, to private development projects achieving a LEED Silver certification. Assuming the property tax is 1 percent of value, this could be worth as much as 5 percent of the building cost, typically far more than the actual cost of achieving LEED Silver on a large project. As a result, a large number of Nevada projects are pursuing LEED certification, including the world's largest private development project, the $7 billion, 17-million-square-foot Project CityCenter in Las Vegas (see Chapter 11).[15] The Nevada law also provides for sales tax abatement for green materials used in LEED Silver-certified buildings. (This law was amended in 2007 to reduce the tax abatement.)

The 2005 federal Energy Policy Act offers two major tax incentives for aspects of green buildings: a tax credit of 30 percent on both solar thermal and electric systems and a tax deduction of up to $1.80 per square foot for projects that reduce energy use for lighting, HVAC, and water heating systems by 50 percent compared with a 2001 baseline standard.[16] In the case of government projects, the tax deduction may be taken by the design team leader, typically the architect.

Productivity Benefits

In the service economy, productivity gains for healthier indoor spaces are worth anywhere from 1 to 5 percent of employee costs, or about $3 to $30 per square foot of leasable or usable space. This estimate is based on average employee costs of $300 to $600 per square foot per year (based on $60,000 average annual salary and benefits and 100 to 200 square feet per person).[17] With energy costs typically less than $2.50 per square foot per year, productivity gains from green buildings could easily equal or exceed the entire energy cost of operating a building.

Here's an example: Research on high-performance lighting by Carnegie Mellon University found median productivity gains of 3.2 percent in 11 studies, or about $1 to $2 per square foot per year, an amount equal to the cost of

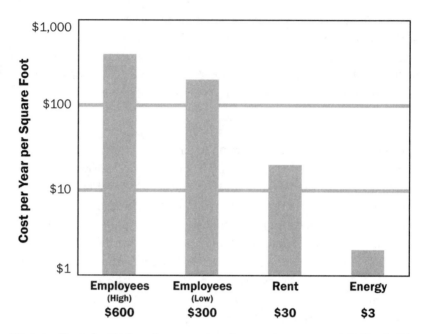

Figure 3.1. Typical cost of employees, rent, and energy in a commercial office building.

energy.[18] This is in addition to a reported average savings of 18 percent on total energy bills from proper lighting. For corporate and institutional owners and occupiers of buildings, that is too much savings to ignore.

Look at it this way. If a building owner could get a 10 percent improvement in productivity from a green building, or about a $30- to $60-per-square-foot increase in output, it would always pay for that company to build a new building and put its employees to work there. In other words, the productivity increase could pay for the building! Even a 5 percent improvement in productivity would pay for half or more of the rent or cost of the new green building. What, then, you might ask, is the business case for a "brown building," one that doesn't have these benefits? (See Chapter 7.)

From another groundbreaking study of the costs of green buildings, Table 3.2 shows the 20-year "net present value" of the various categories of green building benefits.[19] Productivity and health gains provide more than two-thirds of the total benefits of green buildings in this analysis.

Annual Gains from Lighting Improvements

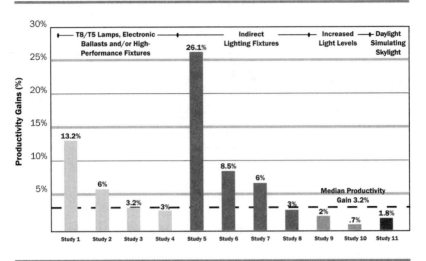

Figure 3.2. Productivity gains from lighting improvements. Courtesy of the Center for Building Performance and Diagnostics, Carnegie Mellon University. eBIDS™, re-drawn with permission.

Risk-Management Benefits

Green building certification can provide some measure of protection against future lawsuits through third-party verification of measures installed to protect indoor air quality, beyond just meeting code-required minimums. With the national focus on mold and its effect on building occupants, developers and building owners are focusing considerable attention on improving and maintaining indoor air quality.

Faster permitting or special permit assistance can also be considered a type of risk mitigation. San Francisco gives faster permit review for projects committing to LEED Gold or Platinum certification. In Chicago the city government has created the position of green projects administrator and is allowing green projects to receive priority processing. For large projects, above minimum requirements, the city waives fees for independent code consultants. Projects with high-level green goals are promised a 15-day permit review.[20] In Austin, Texas, the city fast-tracked the development reviews for a large big-box retailer so that it was able to open 12 months ahead

Table 3.2
Financial Benefits of Green Buildings (Net Present Value, 2003 dollars)

Benefit	Savings per Square Foot
Productivity and health value	$36.90 to $55.30 (70% to 78% of total savings)
Operation and maintenance savings	$ 8.50
Energy savings	$ 5.80
Emissions savings (from energy)	$ 1.20
Water savings	$ 0.50
Total	$52.90 to $71.30

Source:Gregory Kats et al., *The Costs and Financial Benefits of Green Buildings*, 2003, www .cap-e.com/ewebeditpro/items/O59F3303.ppt#1, accessed March 6, 2007.

of schedule; the resulting profit gain paid entirely for the $2.8 million building![21]

Another risk management benefit of green buildings in the private sector is the faster sale and leasing of such buildings, compared to similar projects in the same town. Green buildings tend to be easier to rent and sell, because educated tenants increasingly understand their benefits.

Green buildings are also seen as less risky by insurers. In September 2006, Fireman's Fund, a major insurance company, announced it would give a 5 percent reduction in insurance premiums for green buildings. The insurer also announced its new Certified Green Building Replacement and Green Upgrade coverage.[22]

Health Benefits

Of course, a key element of productivity is healthy workers. By focusing on measures to improve indoor environmental quality, such as increased ventilation, daylighting, views to the outdoors, and low-toxicity finishes and furniture, Figure 3.3 shows that green buildings reduce their occupants' symptoms by an average of 41.5 percent on an annual basis!

Since most companies are effectively self-insured (i.e., their health insurance costs go up when their employees file claims) and most government agencies and large companies are self-insured in reality, it makes good economic sense for them to be concerned about the effect of building design on people's health. In addition, given what we know about the health effects of various green building measures, a company might be inviting lawsuits if

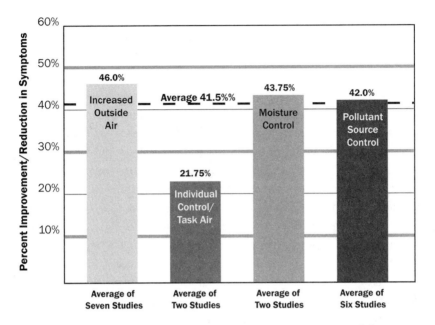

Figure 3.3. Annual gains from air quality improvements. Courtesy of the Center for Building Performance and Diagnostics, Carnegie Mellon University. BIDS™, redrawn with permission.

it didn't pursue all feasible measures to design and construct a healthy building. By having the building certified by an independent third party and by designing well above code-required minimums, a company might have a better defense against employee lawsuits for sick building syndrome symptoms, building-related illnesses, and other ailments.

Public Relations and Marketing Benefits

Stakeholder relations and occupant satisfaction. Tenants and employees want to see a demonstrated concern for their well-being and for that of the planet. Savvy developers and building owners are beginning to realize how to market these benefits to a discerning and skeptical client and stakeholder base, using the advantages of green building certifications and other forms of documentation, including support from local utility and industry programs. This is not "greenwashing"; it is a positive response to a growing public concern for the long-term health of the environment. A good indication of how corporations have embraced this concept is the explosion in green building projects and associated public relations in 2006 and 2007. If you sign up for Google Alerts and enter "green buildings" as a keyword, you will be inundated with six to 12 news stories almost every day from the nation's press.

Environmental stewardship. Being a good neighbor is appropriate not just for building users, but for the larger community. Developers, large corporations, universities, some health-care organizations, schools, local government, and building owners have long recognized the marketing and public relations benefits (including branding) of a demonstrated concern for the environment. Green buildings fit right in with this message. As a result, we expect to see major commitments by corporate real estate executives to greening their buildings and facilities. A good example is Adobe Systems, Inc., a major software maker based in San Jose, California. In 2006, Adobe announced that it had received three LEED-EB Platinum awards for its headquarters towers; not only did it reap great publicity, but the firm showed that it had garnered a net present value almost 20 times its initial investment. (See Chapter 14.)[23]

Many larger public and private organizations have well-articulated sustainability mission statements and are coming to understand how their real estate choices can both reflect and advance those missions. Writing in *Urban Land* magazine, developer Jonathan F. P. Rose notes that "having a socially and environmentally motivated mission makes it easier for businesses in the real estate industry to recruit, and retain, top talent. Communities are more likely to support green projects than traditional projects, and it is easier for such projects to qualify for many government contracts, subsidies, grants, and tax credits. The real estate industry can prosper by making environmentally responsible decisions."[24]

Green buildings also reinforce a company's brand image. Consumer products companies such as Wal-Mart, Starbucks, PNC Bank, or Aveda can improve or maintain their brand image by being associated with green buildings, and so they are moving in this direction. Large corporations, including those that issue sustainability reports every year—and there are more than 1,000 of them—are beginning to see the benefits of building green to demonstrate to their employees, shareholders, and other stakeholders that they are "walking the talk." In fact, as mentioned in the foreword, the first large building to be built at Ground Zero, Seven World Trade

Center, was certified LEED Gold. In September 2006, Governor George Pataki of New York announced that the Freedom Tower, World Trade Center Office Towers 2, 3, and 4, and the World Trade Center Memorial and Memorial Museum will all be designed to achieve LEED Gold certification.[25]

More competitive product in the marketplace. Speculative commercial and residential developers are realizing that green buildings can be more competitive in certain markets, if built on a conventional budget. Green buildings with lower operating costs and better indoor environmental quality are more attractive to a growing group of corporate, public, and individual buyers and tenants. Greenness will not soon replace known real-estate attributes such as price, location, and conventional amenities, but green features will increasingly enter into decisions about leasing space and purchasing properties and homes. Developers are using the precertification available for the LEED for Core and Shell rating system to attract tenants and financing for high-rise office towers in such places as Chicago and Atlanta. One such project mentioned earlier, Hines's 1180 Peachtree in Atlanta, received the 2006 Green Development Award from NAIOP, the National Association of Industrial and Office Properties.[26]

Recruitment and Retention Benefits

One often overlooked aspect of green buildings is their effect on people's interest in joining or staying with an organization. It costs $50,000 to $150,000 to lose a good employee, and most organizations experience 10 to 20 percent turnover per year, at least some of which typically involves people they didn't want to lose. In some of these cases, people leave because of poor physical environments, not just because of the "boss from hell."

In a workforce of 200 people, turnover at this level would mean 20 to 40 people leaving per year. What if a green building could reduce turnover by 5 percent, for example—by one to two people out of the 20 to 40? Taken alone, the value of retaining the employee or employees would be $50,000 to $300,000—more than enough to justify the costs of certifying a building project. A professional services firm, say a law firm, might lose just one good attorney, typically billing $400,000 per year, with a $250,000 gross profit to the firm; that sum would more than pay for the extra cost of a green building or green tenant improvement project that would keep that lawyer at the firm. And what about the impact of a healthy work environment on employees' belief that their employer really cares about their well-being?

Table 3.3 confirms the growing shortage of people to serve the needs of the U.S. economy. Owing to an aging labor force, in 2014 there will be 2.6 million fewer people in the 35- to 44-year-old age group than in 2005, typically the leadership group in most organizations: managers, executives, experienced employees, and senior technical people, usually at the peak of their career. Getting and keeping them will tax the ingenuity and resources of most companies; green buildings can demonstrate that the company or organization and the key employees share the same values. Working in a company that rents or owns green buildings gives employees another reason to tell their friends and spouses why they are staying with an organization.

Financing Green Projects

Whether you are a private developer or a nonprofit school or organization, raising money for projects is always an issue. For private developers, raising both debt and equity capital is the challenge. The rise of socially responsible property investing promises to reward those developers who build green. For example, a large property developer in Portland, Oregon, Gerding Edlen Development, built nearly $1 billion in new projects in 2006. The firm has a strong commitment to building LEED Silver or better buildings in each project.[27]

Investing in green buildings has begun to attract considerable attention as a form of socially responsible investing, a practice that is growing faster than overall investing. "We have yet to see the first public real estate investment fund squarely committed to green real estate," says one expert, professor Gary Pivo at the University of Arizona. "But until such funds are created, there are some other options worth considering. One is to acquire shares in companies that commonly own Energy Star–labeled buildings or have been recognized by Energy Star for their conservation efforts."[28]

Among publicly traded real estate investment trusts (REITs) investing to at least some degree in green buildings, Liberty Property Trust and Corporate Office Properties Trust (COPT) both develop LEED Silver buildings on a speculative or build-to-suit basis for corporate tenants. They say that green buildings are wiser investments because they are cheaper to operate, lease up faster, and attract better tenants.

Table 3.3
The Aging Labor Force

Age Group	2005*	2014 (estimate)*	Change
25–34	32.5	36.8	+4.2
35–44	35.9	33.3	−2.6
45–54	34.2	35.5	+1.3
55 and older	24.1	34.3	+10.2

*All figures in millions

Source: Bureau of Labor Statistics, cited in *Investor's Business Daily*, March 6, 2007, p. 1.

One of COPT's green projects is 318 Sentinel Drive, in the National Business Park in Annapolis Junction, Maryland, which received the 2005 NAIOP Green Development Award. The project, a four-story, 125,000-square-foot office building, was fully leased before construction completion. The Sentinel property is one of 12 projects currently under development that COPT intends to certify under the LEED-CS program; it earned a LEED Gold rating. A companion project at 304 Sentinel Drive received a LEED-CS Silver rating. 318 Sentinel Drive incorporates tenant design and construction guidelines to promote green practices during tenant build-outs, promoting LEED-CI project certification.

The 318 Sentinel Drive project had a $2.84-per-square-foot green construction premium, with an estimated 70-cents-per-square-foot annual energy savings. The company's analysis showed a six-month return on investment, once extra green costs were offset by benefits from energy savings, waste reduction charges, stormwater management (site development) savings, and other green features.[29]

In 2006, New York developer Jonathan F. P. Rose created the Rose Smart Growth Investment Fund to invest in green building projects. The $100 million limited partnership focuses on acquiring existing properties near mass transit. The fund expects to make green improvements to the properties and hold them as long-term investments.[30] The focus on transit-centric developments takes into account the energy savings from enabling greater use of mass transit.

The fund's first project is in downtown Seattle, Washington: a renovation of the 1920s-era Joseph Vance and Sterling buildings, a total building area of about 120,000 square feet, with ground-floor retail and office space above.[31] According to the developer, the office buildings were purchased for $23.5 million and are undergoing $3.5 million worth of practical green renovations to improve energy efficiency and environmental performance. According to the fund, it is "re-branding these buildings as the 'greenest and healthiest' historic buildings in the marketplace, to increase market awareness of the buildings, attract and retain tenants."

For nonprofits and for private colleges and universities, the funding issue is vastly different. They are dependent on private donors to fund most of their new buildings. Many nonprofits have successfully used the greening of their buildings to attract funds for renovation projects. The Ecotrust organization in Portland, Oregon, received a major gift from a single donor to renovate a 100-year-old, two-story brick warehouse into a three-story, 70,000-square-foot modern building with two floors of offices above ground-floor retail. The Jean Vollum Natural Capital Center was only the second LEED Gold-certified project in the United States when it opened in 2001.[32] In 2003, the Natural Resources Defense Council completed one of the first LEED Platinum-certified projects in the world when it opened the Robert Redford Building in Santa Monica, California.

Over the next few years, there is no doubt that many private colleges and universities will find that their green buildings will draw donors from unexpected sources. To accelerate this process, since 2003 the Kresge Foundation's Green Building Initiative has been giving grants of up to $100,000 to nonprofits that will use an integrated design process to build a green building. Kresge also offered a "bonus grant" challenge program for projects that became LEED-certified. By February 2006, the initiative had awarded 64 planning grants totaling $4,146,000, averaging about $70,000 each. One early success was Herman Hipp Hall at Furman University near Greenville, South Carolina, a liberal-arts university with about 2,600 students; Hipp Hall was the first LEED Gold-certified project in higher education in the United States. The bonus grant program is now closed, with a total of $7,200,000 committed to 42 nonprofit organizations, or an average grant of $171,000.[33]

Chapter 4
The Costs of Green Buildings

Understanding the incremental costs of green building is important, because the single most important factor in the development and construction world is cost. Construction costs are "hard," but the benefits of building green are mainly "soft," including projected energy savings, water savings, and productivity gains. Therefore, executing a cost-benefit analysis for each project is crucially important to persuade building owners and developers to proceed with both the sustainable design measures and the LEED certification effort.

The biggest obstacle for green buildings is the perception that they cost more. Jim Goldman, project executive at Turner Construction Company in Seattle, says, "There's still a lot of bad information out there with respect to costs. If you want to kill a green project, there's nothing easier than using [the prospect of higher] costs."[1]

Cost Drivers for Green Buildings

If you're a building owner, a public agency, a private developer, or a corporate real-estate executive, how should you think about the cost of greening your next project? Chapter 3 presented the business case for green buildings by putting the full range of benefits into perspective, often a necessary prelude to considering whether to bear additional costs. But benefits are generally long-term while costs are immediate, so many people tend to shy away from anything that will add costs, no matter what the potential benefits. This chapter addresses the challenge of identifying green building costs and justifying them to clients.

Table 4.1 shows some of the elements of green building design and some construction decisions that may add cost to a project. From this table of "cost drivers," you can see that there is no right answer to the question "How

Table 4.1

Cost Drivers for Green Buildings

Driver	Possible Cost Increases
1. Level of LEED certification sought	Zero for LEED-certified; 1%–2% for LEED Silver, up to 5% for LEED Gold.
2. Stage of the project when the decision is made to seek LEED certification	After 50% completion of construction drawings, things get a lot more costly.
3. Project type	With certain project types, such as science and technology labs, it can be costly to change established models; designs for office buildings are easier to change.
4. Experience of the design and construction teams in sustainable design and green buildings	Every organization has a "learning curve" for green buildings; costs decrease as teams learn more about the process.
5. Types of green technologies involved in the project	Photovoltaics and green roofs are going to add costs, no matter what; it's possible to design a LEED Gold building without them.
6. Level of direction from the owner in establishing priorities for green measures and a strategy for including them	In the absence of clear direction from the owner, each design team member considers strategies in isolation.
7. Geographic location and climate	Climate can make certain levels of LEED certification harder for project types such as labs and even office buildings, as can local codes and labor union resistance to change.

much does a green building cost?" I often tell audiences that the only definitive answer to this question is "It depends!"

Overall, costs associated with green design and construction may exceed 1 percent of construction costs for large buildings and 5 percent of costs for small buildings, depending on the measures employed. Higher levels of sustainable building (for example, LEED Silver, Gold, or Platinum standard) may involve some additional capital costs, based on case studies of completed buildings in the United States. LEED projects also incur additional soft (non-construction) costs for additional design, analysis, engineering, energy modeling, building commissioning, and LEED documentation. For some projects, for example, additional professional services—including energy modeling, building commissioning, additional design services, and the documentation process—can add 0.5 to 1.5 percent to a project's cost, depending on its size.

The 2003 Cost Study for the State of California

A 2003 study by Gregory Kats was the first rigorous assessment of the costs and benefits of green buildings.[2] Chapter 3 presented the benefits assessed by the study. Drawing on cost data from 33 green building projects nationwide, the report concluded that LEED certification adds an average of 1.84 percent to the construction cost of a project. For Gold-certified office projects, construction cost premiums ranged from 1 to 5 percent over the cost of a conventional building at the same site. Table 4.2 shows the results of this early study (2001–3) of green building costs.

Green building advocates frequently resort to rhetoric ("green is good") when promoting their point of view. For owners and developers, however, justifying additional costs traditionally rests on the economic payback, or return on investment, for energy (and sometimes water) conservation measures. Green building standards such as LEED incorporate requirements beyond energy and water use, including indoor environmental quality, daylighting and views of the outdoors, use of recycled materials, and sustainable-site development, so it is often difficult to justify green building investments on the value of utility savings alone.

High Performance on a Budget

A large, developer-driven, build-to-suit project in Portland, Oregon, completed in the fourth quarter of 2006, exposed flaws in the notion that higher levels of performance must always lead to significantly higher capital costs. The 400,000-square-foot, 16-story, $145 million Center for Health and Healing at Oregon Health & Science University received a LEED Platinum rating early in 2007, the largest project in the world to achieve this highest green-building rating. The developer has reported a total cost premium, net of local, state, and federal incentives, of 1 percent.[3] With a full commitment to integrated design and an experienced development, design, and construction team, the total costs for the mechanical and electrical systems were about $3.5 million below the initial budget estimates from the general contractor. At the same time, energy and water modeling indicated a 61 percent savings on future energy use and a 56 percent savings in water consumption. In other words, from a performance standpoint, this project delivered

Table 4.2
Incremental Capital Costs of 33 LEED-Certified Projects

Certification Level	Cost Premium	Number of Projects Analyzed
Certified	0.66%	8
Silver	2.11	18
Gold	1.82	6
Platinum	6.50	1
Average, all certification levels	1.84%	

Source: Gregory Kats et al., *The Costs and Financial Benefits of Green Buildings*, 2003, www.cap-e.com/ewebeditpro/items/O59F3303.ppt#1, accessed March 6, 2007.

"champagne on a beer budget."[4] This project demonstrates the benefits of an integrated design process and an experienced developer and design team willing to push the envelope of building design to produce a high-performance building on a conventional building budget.

The more often developers engage experienced green design and construction firms, and the more often they require their consultants to produce high-performance results (without excuses), the more likely it is that overall project costs will be about the same as the costs for a conventional project that lacks the beneficial characteristics of a high-level certified green project.

Many of the green building measures that give a building its greatest long-term value—for example, on-site energy production, on-site stormwater management and water recycling, green roofs, daylighting, and natural ventilation—often require a higher capital cost. Many project teams are finding that these costs can be paid for by avoiding other costs, such as stormwater and sewer connection fees, or by using local utility incentives, state tax breaks, and federal tax credits.

While it is possible to build a LEED basic Certified (and sometimes LEED Silver) building at no additional cost, as building teams try to make a building truly sustainable, cost increments often accrue. This is especially true when the building owner or developer wants to showcase their green building with more expensive (but visible) measures such as green roofs or photovoltaics for on-site power production, or where there is a strong commitment to green materials such as certified wood products.

The Davis Langdon Cost Studies

As more projects are LEED-certified, it is becoming easier to identify LEED-related and green building–related costs, making it easier to budget for such costs in the next project. It is also becoming cheaper to realize green building goals, especially LEED certification, as more building teams and consultants learn how to achieve these goals within conventional building budgets.

A 2004 study by the international cost-management firm of Davis Langdon offered evidence, based on 94 different building projects of vastly different types, that the most important determinant of project cost is not the level of LEED certification sought, but rather other more conventional issues such as the building program goals, type of construction, and the local construction economy at the time. In this study, the authors concluded that there was no statistically significant evidence that green buildings cost more per square foot than conventional projects, primarily because so many factors influence the cost of any particular type of building.[5] The analysis was updated in late 2006, with one example shown in Figure 4.1. From these results, one should expect more pressure from owners and developers for design and construction teams to aim for high LEED goals, because these buildings are indeed perceived to offer higher value for the money spent.

The study's authors comment, "From this analysis we conclude that many projects achieve sustainable design within their initial budget, or with very small supplemental funding. This suggests that owners are finding ways to incorporate project goals and values, regardless of budget, by making choices. However, there is no one-size-fits-all answer. Each building project is unique and should be considered as such when addressing the cost and feasibility of LEED. Benchmarking with other comparable projects can be valuable and informative, but not predictive."

Davis Langdon also studied the impact of climate zone, for example, on the costs of a research lab; it showed a premium ranging from 2.7 to 6.3 percent for a LEED Gold project and from 1.0 to 3.7 percent for a LEED Silver project, assuming that the same design was constructed in various cities at the same time.[6]

The key cost message to owners and developers (and design and construction teams) is that sustainability needs to be a "program" issue; that

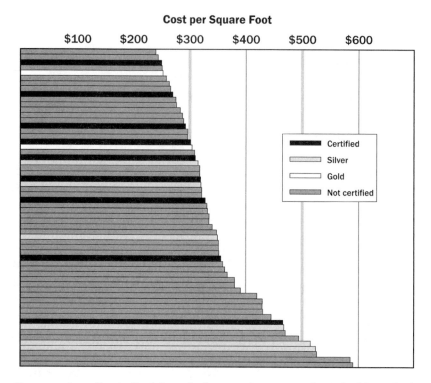

Cost per Square Foot

Figure 4.1. According to Davis Langdon's research, green academic buildings don't always cost more. Courtesy of Davis Langdon, redrawn with permission.

is, it needs to be embedded in the goals of the project and not treated as an add-on cost element. This conclusion is not just a matter of semantics; it goes to the very heart of the question "What is the purpose of this building or project?" If sustainability is not a core purpose, then it's going to cost more; if it is essential to the undertaking, then costs will be in line with non-green buildings of the same type.

Recent examples of academic LEED projects built with no additional cost, however, indicate that design and construction teams are learning how to deliver high performance on conventional budgets. Leith Sharp, director of the Harvard University Green Campus Initiative (profiled in Chapter 9), says, "We've focused a lot of energy on reducing any cost associated with green building design through effective process management. As a result we've just completed a LEED Platinum project that had no added cost."[7]

The 2004 GSA Cost Study

A 2004 federally funded study of the costs of achieving various levels of LEED certification for government buildings looked at both new construction and remodels. It drew somewhat opposite conclusions from the Davis Langdon study and supports somewhat similar conclusions to the work of Kats in 2003 for the state of California. For example, in the California analysis, a $40 million public building seeking a LEED Gold certification might expect to budget about 2 percent, or $800,000, extra to achieve this rating.

Table 4.3 shows the results of the 2004 study, which was undertaken for the U.S. General Services Administration (GSA). It carefully detailed two typical projects, a new federal courthouse (with 262,000 square feet and a construction cost of $220 per gross square foot) and an office building modification (with 307,000 square feet and a construction cost of $130 per gross square foot). At that time, the study's estimates of the additional capital costs of both types of GSA projects ranged from negligible for LEED-certified projects up to 4 percent for Silver certification and 8 percent for Gold.[8]

Soft costs (i.e., nonconstruction costs) for design and documentation services were also estimated in the "GSA LEED Cost Study," and ranged from about 40 to 80 cents per square foot (0.2 to 0.4 percent) for the courthouse and 35 to 70 cents per square foot (0.3 to 0.6 percent) for the office building modernization project. One caution: the added percentage of total cost may be higher for smaller projects. Therefore, each building team should look at every cost that a project will incur, from permitting to site development to furniture and fixtures, before deciding that a particular green measure is "too costly." Deciding which costs are going to provide the highest value in a given situation is a primary task of the architect, working in concert with the client, the building owner or developer, and the builder.

More recent work in 2006 by Davis Langdon on 130 projects resulted in these conclusions: Most projects by good design teams have "embedded" 12 LEED points (out of 26 needed for certification), and most could add 18 points to get certified with minimal total cost, through an integrated design approach.[9] Of 60 LEED-seeking projects that were analyzed, over half received no supplemental budget to support sustainable goals. Of those that received additional funding, the supplement was typically less than 5 percent, and supplemental funding was usually for specific enhancements, most commonly photovoltaics.

Table 4.3
Incremental Costs of LEED-Certifying Two Prototypical GSA Projects

Level of LEED Certification	Range of Green Cost Premiums (% of total construction cost)	
Building Type	New Courthouse	Office Modernization
Certified	−0.4% to 1.0%	1.4% to 2.1%
Silver	−0.0% to 4.4%	3.1% to 4.2%
Gold	1.4% to 8.1%	7.8% to 8.2%

Integrated Design Reduces Costs

If you were to ask experienced architects and engineers, developers, and builders how to reduce the costs of green buildings, I think the first thing they would all say is that an integrated design process, similar to that shown in Figure 4.2, is essential. If time is not taken to bring together all of the relevant parties and study alternatives before fixing on a final design, a project may miss opportunities to make single systems carry out multiple tasks. Without an effort to integrate the various design disciplines, for instance, individual subsystems (such as the HVAC system) may be optimized, but the system as a whole may be "pessimized."[10] In other words, a project might pay more for a more efficient chiller for a building, and get more energy savings. But if the team took the same amount of money and spent it on conservation, they could have achieved three to ten times the energy savings of just an efficient air conditioning system.

Gail Lindsey, an experienced green architect based in North Carolina, shares her experience with cost management:

Early questioning is essential. The best thing that I can do is ask questions. For example, I recently went to an interview for a waste facility project. The client wanted a building for their offices and space for public education. The conceptual design proposed a brand-new building. But when I visited the site, I noticed that the old building had a lot of cool old sculptural features. I suggested that they move those old pieces outside into a garden and use them to tell the story of what they used to do. I also suggested that they renovate the existing building and use it for an auditorium and public education center. The client loved the idea because it will help to pre-

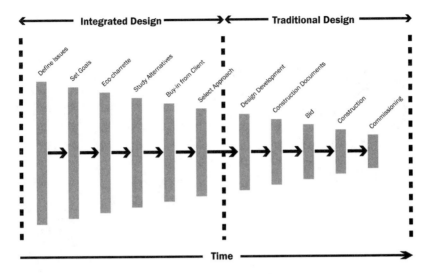

Figure 4.2. The opportunities for integrated design diminish over time.

serve the history of the place, the history of waste, and how they learned from their past mistakes.[11]

This story illustrates a key precept of integrated design: asking the right questions at the right time. Integrated design follows several basic steps. It begins with the project team holding goal-setting sessions in which green building measures are introduced. Either concurrently or soon thereafter, the project team holds an eco-charrette, to get the best ideas out in the open for everyone's consideration. With an experienced facilitator, this process often results in lower overall project costs and much higher building performance. Figure 4.3 shows Gail Lindsey facilitating such a charrette for a public-sector project.

The integrated design process, particularly for a LEED-registered project, typically covers the following steps:

- Analyzing green building and LEED-related design tasks, with specific assignments to each design team member
- Coaching and facilitation by an experienced green building expert
- Modeling key energy-using systems, typically by the mechanical engineer; this process may include daylighting modeling, with a

Figure 4.3. Opening charrette session with the facilitator, Gail Lindsey, setting goals and expectations and reviewing the agenda. Photo by Judy Kincaid, courtesy of Gail Lindsey.

lighting designer or electrical engineer, and often involves modeling initial and life-cycle costs of various alternative methods for achieving comfort, health, and productivity in the building

- Researching materials, usually done by the architect in conjunction with the contractor
- Preparing "green" specifications for the construction team
- Construction-period monitoring to ensure that green goals and measures are not compromised, often in partnership with the general contractor
- Commissioning the building near completion to make sure that all energy-using systems are working according to design intent
- If going for LEED certification, documenting the achievement of specific LEED requirements, often done by a specialized green-building consultant

Each of these steps has specific cost and schedule implications, and each needs to be thought about from the beginning of the process if green buildings are to stay within their budgets, which are often established well in advance of the decision to seek LEED certification.

Relating her own experience with building teams in western Pennsylvania, Rebecca Flora, executive director of the Pittsburgh-based Green Building Alliance, says:

> We're finding that there is still a limited amount of knowledge of how to do green projects well, particularly as it relates to integrated design capacity. People are doing the projects and getting the LEED certification, but they're not necessarily delivering the most effective and efficient results.
>
> To help control costs, the first thing we do is to help people understand that green building should not be a LEED point-chasing game. We ask them to step back for a moment, and we ask, "What do you value? What's important to you? What kind of building do you want? How does it relate to who you are as a company or organization?" We ask them to focus first on their values and then rethink how to use the LEED system as a tool to help achieve those values and goals. What I've found is that it's often being done in reverse, which is not a good approach.[12]

If you're just setting out to build your first green building, green development, or green renovation project, the most important advice is this: Establish your goals for the project; do your homework by visiting other projects and learn from their experiences. Retain a knowledgeable green building consultant to help you manage a building process that is goal-focused, not "point-focused."

Chapter 5
The Future of Green Buildings

In December 2006, the largest advertising agency in the United States, JWT Worldwide, published a list of 70 trends to watch in 2007.[1] In seventh place was "sustainable construction/green buildings." This trend is unmistakable. In 2006, just about every major business magazine and most large newspapers published cover stories and multiple articles on the "Green Trend," many of them focusing on green buildings.

In 2006, Wal-Mart announced a $500 million commitment to energy-efficiency upgrades to its stores; it had previously completed two green-building experimental stores in Colorado and Texas. The Lowe's home improvement chain completed a LEED-certified project in Austin, Texas. PNC Bank, a large mid-Atlantic financial institution, has LEED-certified nearly 40 bank branches. Private businesses all over the United States and Canada are beginning to see the value of "greening" their buildings.

Green Building Growth Rates by Market Sector

A recent survey conducted for the U.S. Green Building Council projected market growth for various building sectors, shown in Table 5.1.[2] Note that the "education" sector includes both the higher education and K-12 sectors. What's notable about the table is that the sectors projected to grow the fastest are those that have seen the most activity so far: education, government, institutional, and office. Other market sectors such as health care, residential, hospitality, and retail are still finding their way into green buildings. But when Starbucks announces that it plans to build 10,000 stores over the next four years, it won't be long before the company decides that its customers and employee-associates want green stores.[3] The same holds for other major retailers, hotel chains, health care providers, and large homebuilders. For these market segments, the green building revolution is just getting started!

Table 5.1
Projected Annual Growth Rates for Green Buildings

Market Sector	Growth Rate
Education	65%
Government	62%
Institutional	54%
Office	48%
Health care	46%
Residential	32%
Hospitality	22%
Retail	20%

Source: *Education Green Building SmartMarket Report,* McGraw-Hill Construction Research & Analytics, 2007, available at www.construction.com/greensource/resources/smartmarket.asp.

Green Building Market Drivers

A number of important trend factors, shown in Table 5.2, favor the continued rapid growth of green buildings over the next five years.

More Commercial and Institutional Green Projects

First, the commercial and institutional green building market continues to grow by more than 50 percent per year (see Figure 1.2). In 2006, cumulative LEED-NC registered projects and project area grew by 50 percent, and LEED-NC certified projects grew by nearly 70 percent. LEED statistics indicate considerable growth potential ahead for commercial green buildings as well as high-rise and midrise residential projects (a dozen or more of the LEED-NC certified projects are in fact midrise to high-rise multifamily residential units, both apartments and condominiums).

The growth of the market tends to accelerate; as more green projects are built, costs are reduced, leading to more cost-effective projects, which tips the scales in favor of building even more projects. Greater publicity for green buildings leads to more pressure on companies to specify green design for their next building project. For these and many other reasons, I expect the exponential growth of the green building market, which began in 2000, to continue for the foreseeable future, at least through 2012.

In 2006, the LEED rating system registered more than 1,100 new projects, totaling nearly 140 million square feet of space, averaging about 120,000 square feet of gross building area per project. I predict that the total

Table 5.2
Drivers for Green Building Growth

Driver	Expected Importance to 2012
1. Growing evidence for the business case benefits of green buildings	Significant driver; productivity gains and utility savings can easily balance most cost increases
2. More commercial and institutional green projects	Significant – will totally transform the building industry within next five years
3. Energy Policy Act of 2005 (assuming extension past 2012)	Increasing over time, as economics of renewable energy gets better each year
4. New local government, utility and state government tax incentives for green buildings and renewable energy	Significant influence, particularly if they provide for governments and nonprofits to pass on the benefits to the private sector
5. Higher oil and natural gas prices	Significant, especially for changes in consumer psychology
6. Movement back into the cities	Moderate impact, but will open up new markets for urban infill with green projects
7. Changes in cultural patterns, to favor more environmentally friendly lifestyles	Moderate impact, a long-standing trend that will increase the market for green home improvements and healthier buildings
8. More green homes on the marketplace, leading to growing demand for them	Significant, since residential construction revenues, even in 2007, are larger than commercial and institutional
9. Local government incentives and mandates for green buildings	Small at this time, but potentially huge impact on private sector's willingness to "go green"
10. Growing awareness of the role played by buildings in carbon dioxide emissions	Potentially large growth in building energy conservation investments
11. Growing pressure on companies to conduct sustainable operations	Potentially moderately positive impact on the demand for green offices
12. Slowdown in homebuilding market causes builders to "build green" for competitive reason	Low to moderate impact, owing to poorly articulated buyer demand for green homes

number of LEED-registered projects will increase more than threefold through 2010, and will continue to increase at more than 25 percent per year even through 2012.[4]

By the end of 2006, the USGBC system had certified more than 660 LEED projects in its four rating categories. Growth in LEED-certified projects means that people everywhere will continue to see more information about green buildings in their cities and towns. I believe this information will translate into significantly increased activity in both the commercial and the residential green building markets, both for new homes and for conservation retrofits.

The USGBC believes that we are on the cusp of an "explosion" in green building activity that could increase these estimates dramatically within the next three to five years. That growth would represent far more "revolution" than "evolution." But everyone agrees that green building growth will far outpace the general growth of the building industry over the next five years. For example, commercial construction in 2007 is predicted to increase 12.7 percent, after a 13.5 percent increase in 2006. Residential construction (including both new housing and remodels) in 2007 is predicted to decrease 7.8 percent, after a 1.8 percent decrease in 2006.[5]

Tax Incentives

Both the federal Energy Policy and Conservation Act of 2005 (and its extension passed by Congress in 2006) contain increased incentives for residential solar electric and water heating systems, as shown in Table 5.3. And the law provides a tax credit for homebuilders of $2,000 per energy-efficient residential unit; that incentive should spur them to build more such homes.

The array of new state and federal solar photovoltaic incentives will likely produce a rapid rise in small (1.0 - to 2.5-kilowatt) solar electric and rooftop solar water-heating systems—the most visible way for homeowners to show that they are doing something to save energy. California Governor Arnold Schwarzenegger's solar initiatives have played a role in kick-starting the solar industry in his state, the nation's largest market. In addition, New Mexico passed a major green-building tax credit in 2007, and Oregon has a 35 percent tax credit for solar energy systems.

Higher Oil and Natural Gas Prices

By 2007, prolonged oil prices above $50 to $60 per barrel had changed the psychology of consumers and businesses for the first time in a generation. The new reality of energy is that it's a seller's market, and prices will climb as new supplies become harder to find and extract. Over time, this will likely translate into higher electricity and gas prices for residential use and more interest in investing in conservation.

In fact, this shift is already taking place. For example, market studies for the Seattle area's King-Snohomish Master Builders Association in 2003, well

Table 5.3

National Energy Policy Act of 2005: Key Provisions for Commercial Green Buildings

Affected Technology	Tax Credit
Photovoltaics	30% (residential limit is $2,000 credit)
Solar thermal systems	30% (residential limit is $2,000 credit)
Microturbines	10% (up to $200/kW credit)
Energy conservation investments for HVAC, envelope, lighting, and water heating systems	$1.80/square foot (federal tax deduction if exceeding 50% savings vs. ASHRAE 90.1-2001 standard); up to $0.60 per square foot for lighting retrofits alone
New homes exceeding 50% energy savings vs. model code	$2,000 credit for site-built homes

Source: IRS Bulletin #2006-26, June 26, 2006, www.irs.gov/pub/irs-irbs06-26.pdf, accessed June 3, 2007.

before the current rise in energy prices, showed a willingness by homebuyers to pay 1 percent more, for example, about $2,500 on a $250,000 home, for a new residence with an energy-efficiency package. By 2007, it seems likely that the willingness to pay more may have increased to something approaching $5,000, especially with awareness of the need to combat global warming with less wasteful homes.

Movement Back into the Cities

Over the past four decades, America has experienced the emergence of a new demographic segment made up of people working in knowledge-intensive businesses. The rise of this "creative class," first chronicled by Richard Florida in 2002,[6] has the potential to change American demographic patterns as dramatically as the rise of Levittown and the suburban lifestyle did after World War II.

An increasing trend for creatives and baby boomers is to relocate into one of the top 30 major metropolitan areas. They want connectedness, they want the amenities of urban living, and they don't want to commute for hours each day for the privilege of mowing a patch of grass on Saturdays. This trend is already evident in Atlanta, Chicago, Boston, New York, Portland, Seattle, and San Francisco.

Boomers and creatives are especially well represented in the Lifestyles of Health and Sustainability (LOHAS) market segment of American consumers, said to encompass up to 30 percent of the U.S. population.[7] LOHAS consumers, 60 percent of whom are women, have a particular interest in health and fitness, the environment, personal development, and sustainable living. And the metropolitan areas that attract them are also home to more-sophisticated builders who understand the need for green homes, condos, and apartments.

This trend alone will lead to more energy-efficient homes and remodels, with a heavy focus on already existing urban landscapes. The continued movement of boomers back into urban cores can be expected to bring more discriminating buyers to urban infill housing and condo developments, giving an advantage to builders with a stronger "green" product differentiation. Boomers remaining in their existing homes will want to upgrade them to be energy efficient, both to save on future utility costs and to show sensitivity to such issues as global warming and environmental protection.

More Green Homes on the Market

The growing number of successful green-home developments with a strong focus on solar and conservation features, in all major growth regions, including Florida, California, and the rest of the Sunbelt, will give developers confidence in their ability to deliver a high-performance green development on a conventional budget. A good example is Shea Homes in San Diego. The country's 10th-largest builder, Shea developed a package of energy conservation and solar technologies in 2001. Their new product line, the High Performance Home, meets the requirements of an Energy Star home, meaning it is designed to expend 15 percent less energy on heating, cooling, and water heating than a similar home built to 2004 International Residential Code standards.[8] (In 2006, nearly 175,000 new homes were Energy Star certified.)[9] High Performance Homes are fitted with advanced features, including radiant barrier roof sheathing that reflects heat away from the attic, as well as thermostatic expansion valves that are designed to improve HVAC system performance. In addition to these energy-efficiency measures, these homes incorporate passive solar thermal water heating as well as solar photovoltaics for electricity production.[10]

The LEED for Homes rating system, now in its pilot phase or beta test, with 300 projects and about 6,000 homes, will roll out a standard version in the fall of 2007. Given the success of the LEED for New Construction (LEED-NC) rating system and the growing recognition of the LEED brand name, LEED-H should begin to affect the residential market significantly in 2008 to 2010. Other local programs, such as the homebuilders' Built Green Colorado (licensed to builders' associations in seven states now) and local utility programs, as well as the voluntary certification program of the National Association of Home Builders (NAHB), should keep the new-home energy-efficiency market growing rapidly.

Local Government Incentives

More cities that have subscribed to climate change initiatives will begin to require residential projects to construct green buildings—especially when they are large developments with major infrastructure impacts. In 2006, Washington, D.C., required all new commercial buildings over 50,000 square feet to meet the LEED standard by 2009. Also in 2006, Boston announced that it would put green building standards into its building code.

These requirements and policy directions for commercial buildings will spill over into the homebuilding market throughout the next half-decade. In 2004 to 2006, many states, large universities, and cities began to require LEED Silver certification (or better) from their own building programs. The increasing use of voluntary certification programs by homebuilders, such as the NAHB's Model Green Home Building Guidelines and the various utility programs, can perhaps be viewed as a way to forestall legislative action by states and cities; the green building trend is likely to overwhelm these efforts over the next five years.

Growing Awareness of Carbon Dioxide Emissions and Global Warming

The U.S. Environmental Protection Agency's Energy Star program will also be used to promote energy-efficient and zero-net-energy, or carbon-neutral, buildings. We will begin seeing buildings routinely cut energy use to 50 percent or more below 2006 levels through integrated design and innovative technological approaches.

With the growing awareness of the carbon dioxide problem and the contribution of buildings and urban settlement patterns to global warming, architects and others in the design and construction industry have begun to propose positive actions. One sign of this is the position statement adopted by the American Institute of Architects (AIA) in December 2005, calling for a minimum 50 percent reduction in building energy consumption by 2010.[11] In its statement, the AIA supported "the development and use of rating systems and standards that promote the design and construction" of more re-source-efficient communities.

The attention given in 2006 and 2007 to the dramatic call for energy-use reduction by a new nonprofit, Architecture 2030, will also affect homebuilding in the next five years.[12] By showing for the first time the enormous contribution of residential and commercial buildings to carbon-dioxide emissions, Edward Mazria, a well-known architect who founded Architecture 2030, managed to escalate the discussion about green buildings from a "nice idea" to a planetary imperative. Through his influence, the entire architecture profession was put on notice that energy-efficient, green buildings are no longer just one option among many for a new building or renovation, but a "front and center" priority. Collaborating with key players in the building industry, Architecture 2030 issued the "2030 Challenge," a program and set of guidelines to reduce energy use in buildings by 90 percent in 2030, compared with a 2003 baseline. The first step is a goal to reduce energy use in new buildings by 50 percent compared with the 2003 average energy consumption. By mid-2007, the US Conference of Mayors and the American Institute of Architects had formally adopted these guidelines.

Pressure on Companies to Conduct Sustainable Operations

The burden of more socially responsible activities increasingly falls on public companies, major commercial developers, and homebuilders. For example, just to get projects permitted, built, and sold, companies will increasingly have to build green buildings. To recruit top talent, the source of growth in revenues and profits, green buildings will form an integral part of a company's sustainability "story."

The top 10 homebuilders now account for more than 25 percent of all new homes in the country.[13] Look for the corporate governance and socially responsible investing movements to influence how these large homebuilders plan, design, and market their homes. More capital is flowing into socially responsible real estate investment funds, and these will in turn influence how green projects are conceived, developed, leased, and sold.

The Competitive Advantage of Green Homes

The slowdown in the homebuilding market in 2006 and 2007, likely to last for several years, may spur more builders toward constructing green homes and finding a point of differentiation that will resonate with an increasingly educated, socially conscious, and environmentally concerned consumer base.

People are already responding to the idea of low-energy-use homes, for both economic and social reasons. It won't be long before major home-builders start retooling their models to be more energy efficient and to be certified as such by some reputable organization. Strong evidence for that belief is the fact that Energy Star homes certified 174,000 single-family residential units in 2006, 12 percent of the nation's individual site-built housing starts.[14]

The Larger Picture

Reducing carbon dioxide emissions from the buildings sector is critical to our ability to combat global warming. Energy-efficient design and operation of buildings, along with on-site renewable energy production, are a strong part of the answer to the challenge to Americans to reduce their ecological footprint.

Figure 5.1 shows the divergence in carbon dioxide emissions between now and 2050 under two scenarios: "business as usual" and with a strong carbon-release mitigation program. It demonstrates how important green buildings are to the efforts to bring carbon dioxide emissions back to 1990 levels, as required by the Kyoto Protocol, so that we can stabilize carbon dioxide concentrations in the atmosphere.

Jim Broughton is a business development manager in Houston with a manufacturer of energy-efficiency equipment for buildings, power generation and industrial processes. From his vantage point, he sees a dramatically altered future for property holdings:

> The asset value of buildings that are not energy-efficient will get hammered if owners do not build or renovate for low energy use—particularly as energy costs rise. Buildings are responsible for about 40% of our nation's carbon emissions, primarily because of consumption of electrical power. Given this fact, carbon dioxide emissions regulations will be focused on power producers who may, in turn, force building owners to conserve by linking power rates to the building's carbon footprint. In addition to present tax incentives for reducing energy consumption, there is a strong pos-

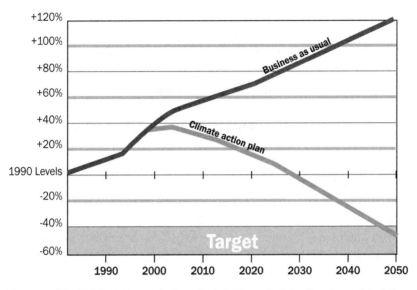

Figure 5.1. The U.S. building sector's projected CO_2 emissions. Courtesy of Architecture 2030, redrawn with permission.

sibility that regulators will consider a carbon tax disincentive to stimulate renovation of high energy-use buildings. As owners and property managers realize carbon dioxide regulations are likely and buildings will be a prime target, renovations of existing buildings for energy-use reductions should accelerate dramatically.[15]

Barriers to Green Buildings and Green Development

Still, there are barriers to the widespread adoption of green building techniques, technologies, and systems, some of them related to real-life experience and the rest to the perception in the building industry that green buildings add extra cost (see Chapter 4). Senior executives representing architectural and engineering firms, consultants, developers, building owners, corporate owner-occupants, and educational institutions have positive attitudes about the benefits and costs of green construction, according to the 2005 Green Building Market Barometer, a survey cited in Chapter 3.[16]

Another survey of the building industry, published in 2006, revealed similar findings:[17]

- 57 percent of the 872 building owners and developers surveyed said it was hard to justify the greater initial costs of green buildings.
- 56 percent said green buildings added significantly to the initial cost.
- 52 percent said the market was not willing to pay a premium for green buildings.
- 36 percent said the certification process was too complicated, with too much paperwork.
- 30 percent said the market was not comfortable with new ideas or new technologies.
- Only 14 percent did not see sustainable design as a market barrier.

Jim Goldman is a project executive with Turner Construction Company in Seattle and was co-chair of the national committee for LEED-NC. He has had a front-row seat at the green building revolution over the past seven years, delivering green projects to institutional and commercial building owners. He says, "In private work, the biggest barrier is the unequal distribution of benefits between developers and tenants." Developers have to put up the money, but tenants reap most of the benefits. Another barrier, says Goldman, "is the amount of time within the building cycle. During the design phase, the owner isn't necessarily committed to green building; and because of integrated design, it can take some time to get optimal answers," but time is often in short supply. Goldman also says that cost is always a barrier—both construction cost and the cost of services for studying green options and for certifying the projects. Nevertheless, he says, "in five years green building will be ubiquitous."[18]

Triggers for Green Building

The top triggers for green building among building owners are shown in Table 5.4.[19] From this list, it's easy to see that the prime motivator for owners is reducing energy costs. As a result of the new awareness of rising energy costs for electricity, oil, and natural gas, we expect more building owners and developers to be urging their design teams to cut energy use 30 percent or more below the ASHRAE 90.1-2004 standards found in LEED version 2.2.

Table 5.4
Green Building Triggers for Building Owners

Key Issue	Percentage of Owners Mentioning Issue
Energy cost increases/utility rebates	74%
Achieving superior energy performance	68%
Lower life-cycle operating costs	64%
Have a positive environmental impact	60%
Easier to get LEED certification now	54%
Secure a competitive advantage	53%
Respond to government regulations	53%
Secure productivity benefits	53%

Source: *Education Green Building SmartMarket Report*, McGraw-Hill Construction Research & Analytics, 2007, available at www .construction.com/greensource/resources/smartmarket.asp.

Over the next few years, I predict that securing competitive advantage and gaining access to good investors will move up to the top of the list of triggers. As Hines' Jerry Lea says, "We were the first to create an investment fund for green buildings. We had investors approach us and ask if we would participate in such a fund. We created the fund with CalPERS [in 2006, for $123 million], the California state employees pension fund. It's been very successful and we anticipate that another green fund will follow it, simply because it has been successful."[20]

Beyond LEED

Many leading voices in the green building industry are beginning to look at how to move beyond LEED requirements, toward buildings and neighborhoods that are "restorative" or "regenerative" (or "biophilic"[21]), providing all of their own power (at least on an annual average) and most or all of their water, along with restoring habitat and, in some cases, restoring natural stream drainage patterns. Many of these projects aim to use renewable energy systems to achieve their goals. At least through the end of 2008, the solar energy tax credits contained in the Energy Policy Act of 2005 should facilitate many more projects with integrated photovoltaics, solar water heating, and similar approaches to using "free" on-site resources.[22]

As to the merit of going beyond LEED, architect Gail Lindsey says, "Much of the green development that's going on now is at the most basic level; it is really about doing less bad, attempting to slow down the damage. We need to move on to the restorative and regenerative levels—ultimately, make the place better than it was before."[23] Programs such as the Living Building Challenge of the Cascadia Green Building Council aim to encourage architects and engineers to create buildings that have a small to negligible ecological footprint.[24]

The USGBC plans to change LEED significantly by 2008 so that it focuses more heavily on reducing carbon dioxide emissions from buildings, moves away from a "one size fits all" system toward one that is more responsive to regional environmental and energy use issues, and takes into account the life-cycle assessment of building systems and building materials. While I do not expect the LEED system to disappear anytime soon, I expect that it will become more flexible and even more embedded in building codes and standard practices of architects, engineers, and builders. In that way, the USGBC's goal of market transformation of the building industry will see its full realization.

Chapter 6
The International Green Building Revolution

While the United States is the global leader in green buildings, based on the rapid adoption of the LEED system, some European countries have been using green building assessment tools for the past ten years. Other countries have also moved ahead to develop their own green building rating systems and further transform the building industry.

European assessment tools include the United Kingdom's BREEAM system,[1] which has certified hundreds of thousands of buildings,[2] and GB Tool, developed and owned by Natural Resources Canada, a federal government agency. The green building revolution is just picking up steam in Europe, however. Most of these green building evaluation tools are the products of governments and research universities, and there has often been a "disconnect" between them and the practicing world of architects and engineers.

LEED's particular strength has been as a product of collaboration between the often divergent incentives, motivations, and even vocabulary of building industry practitioners, government agencies, and a number of environmental nonprofits, such as the Natural Resources Defense Council. More than any other tool, LEED is a guide for sustainable design that can be used by architects, engineers, contractors, building owners, and developers during the design and construction process.

Elsewhere around the world, Australia has the popular Green Star rating system, Japan has the CASBEE system, and Canada has its own version of LEED. Both Canada and India have licensed the USGBC's LEED rating system for adaptation to their own building environments.[3]

Table 6.1

Status of Green Building Activity in Selected Countries

Country	Ranking/Score
United States	59
Hong Kong	57
Taiwan	55
China	49
Australia	47
(tie) New Zealand/United Arab Emirates	45
India	44

Source: Australian Trade Commission (Austrade), presentation given by Elizabeth Gordon, Senior Trade Adviser, Government of Australia, at the Green Cities '07 conference, Sydney, Australia, February 2007.

Global Green Building Status

Table 6.1 shows the status of green building in eight countries, ranked according to a number of variables, including starting date of green building activity, government commitment, strength of industry association, corporate business commitment, membership in the World Green Building Council, existence of a green building rating system, number of green buildings, and short-term outlook for green building growth. A higher score indicates a higher level of green building activity. While admittedly arbitrary, it does give a sense of where the U.S. green building revolution stands in the entire pantheon.

The World Green Building Council

Leading the charge for the LEED approach in the international arena is the World Green Building Council (World GBC),[4] formed in 1999 by David Gottfried, a co-founder of the USGBC. Currently consisting of ten member countries, including the United States and Canada, the World GBC is taking the green building message around the world.

Kevin Hydes of Stantec Consulting in Montreal became the chair of the World GBC in 2007. He reports seeing a massive uptake in green-building policy and business practice over the past few years, driven primarily by the climate change agenda. Barriers are coming down, Hydes says, as the role of carbon dioxide emissions in driving climate change is becoming understood by the public. Cost has become less of a barrier because of improvements in green building design practice and better communication of results. Hydes believes that "the main barrier emerging is simply the size of the problem that we face and the capacity of the building industry to tackle it."[5] As a result, he believes that the strategies unfolding globally are those that focus on performance of the rating tools themselves, speed of introducing green buildings into industry, and the ability to "scale" responses quickly enough.

The World Green Building Council is becoming a catalyst for action in many countries. According to its executive director, Huston Eubank, an American architect based in Montreal, "The main thing that the World GBC is doing to help form new chapters is providing information and moral support. We provide a road map that distills a lot of good experience about the sequential steps required to successfully launch a country's green building council." Each country is unique, says Eubank, and each has its own catalyst for the green building movement.

> The movement in Malaysia, where the government does a high percentage of the construction, started because they had a brand-new hospital that had serious indoor air quality problems. Basically it was a simple situation; they hadn't opened the hospital yet and weren't operating the building systems, so they had a lot of mold growth. That focused a lot of national attention on that issue, and it was very embarrassing for the government. In Malaysia, in spite of having energy efficiency and water conservation agencies, the indoor air quality issue is what drove them to green building. In the process of forming a council, they realized it is a great way to increase the synergy and visibility of all their existing efforts.[6]

Canada

Because of its proximity to the United States and the strong cross-border trade in architectural and engineering services, Canada is far along in developing a domestic green building industry. The Canadian Green Building Council had more than 1,300 members as of early 2007, a number that in relative terms is bigger than the USGBC membership. More than 60 percent of the membership is from the provinces of British Columbia and Ontario.[7]

British Columbia was an early adopter of green building standards; for example, the City of Vancouver adopted a policy in 2004 that all public buildings had to achieve LEED Gold certification (at that time, under the U.S. system). It was the first municipality in North America to adopt this high standard for its own buildings.

As of early 2007, more than 420 projects were registered for certification under LEED for Canada or BC LEED, the provincial standard in British Columbia. Given that Canada has about one-tenth of the U.S. population, this is close to the relative level of U.S. activity. Prior to the advent of LEED for Canada, 17 LEED-NC projects were certified under the U.S. standard. As of March 2007, more than 60 Canadian projects had already been certified under either the U.S. or Canadian LEED standards, including the first LEED for Canada Platinum-rated project, the Operations Centre at the Gulf Islands National Park Reserve, an 11,600-square-foot building. The project uses an ocean-based geothermal heating system: ocean water is pumped into the building and passes through a heat exchanger and heat pumps to extract and upgrade the available heat energy to heat the building. Photovoltaic panels provide 20 percent of the building's annual energy needs. The Operations Centre is designed to use only 25 percent of the annual energy of a comparable building.[8]

For the future, the major driver of green buildings in Canada is likely to be federal and provincial policies to reduce Canada's greenhouse gas emissions, reports Thomas Mueller, executive director of the Canada Green Building Council.[9] He says the barriers to green buildings include higher costs, lack of industry knowledge about how to create green buildings on conventional budgets, the lack of good data on green building markets, and institutional barriers such as building codes and local regulations. In Canada, British Columbia has been the clear market leader in adopting green buildings, but activity in Ontario (especially around the Toronto area) is picking up quickly, with a third major node of activity in Alberta.

A 2006 international study for the Canada Mortgage and Housing Corporation, "Sustainable Building Policy Initiatives,"[10] noted that while national governments provide leadership to the green building movements in Europe and Asia, in North America the movements are led by municipal government, nonprofit, and private-sector initiatives. For years, national policies elsewhere strategically managed national priorities of energy, emissions, and water. The study found that Canada is now lagging in this indus-

Figure 6.1. Designed by Larry McFarland Architects Ltd., the Operations Centre at the Gulf Islands National Park Reserve in British Columbia received a Canadian LEED Platinum certification. Photo by dereklepper.com, courtesy of Larry McFarland Architects Ltd.

try sector from a broad national perspective, although some municipalities and developments are working to be keenly green. Using per-capita carbon dioxide emissions as an indicator of efficiency, Canada, the United States, and Australia have far to go in increasing energy efficiency, since they have much higher emissions rates than the European Union countries.

China

China and India, two of the biggest potential markets for the green building industry, are busy developing their own approaches to green buildings. I attended China's first Intelligent and Green Building national conference in Beijing in March 2005, which had about 1,500 delegates. As the host of the 2008 Beijing Summer Olympic Games, China is moving quickly to build a number of very large green buildings, which is in turn spurring local efforts to learn about sustainable design and green buildings and to adopt them as quickly as possible. At the Intelligent and Green Building conference, for example, I learned about China's focus on energy efficiency in buildings. Given the rapid growth of energy use in China and the difficulty of growing electricity supply fast enough to meet surging demand, China's government chose to focus on building energy efficiency as its primary approach to green buildings. In cities like Shanghai and Hong Kong, home to many foreign companies that value the full range of green building benefits, some office developers have begun to certify Chinese projects against the U.S. LEED standard.[11]

A major new city for 3 million people is being designed as the world's first "zero-net-energy" town. The project, Dongtan Eco-City, adjacent to Shanghai on Chongming Island at the mouth of the Yangtze River, is a good example of sustainable town planning. A collaboration between the Shanghai Industrial Investment Corporation and the international planning and engineering firm Arup, Dongtan Eco-City is still in the planning phase. In the first phase, designed for 50,000 people on about 1,500 acres (630 hectares), there is a balance of 54 percent residential space and 46 percent commercial and industrial space.

Planning is focused on capturing and purifying water, generating no particulate emissions, promoting ecologically sensible waste management and recycling, reducing landfills that damage the environment, and creating combined heat and power systems that are linked to the use of renewable energy from solar, wind, and biomass, creating clean and reliable energy.[12] Planners expect to reduce the ecological footprint of Dongtan to about one-third that of Shanghai, if all proposed measures and systems are adopted.[13] Water consumption would be reduced by 43 percent and wastewater generation by 88 percent, providing a high level of wastewater reuse. Energy usage would be reduced by 64 percent, and emissions from power production would be eliminated, saving 350,000 metric tons of carbon dioxide emissions annually. Building a compact city with abundant public transit and reduced daily travel requirements would further reduce emissions from transport by 400,000 metric tons yearly. Other sustainable communities under design in China include Silo City (Coastal Greenland Real Estate Group), Linked Hybrid (Modern Real Estate Group), and the 2008 Olympic Village project (Guo Ao Investment and Development Company).

The green building consulting firm EMSI, headquartered in Washington, DC, entered China in 2001 and has since been involved in most of the more than 25 commercial green building and sustainable community projects. EMSI's president, Kenneth Langer, points out that the LEED rating system, which offers the greatest international recognition, has been used by every real estate developer and multinational company pursuing green building certification for their projects in China.[14]

Langer reports that the green building movement in China is still at an early stage, with the first projects becoming LEED-certified only in 2004. He points out that projects pursuing certification are very large, visible buildings in major cities, and that the demand for green building services is growing fastest among large *Fortune 500* companies, such as GE, Dow Chemical (R&D Center), Otis Elevator, Trane, Johnson Controls, Interface, Plantronics, and Carrefour, China's largest retailer. For Chinese developers of speculative office buildings, the primary drivers are the public relations and marketing benefit that would help them to secure international corporate tenants. One such project, the first to be awarded LEED certification (LEED-NC Silver), is the Frazer Place Service Apartments in Shenzhen, China, shown in Figure 6.2.

Langer believes that some of the barriers to green development are lack of technical know-how of the powerful and numerous local "design institutes"—quasi-public firms that do most of the architecture and engineering in China—the intense focus on keeping initial capital costs as low as possible and the lack of green building technologies and materials. In 2006 the Chinese central government issued its first draft of a national green building rating system and is currently establishing a national green building council. Langer expects these developments to accelerate demand for green buildings in China, and he predicts that green buildings will account for 2 percent of the new commercial building market by 2012. Given that nearly half of the world's building will occur in China between 2005 and 2015, even 2 percent of that market would be huge.[15]

India

In 2004, India certified the first LEED Platinum building in the world, the 20,000-square-foot CII-Sohrabji Godrej Green Business Centre in Hyderabad, the headquarters building for the Indian Green Building Council. In 2007, the Indian Green Building Council announced its own national

Figure 6.2. Frazer Place Service Apartments is the first building in China to receive LEED certification from the USGBC. Courtesy of EMSI.

rating system, similar to LEED, created under license from the USGBC. The Indian system was developed in close cooperation with the Confederation of Indian Industries (CII).[16]

U.S. green building consultant Kath Williams has worked for several years with the Indian green building movement. She reports that green building in India, "is in the awareness stage. If you look at a change process, the first step is awareness. When the president of India came to inaugurate the Green Business Centre—the first green platinum building there—that was attention-getting. In the U.S., the government has been supporting green building basically for the last 10 years and before that supporting energy efficiency and energy codes development. It's finally getting noticed. So all of the ground work that the U.S. has done is finally paying off. But for the general public in India, it's still at the early awareness stage."[17]

In India, industry is the leader. According to Williams, "The Confederation of Indian Industries is the number-one organization that's taken the lead on sustainable development and is pushing it forward. Those are all of the big industries—there are 4,000 big companies. The government has been supportive, but the leadership has come from industry. They established the Green Building Council and set up the Green Business Centre in Hyderabad."

The Indian Green Building Council projects 10 million square feet of green buildings by the end of 2008, up from 4 million at the end of 2005.[18] At an average of 100,000 square feet, this would indicate 100 such buildings in 2008, with 45 buildings added in 2008 alone. The council's goal is to have 100 such buildings being constructed per year by the 2010 to 2012 period. The country's "LEED-India" rating tool became the official standard on January 1, 2007.

Australia

Sydney, Australia, hosted the inaugural Green Cities conference early in 2007, sponsored by both the Green Building Council of Australia and the National Property Council of Australia, representing that country's powerful development industry.[19] At Green Cities '07, I observed great interest in promoting green buildings to handle the country's looming energy shortages and severe water shortages.

The Australian conference attracted 900 delegates from the design, construction, and development industry, a per-capita turnout that rivaled the USGBC's annual Greenbuild conference in Denver in November 2006.[20] The Green Building Council of Australia has adopted a system similar to LEED, called Green Star, that rates buildings from one to six stars. Three extraordinary projects are the Five Green Star–Office as Built speculative office building in Sydney known as 30 The Bond, and the first two Six Green Star (equivalent to LEED Platinum) buildings, both in Melbourne: Council House

Two, for the City of Melbourne, and 40 Albert Road. All would fit right in with LEED Platinum buildings anywhere in the world.

The 135,000-square-foot Council House Two project, Figure 6.3, diverts sewage flows from under the street, treats them, and reuses them for the building's toilets, a creative solution to Australia's major drought conditions. To keep out the strong northern sun in summer, the project features solar-powered movable louvers on the west facade. The project also has a green roof, with six vertical-axis wind turbines on top of the building. As of early 2007, more than 100 projects in Australia had registered for Green Star certification.[21] Also early in 2007, the New Zealand Green Building Council announced that it would adopt the Australian Green Star rating system.

Spain

The Spain Green Building Council was formed in 1998. The first LEED building in Europe was certified in Spain in 2005: the Alvento Business Park project in Madrid, a two-building, 355,000-square-foot, seven-story speculative commercial office development. Completed in 2003 by Spain's largest developer, Metrovacesa, both buildings certified at LEED Silver level. Costing $232 per square foot, the buildings house nearly 3,000 people and were fully leased within the first year, in an environment where other office buildings were partially vacant.[22] The modeled energy usage was 31 percent less than the usage in a conventional building, and water usage was estimated at 44 percent less than the usage in a standard office.

The founder and president of the Spain Green Building Council, Aurelio Ramírez-Zarzosa, reports that the European market is 10 to 15 years behind the United States, but many firms now starting projects in major cities are proposing to have them LEED-certified.[23] At present, he considers perceived higher costs and lack of education about sustainable design to be the primary barriers to the rapid growth of green buildings in Europe. He says that things have changed significantly since 1998, and he perceives an acceleration that began in late 2006: Since then, there have been more than twenty private companies and government bodies applying for or having an interest in LEED buildings, not only in Spain but in Italy and France as well. An example is the architect Cesar Pelli's tower for Iberdrola's headquarters in Bilbao (the firm is a major utility with wind farm operations in the U.S.).

Figure 6.3. The Council House Two building in Melbourne is a Five Green Star certified building, equivalent to LEED Gold. Courtesy of the City of Melbourne.

There is also an office complex by British architect Richard Rogers for Abergoa's headquarters in Seville (the firm is a major bio-ethanol producer with a big operation in the U.S.). The driver for the private sector is building certification and, in some cases, design firms observing that this is what companies want. "The companies want to get the medal [certification] to differentiate them," he says, "to get recognition by a third party because it is prestigious, something that is international. The driver is LEED, because it is international (and because the governmental system in Europe does not address the industry interests and needs), and they see that there are a lot of buildings that have been built that way [LEED]."[24]

Ramírez also reports that an early March 2007 visit to Madrid by Al Gore to show his film *An Inconvenient Truth* really shook up the Spanish building industry; as a result, he expects to see a renewed focus on energy-efficient and green buildings in the next three years. He also believes that LEED's provenance as an industry-developed system is viewed favorably by the Spanish and European design and construction industry, which reacts negatively to anything that comes from government mandates.

Chapter 7
The Revolution in Commercial Development

The green building revolution is a tidal wave approaching the commercial building and development industry. Any commercial green building project started today that does not explicitly incorporate green features and certify itself according to a recognized, third party–validated standard will be functionally obsolete the day it opens and may be economically disadvantaged the rest of its lifetime. At this time of rapid convergence between green building technology, green building certification, and a growing awareness of green buildings' benefits, a building owner's entire portfolio may be at risk without a clear commitment to green building.

According to Rod Wille of Turner Construction, the nation's largest commercial builder, the momentum for green building has expanded from government to the private sector:

> Government certainly was an early driver. But as I look around at federal government and other public entities, I find they are still floundering— they may have policies at the highest level, but a lot of their management people still don't necessarily embrace it. On the other hand, major universities, some school districts, and certain developers are now totally embracing it—again, maybe not for all of the triple-bottom-line reasons, but they have certainly made it their policy—whether it's their campus policy or a policy for new development—so those people are taking over and driving the market.

More and more government agencies in cities and states are adopting policies, but a lot of them are executive orders, and they are not being implemented at the project level because people are just being told to do it rather than having a personal commitment.[1]

Commercial Market Size

Table 7.1 shows the size of the commercial (nonresidential) building market, about $352 billon per year. Office (including government offices) and commercial uses account for about 42 percent of the total, education about 26 percent, health care about 13 percent, and all other uses about 19 percent of total construction cost.[2] Government buildings of all types are about 37 percent of all nonresidential building construction, about $129 billion per year. To give a measure of perspective, the residential construction market in the United States was $595 billion in 2006, about 70 percent larger than the total nonresidential market.[3]

Which Sector Builds the Most Green Buildings?

But what about cost? If green buildings cost more and certification costs are onerous, we would expect that most of the activity in green buildings would be found in government agencies, schools, and universities: institutions that can afford to take the long view and invest more money up front to save money on operating costs year after year. That was certainly the case early in the development and use of the LEED system, when only about one-third of the project owners (by area, or value) were private corporations. Lately, however, the pendulum is swinging: private companies and private developers now represent the majority of LEED projects (ranked by building area, or value) applying for registration in 2006 and 2007.

In fact, the largest user of the LEED system is not a corporation or university, or even a government agency; it is a privately held development firm in Portland, Oregon. With more than 30 LEED-registered projects either completed or in process, Gerding Edlen Development began its green building "learning curve" in the mid-1990s. Key members of the firm just felt it was the right thing to do. Early developments were build-to-suit projects with green features, such as energy-efficient underfloor air-distribution systems, for private corporations and government agencies.

In the late 1990s, the firm acquired a $19.5 million, five-block parcel of land just north of downtown Portland that housed a former Blitz-Weinhard brewery. Ignoring advice from a number of out-of-town real estate professionals, Gerding Edlen decided to build a two-and-a-half-block underground

Table 7.1
Nonresidential Commercial Market, 2006

Building Type	Market Size (in billions)	Percentage of Total
Educational	$92.4	26.2%
Commercial	$85.5	24.3%
Office	$61.2	17.4%
Health care	$46.0	13.1%
Amusement/recreation	$23.3	6.6%
Lodging	$22.9	6.5%
Public safety	$12.1	3.4%
Religious	$ 8.2	2.3%

Source: U.S. Census Bureau, www.census.gov/const/www/C30index.html, accessed March 22, 2007.

parking garage and to take a mixed-use approach to development. Over a period of six years, they built a 15-story high-rise condominium project, The Henry (after Henry Weinhard); a 16-story apartment building, The Louisa (Henry's wife); two 10-story office towers, and a four-story office/retail building. On half of one block, they renovated an 1890s-era National Guard armory into the Gerding Theater, a performing arts center that opened in 2006 as the first LEED-NC Platinum Historic Register project in the country.[4]

The firm is values-driven, but commercially very savvy. Led by partner Mark Edlen, a former top local commercial real-estate broker, the firm successfully leased 500,000 square feet of space during a period (2002 to 2004) when the local real estate market was losing a net one million square feet of leased space. They did it not so much by stealing tenants from other office and residential buildings as by creating value in a new type of urban mixed-use development, a place where people would want to invest their money and locate their businesses and homes. The two office towers sport operable windows and energy-conserving lighting fixtures, and one of the towers has a green roof and photovoltaic panels on the facade and roof.

Dennis Wilde, a partner at Gerding Edlen, says, "We believe people are an important part of sustainability. Creating great places where people can do it all—live, work and play—is a sustainable pattern of development."[5] Their Brewery Blocks development now abuts a major gentrification development zone in Portland called the Pearl District, a mecca for visitors and residents alike. Retail tenants in the Brewery Blocks include Anthropologie, Diesel, P. F. Chang's Bistro, and Whole Foods, all national retailers locating in Portland for the first time.[6]

Gerding Edlen's commitment is to target LEED Silver or better in all their buildings. The Louisa apartments are LEED Gold (and were 40 percent leased before construction completion); The Henry condos (which sold out nine months before construction completion in 2003) are LEED Gold; and two of the three office buildings are targeting LEED-CS Silver and the third, Gold.[7] This is the key message for other developers: you can be values-driven and commercially successful at the same time. Dennis Wilde says simply:

> Tenants and buyers won't pay more for high-performing buildings. So we can't go into the marketplace and command higher rents or higher sale prices. That means we are typically spending more than our competitors for an equivalent building—by about 1 to 2 percent more—not a lot, but it adds up. . . . The benefit we do get is that it differentiates us in the market-place; the energy-saving features might help make a difference in the sale, but only if our price points are the same. We are able to perhaps lease up space faster, but our pricing has to be comparable to other Class A office buildings in a given district. However, as the overall market slows down, I think it [sustainable, energy-efficient design] does give us an advantage.[8]

In Boise, Idaho, the Banner Bank building is a LEED for Core and Shell Platinum-certified speculative commercial office building completed in 2006 by the Christensen Corporation.[9] The project features 65 percent less energy use and 60 percent less water use than a comparable standard development. Built at a construction cost of $128 per square foot, this 195,000-square-foot, 11-story art deco building in downtown Boise shows a $1.5 million increase in asset value (based just on energy savings), with a 32 percent return on the incremental investment to build to LEED Platinum standards.

The large operational saving allows the owner to charge rents comparable to much older buildings and still reap a handsome profit. The project incorporates such efficiency measures as a geothermal heating system, smart lighting controls with occupancy sensors, and underfloor air ventilation. Developer Gary Christensen comments, "If we hadn't committed to a high level of LEED certification, it would have been easy to cut corners here and there. But when you have that plaque, you know that the project was held to a high standard. We take great satisfaction in that."[10]

Figure 7.1. The Banner Bank building in Boise, Idaho, is a LEED-CS Platinum-certified commercial office building. Alpha Image Photography by Giuseppe Saitta, courtesy of HDR, Inc.

The Portland and Boise projects are just two examples of the hundreds of green commercial developments all over the country that are completed, under construction, or in the planning stage. Commercial offices constitute about 25 percent of all LEED-registered projects, according to the USGBC, and they keep getting larger. For example, in New York City, Bank of America has teamed with the Durst Organization, a local developer, to construct what is expected to be the world's largest LEED Platinum building when it's completed in 2008: the 54-story, 2.2 million-square-foot Bank of America Tower at One Bryant Park. Located in the Times Square area (as is Four Times Square, the Durst Organization's breakthrough green building of the 1990s), the Bank of America Tower will contain a host of green building technologies, including on-site power generation and a rainwater harvesting system.

Designed by the firm Cook+Fox, the project has attracted worldwide attention. Architect Richard Cook says:

The green building movement has reached a watershed. With sustainability poised at the forefront of mainstream consciousness, green building has affected everything and has become a global imperative. Our clients

Figure 7.2. The 54-story, 2.2-million-square-foot Bank of America Tower at One Bryant Park in New York City is expected to become the world's largest LEED Platinum building upon completion in 2008. © dBox for Cook+Fox Architects.

are interested in sustainability because of an increasing awareness of the impacts on our children's generation, the health and productivity paybacks, and competition in the marketplace. To many, the perceived increase in first costs for implementing green strategies has been a barrier. However, as energy costs rise, paybacks on green technologies are becoming shorter. A second barrier has been resistance to change among the client base, construction industry, and consultants. But we also see this inertia disappearing very fast. Currently we are exploring green design at all scales, from a 2.2 million square foot office tower to our own 12,000-square-foot LEED Platinum office space.[11]

The Business Case for Green Commercial Development

Table 7.2 shows the business case for green commercial development. The largest issue for speculative developers (those who build space without having all tenant leases at the beginning) is the divergence in returns between themselves and the tenants. The tenants get most of the productivity and health benefits; in the case of triple-net leases, the tenants also reap the benefits of energy savings. The developer has to deal with the initial costs, which for the first few projects might be higher than for a conventional building. What are the benefits, then?

There are many, though not all apply in every case. Some are benefits that may happen in the future, but can't be quantified now. For example, there is neither good data on the resale value of green buildings to show that they command a higher price, nor data indicating that tenants are willing to pay higher rents to get the value of increased productivity and reduction in health problems. But this very paucity of data creates opportunities for leadership: if you're in business and wait until all the facts are in and commonly agreed upon, you've lost most of the potential rewards. Leaders act when others are sitting on the sidelines, and as we've seen, there are plenty of bold leaders in the world of green commercial buildings.

The Business Case for Brown Development

Commercial real estate is still a tough world for developers, one that is fast-changing. While there is ample evidence of successful green developments

Table 7.2

The Business Case for Speculative Green Commercial Buildings

Greening a speculative commercial building and achieving LEED for Core and Shell (LEED-CS) precertification can help a developer:

- Obtain marketing advantages in most markets; word of mouth and "buzz" can be powerful factors in commercial leasing
- Secure access to more sources of project financing (through programs such as Bank of America's)
- Gain access to more potential investors (through socially responsible property investing)
- Lease the project faster by selling the productivity and health benefits to prospective tenants
- Add value to the property through energy and water savings that increase Net Operating Income (with an increase in valuation of about 16 times the annual savings!)
- Acquire better-quality tenants who are likely to stay in the building longer
- Obtain greater public relations benefits
- Secure lower costs for commercial insurance from some companies
- Reduce the risk of lawsuits over "sick building syndrome" because of the attention to indoor air quality
- Boost employees' morale and make recruitment and retention of key people easier
- Take advantage of local incentives for green development, such as fast-tracking of permits and higher floor-to-area ratios that cut time-to-market and increase allowable building heights, resulting in more leasable area
- Take advantage of federal and state incentives, including tax credits, tax deductions, and property and sales tax abatements
- Take advantage of utility incentives for renewable energy
- Make use of third-party funds for more expensive capital investments, such as solar power and on-site power production

by experienced real estate companies, there is also the potential for missteps: timing the market poorly by bringing more supply online when the market is losing tenants; spending too much on green features that prospective tenants or owners don't perceive as adding value; putting a green development in an unattractive location. Conversely, it's certainly possible for conventional, non-green development to be successful, because the three basic laws of real estate development haven't been repealed: location, location, location. But by doing non-green development, a firm takes on the risk that the property will be valued less over time compared to neighboring green buildings.

Now imagine you're a real estate broker trying to make a sale, i.e., get a lease commitment from a major corporation. Your sales presentation goes something like this:

Mr. or Ms. Client: I have a building for you in which your employees will have poor daylighting and limited views of the outdoors, and of course they'll have to endure several months of toxic fumes right after occupancy, before they diminish. And did I mention, there will be lower productivity and the likelihood of greater health problems, because we've skimped on indoor air quality measures, lighting controls, and individual temperature controls. For these and other reasons, your key employees will be looking for another job just as soon as they realize what kind of space this is and how it expresses your company's true values. Of course, with our triple-net lease provisions, you'll be paying an extra dollar per square foot for utilities, costs that will likely increase dramatically in the future. Now here's the good part: we have a beautiful lobby to impress your clients and executives, and you're going to save 50 cents a square foot on the rent, about $100 a year savings for each valuable employee who costs you $50,000 on average each year. Do you have any questions?

Wouldn't you feel a bit ashamed, as a real estate professional, to offer such a deal to your clients? Yet it's being done every day, if not exactly in those words (!), because that's the only available leasable space on the market. If it were me, I'd rather be advocating the business case for a green building any day. Wouldn't you?

LEED for Core and Shell Helps Developers

LEED-CS was created explicitly to meet the needs of developers, for one good reason. Most developers can't wait until a building is built and occupied for it to be certified, a requirement under the LEED-NC system. They need the certification to do marketing to get tenants, and to use the tenant leases to attract both equity and debt capital. So LEED-CS created a precertification to Certified, Silver, Gold, and Platinum levels based on the project's design. When the project is finished, the developer submits paperwork for a final rating. The USGBC hopes, and expects, that the developer will also encourage tenants to follow the LEED-CI guidelines for build-out of their spaces, so that the entire building will have the same environmental benefits of a LEED-NC building.

As a major U.S. commercial developer, Hines has been a significant user of the LEED for Core and Shell system. Jerry Lea of Hines says,

LEED-CS has confirmed the quality of projects that we've been doing. The first two projects that got certified under the Core and Shell system were well into construction before that rating system was even created, and we were able to get those two buildings certified—one Silver and the other Gold—while they were in construction. In other words, we didn't design these buildings to get certified under the rating system because the rating system didn't exist when we were doing the design. It has confirmed that the good-quality building that we're doing can get LEED-certified. Basically, all of our spec buildings are getting certified to one level or another.[12]

The Revolution Comes to Corporate Real Estate

So far we've been discussing the business case for speculative real estate development. Yet a great proportion of buildings are built for corporations' own needs—whether directly, through a company's purchasing real estate or constructing a new building, or indirectly, by hiring a developer to build for the company. Many large corporations are building their own LEED-certified buildings, including Herman Miller, Ford, Toyota, Honda, Goldman Sachs, and Bank of America.

Build-to-suit is also quite common as a method for companies to acquire new buildings. One company that has approached the corporate build-to-suit market in a systematic and disciplined way is Workstage LLC, based in Grand Rapids, Michigan, which constructs LEED Silver suburban office buildings for major corporate clients in the Midwest, as well as projects for public and private universities. The key to Workstage's approach is to create office buildings the way a factory would produce goods, by having an interchangeable "kit of parts" that yields a green building at a conventional cost.[13] According to Workstage, "Above all else, buildings and their interiors should be designed for the people who work and live inside them. The building gives individuals what they want: control over their own air, light, acoustics, technology access, and work tools. The productivity, effectiveness, and efficiency that people bring to their daily work are in direct proportion to their satisfaction with their environment and work tools."[14]

For Royal Caribbean Cruises Ltd., Workstage built a $44 million, 162,000-square-foot call center in Springfield, Oregon, to house nearly 1,000 employees. When constructing a call-center facility, owners have traditionally fo-

Figure 7.3. Developed by Workstage, LLC, the Royal Caribbean call center in Spring-field, Oregon, is a cruise ship–themed building with a LEED Gold certification. Photo by Johnny Quirin, courtesy of Workstage.

cused only on minimizing the cost per cubicle. Royal Caribbean believes that since it spends far more on salaries than on buildings, it should offer a great place to work. The architects created an office filled with fresh air and natural light, supporting the company's commitment to the health and well-being of its employees. Occupied in 2006, the building earned a LEED-NC Gold rating. The elegant design, which has a cruise-ship theme, stands as a testimony to the universal appeal of sustainable building.[15]

Gary Saulson is senior vice president and director of corporate real estate at PNC Bank in Pittsburgh, the nation's 15th-largest bank, with 800 branches in 40 states. He has spearheaded the bank's effort to LEED-certify more buildings than any other corporation. By early 2007, the bank had certified 12 buildings and was well on the way to certifying dozens more. Each daylit, 3,600-square-foot LEED-certified branch costs about $1.3 million to build. Saulson expects the payback on the initial extra investments in two to five years.

PNC plans to construct 80 similar branches over the next five years throughout the mid-Atlantic region, based on the standards implemented for the first two LEED-certified units in Pennsylvania. Under the USGBC's "volume build" program, in which a retailer certifies most of the building elements of a prototype design just once, then provides evidence of construction completion, certification costs are expected to run far less than the current $3,000 per unit, or 0.25 percent of capital cost.[16]

Beginning with the 650,000-square-foot LEED Silver PNC Firstside Center in Pittsburgh in 2002, PNC has consistently worked to get LEED Silver buildings built at conventional costs. Energy savings in the branches are averaging 25 percent. PNC now has 43 green branches completed or under construction and plans to build at least 80 more as it expands throughout its service areas of the mid-South and the East Coast. All the green branches are freestanding, and many are in shopping center locations.[17]

Visteon Village, a new manufacturing site in Van Buren Township, Michigan, created for one of the world's largest auto parts suppliers, sits on a 265-acre suburban site that once was a gravel pit. Completed in 2005, the 800,000-square-foot corporate headquarters received LEED certification. It comprises seven buildings laid out like a village, complete with a central energy plant and a nature trail. The site now includes a lake, wetlands, and walking trails, with development on only 30 percent of the site. In addition to planting 5,000 new trees, the project includes structures designed to have minimal impact on the environment, including the use of recycled products and reuse of on-site materials.[18]

Industrial Buildings

Industrial construction was estimated at about $40 billion in 2007.[19] A good portion of this construction consists of buildings that can be renovated or built to LEED standards. An early example of a LEED-certified industrial building is the Oatey Distribution Center in Cleveland, Ohio.[20] With an additional investment of $300,000 on this $8 million project (about 3.8 percent), heating savings alone are estimated at $75,000 per year, a 43 percent savings. The building uses a graywater collection and reuse system to save 100,000 gallons per year of potable water.

There are many other examples of LEED-certified industrial projects. In fact, as of early 2007, more than 115 industrial projects were registered for eventual certification under the LEED program.[21]

Figure 7.4. Designed by SmithGroup, the Visteon Village manufacturing plant in Van Buren Township, Michigan, contains seven buildings laid out like a village, complete with a central energy plant and a nature trail. Justin Maconochie Photography, courtesy of SmithGroup.

Socially Responsible Property Investing

Another factor that may accelerate the rise in green commercial development in the near future is a relatively recent phenomenon, the growth of socially responsible property investing (SRPI). The growth of real estate investment trusts (REITs) since the mid-1990s has securitized the commercial real-estate sector and made investment in REITs a way for small investors to become real estate moguls. In the past two to three years, some large pension funds and REITs have begun to focus on green buildings as a great investment opportunity.

Liberty Property Trust and Corporate Office Properties Trust stand out for their commitment to investing in LEED Silver-certified buildings. Liberty's One Crescent Drive project is a four-story building at the Navy Yard Corporate Center in Philadelphia, designed by world-renowned architect Robert

Figure 7.5. Located on a decommissioned U.S. naval base in Philadelphia, One Crescent Drive is a LEED Platinum-certified project. Photo by Brian Cohen, courtesy of Liberty Property Trust.

A.M. Stern. Situated within a Keystone Opportunity Improvement Zone, One Crescent Drive offers qualified businesses substantial city and state tax abatements through 2018. It has a sustainable, green design that provides a more efficient and higher-quality workplace environment than a comparable conventional building, and it has been certified as LEED Platinum.[22]

In mid-2006, Liberty had more than a dozen LEED projects in the works, including the Comcast Center in Philadelphia, which is currently the tallest building in the world seeking LEED certification.[23]

In 2006, the California Public Employees Retirement System (CalPERS) formed a joint venture with Hines, the Hines CalPERS Green Development Fund, and contributed $123 million in equity toward future green real estate development. CalPERS Green will likely develop three to four new office buildings, which could be build-to-suits for one user or speculative space. Construction has begun on the fund's first project, Tower 333 in Bellevue, Washington, intended to be the West Coast's first LEED-CS precertified office project.[24]

Professor Gary Pivo heralds the growth of SRPI. "If 10 percent of the more than $2 trillion in socially responsible investing today were in real estate," he hypothesizes, "it would equal nearly 75 percent of the entire REIT equity market capitalization in the U.S., which was around $300 billion at the end of 2004. Clearly, then, the potential scale of a socially responsible property investment market may be very substantial."[25] The implication that tens of billions of dollars of socially responsible investment money are potentially waiting to go into green real estate should give most serious developers yet another reason to embrace green buildings.

In March 2007, Bank of America committed $20 billion of new investment to build and support energy-efficient technologies and green buildings. The bank's program to fight global warming over the next decade includes financing companies that develop low-emissions technology, lending money for green building projects, and creating the ability for customers to trade carbon credits. The bank will spend $18 billion on commercial green lending and finance, while another $2 billion will be spent on consumer programs and efforts to reduce the greenhouse gas emissions and environmental impact of its own operations. These include $1.4 billion to ensure that all new offices and bank branches meet green building standards and $100 million on energy-efficiency upgrades in older facilities.[26]

Not to be outdone, in April 2007 Citibank committed $50 billion of investments, financings, and other activities to encourage the commercialization and growth of alternative energy and clean technology. The company also earmarked $1 billion for the Clinton Climate Initiative, a project to implement the new Energy Efficiency Building Retrofit Program.[27]

Look for the movement toward socially responsible property investing to gain steam in the next few years, as green buildings begin to demonstrate not only superior environmental value but also higher investment returns to owners.

Chapter 8
The Revolution in Government and Nonprofit Buildings

The federal government, along with state and local governments and the nonprofit sector, has played a key role in the green building revolution. The U.S. Department of Energy provided the initial funding to help the USGBC create the LEED rating system in the late 1990s. For the first five years of the LEED program (2000–2004), more than half of the registered projects, and many of the certified projects, were for government agencies or nonprofit entities. Since 2005, the ratio of the area in public to private projects has shifted from 2:1 to about 50:50, and private projects tend to have a larger average size.[1]

The Government Buildings Market

By itself, nonresidential public building construction is a considerable market, estimated at $129 billion in 2006, or 37 percent of the total nonresidential construction market of $352 billion.[2] Public nonresidential construction increased 7.5 percent in 2006, indicating steady growth of this market, fueled by rising tax revenues from the five-year domestic economic expansion. In certain sectors, public construction dominates: public agencies spent 83 percent of all educational construction funds and built 60 percent of all recreational projects and 100 percent of public safety projects. Government agencies built 19 percent of all offices and 23 percent of all health care facilities. (Many of the latter are built by nonprofit hospitals and agencies.)[3]

Green Building Drivers
Why is the government so active in green buildings? There are two essential reasons. The government is in many ways less sensitive to initial costs

than the private sector, because its requirements are different. There are no investors to please, only various stakeholders, including legislators and agency officials. So, to promote energy-efficiency and sustainability policies, government agencies make capital investments that (1) demonstrate to the private sector, for example, how to do green buildings and (2) can be justified on a "life-cycle-cost" accounting basis. Also, the government is a long-term owner/operator of facilities. The government isn't going out of business, and agencies will pay the operating costs, health care expenses, and turnover costs well into the future, so a current investment to create future benefits is consistent with the government's responsibilities and outlook.

Don Horn has long been active in the green building efforts at the U.S. General Services Administration (GSA). "GSA is committed to incorporating principles of sustainable design and energy efficiency into all of its building projects," he says. "Our approach has been to integrate sustainable design requirements as seamlessly as possible into our existing design, construction, property management, and leasing processes."[4] Horn reports that GSA had approximately 60 projects registered and working toward LEED certification as of March 2007, and that 19 GSA projects had already received certification. Of GSA's approach, he says:

> Our approach to sustainable design has been to incorporate requirements throughout our guidance and standards. It is difficult to identify specific items as costs for building green when most can be related to the expectations of quality in our projects. In general, we have not allocated any extra money for building green or LEED. What we've accomplished has been within our existing project budgets. We have found that firms experienced in green building and sustainable design can meet our goals and expectations without difficulty. Inexperienced firms sometimes find it difficult to balance the many project objectives we require.

Government buildings present different dynamics than private-sector design and construction. Often the design and construction cycles are longer, because money may be allocated by a legislative body, first for studies and design, then later for construction. In the state of Washington, for example, it often takes three two-year legislative sessions to get construction money allocated for public colleges and universities and for state-owned buildings.

Like government, the nonprofit sector has to please various stakeholders: donors, staff, the press, and beneficiaries of their services. The nonprofit sector has a different dynamic than government, however. Many nonprofits believe that they should be leaders in demonstrating the benefits of green design to the public and to a somewhat skeptical private sector. Therefore, they use green buildings as a way to communicate a message—for example, that a healthy environment and a productive economy are not incompatible objectives.

Green buildings also provide fund-raising opportunities that many nonprofits have seized. For example, the Jean Vollum Natural Capital Center in Portland, Oregon, was the second LEED Gold-certified building in the country. Ecotrust, the nonprofit that sponsored the project, raised most of the money from one donor to renovate a 100-year-old warehouse into a modern office building. From a program or policy standpoint, they also wanted to show the public that investing in older buildings and older neighborhoods was an appropriate way to create a "conservation economy" in the Pacific Northwest, their region of concern.[5]

Integrated Design for Public Projects

John Boecker, an architect in Pennsylvania and one of the green-design pioneers in the mid-Atlantic region, led the design team that in 2001 created the first LEED Version 2.0 Gold-certified building in the country, the Pennsylvania Department of Environmental Protection's Cambria office building. Of the difficulties he has and still encounters in promoting integrated design in government projects, Boecker says:

> The biggest impediment I face is helping people fight their conditioning in order to shift their mindset and their process, because green building and integrated design requires a change in both (mindset and process). The solution to addressing this rather ubiquitous inertia against change is education and getting everybody on board. In short, this requires the three E's: you have to address Everything, with Everyone, Early. Accordingly, chances of success are significantly improved by getting building professionals (contractors) to become members of the team, along with the project's design professionals, before anybody even starts to design.

The overarching goal of integrated design, then, is to augment perform-ance while neutralizing first-cost—that way, there's no need to discuss in-creased costs, and as a result, any discussion of "paybacks" becomes moot. That's always our goal. Simply stated, integrated design is the key to creat-ing high-performance buildings cost effectively and to do so without changing the completion date or protracting the project design schedule by reallocating time within the same schedule; in other words, by focusing more effort up front in conceptual and schematic design, decisions are reached that allow for the time required in the construction documents phase to be reduced.[6]

GSA's Don Horn echoes these sentiments. Citing lessons learned from dozens of projects, Horn says there are three keys to delivering governmen-tal green building projects on established budgets:

- Start early in the project with sustainable design goals; adding goals or requirements later will only cost more.
- Use an integrated, whole-building approach to take advantage of synergies between design strategies and to avoid cuts during "value engineering."
- Include property management representatives throughout the proj-ect so they understand the bigger picture and can offer suggestions from their experience.

LEED Use by Government Agencies

All around the country, government bodies are deciding to build LEED for New Construction projects. Through the first six years of the LEED-NC pro-gram, 2000 to 2005, the federal government registered 8 percent of all proj-ects, state government registered 12 percent, and local government regis-tered another 21 percent, for a total government allocation of 41 percent through early 2006. The nonprofit sector, including many private schools, colleges, and universities, registered 21 percent of all LEED-NC projects. Through September 2006, 31 percent of all LEED-certified projects (under the four major rating systems) were government projects, and 18 percent came from the nonprofit sector.[8] In sum, government and nonprofits accounted for 62 percent of all registered projects and nearly 50 percent of all certified projects as of the third quarter of 2006.

At the federal level, the General Services Administration tries to build LEED-certified buildings for most projects, especially through its Design Excellence program for new federal buildings and courthouses. The Department of Defense has completed a number of LEED projects, and the U.S. Army has officially adopted LEED as its evaluation standard for new construction. The National Park Service has built a number of new visitor centers to LEED criteria.[9] In Montana, the joint border crossing called Sweetgrass/Coutts Port of Entry is LEED-certified, as is the EPA's National Computer Center in Morrisville, North Carolina (Silver), and the Bureau of Land Management's Science Center in Escalante, Utah (Gold).

Table 8.1 shows all of the federal projects that had been LEED-certified through the end of 2006. It lists 44 projects, for 12 agencies, for 11 different building types. Federal sources estimated that 250 additional LEED-registered projects were in process at the end of 2006.[10]

As a policy, many state governments, by both legislation and executive order, have decided to build LEED Silver or better buildings. By ordinance or policy, many leading cities have commitments to green construction, including Seattle, Portland, Denver, Salt Lake City, Tucson, Phoenix, and San Jose and Pasadena, California. Table 8.2 shows government initiatives in the United States and Canada, as of June 2006.

Exemplary Government and Nonprofit Projects

Completed in 2006, the new Eugene, Oregon, federal courthouse is the centerpiece for revitalizing the downtown area and is a good example of a government green building project that achieved a LEED Gold certification. Commissioned by the General Services Administration under its Design Excellence program, the 270,000-square-foot, $72 million project engaged the well-known Thom Mayne of the firm Morphosis as the design architect.

In the courthouse, the HVAC design includes an underfloor air distribution system serving most of the spaces, including the six courtrooms. Radiant slabs for heating and cooling, coupled with displacement ventilation, serve the lobbies and public spaces. A heat-recovery chiller in the HVAC central plant uses rejected heat from the computer server room loads for the

Table 8.1

Characteristics of 44 Federal LEED-Certified Projects

Agencies Represented (Projects)	Building Types (Projects)
Department of Defense (10)	Office (15)
Department of the Interior (7)	Laboratory (9)
General Services Administration (6)	Hangar/warehouse (4)
Environmental Protection Agency (5)	Courthouse (4)
Department of Energy (4)	School (3)
Department of Commerce (2)	Recreation (2)
Department of Transportation (2)	Visitor center (2)
NASA (2)	Military dormitory (2)
Social Security Administration (2)	Transit station (1)
Department of Human Services (2)	Prison (1)
Department of Justice (1)	House (1)
Department of Labor (1)	

Source: U.S. Dept. of Energy, Office of Energy Efficiency and Renewable Energy, "Federal Build-ings Certified by the U.S. Green Building Council LEED Rating System," April 2007, www1 .eere.energy.gov/femp/pdfs/fed_leed_bldgs.pdf, accessed March 30, 2007.

water heating system. Condensing boilers maximize the efficiency of the water heating system and keep water loop temperatures low enough for the heat-rejection chiller to work efficiently.[11]

The Natural Resources Defense Council constructed the 15,000-square-foot Robert Redford Building in Santa Monica, California, to demonstrate green building principles. Completed in 2003, the project was one of the first three LEED-NC (version 2.0) Platinum buildings in the United States. Surpris-ingly, all three were built in Southern California, and all were certified within a few months of each other. Designed by Moule and Polyzoides Ar-chitects, NRDC's headquarters uses 44 percent less energy than a conven-tional building of its size in California, gets 100 percent of its energy from carbon-free green power, and consumes 60 percent less potable water than a standard building.[12] The offices are cooled through natural breezes com-ing off the nearby Pacific Ocean. The windows are designed to block solar radiation and reduce the amount of heat gain into the building, thereby minimizing the need for air conditioning. A 7.5-kilowatt photovoltaic array on the roof provides 20 percent of total energy use and ensures that this building will generate zero carbon-dioxide emissions.[13]

In Santa Clarita, California, HOK Architects built a straw-bale mainte-nance facility for a local transit department, the first LEED Gold-certified

Table 8.2

Government Initiatives to Promote Green Buildings

The following governments and government agencies have passed legislation, executive orders, ordinances, policies, or other incentives for buildings to meet LEED criteria.

Federal

Department of Energy	Department of Defense
Department of Interior	U.S. Environmental Protection Agency
Department of State	U.S. General Services Administration

State

Arizona	Michigan
Arkansas	Nevada
California	New Jersey
Colorado	New Mexico
Connecticut	New York
Illinois	Oregon
Maine	Pennsylvania
Maryland	Rhode Island
Massachusetts	Washington

County

Alameda County, CA	County of San Mateo, CA
Cook County, IL	Sarasota County, FL
King County, WA	Suffolk County, NY

City

Acton, MA	Eugene, OR	Pleasanton, CA
Albuquerque, NM	Frisco, TX	Portland, OR
Arlington, MA	Gainesville, FL	Princeton, NJ
Arlington, VA	Grand Rapids, MI	Sacramento, CA
Atlanta, GA	Houston, TX	Salt Lake City, UT
Austin, TX	Issaquah, WA	San Diego, CA
Berkeley, CA	Kansas City, MO	San Francisco, CA
Boston, MA	Long Beach, CA	San Jose, CA
Boulder, CO	Los Angeles, CA	Santa Monica, CA
Bowie, MD	New York, NY	Scottsdale, AZ
Calabasas, CA	Normal, IL	Seattle, WA
Calgary, AB (Canada)	Oakland, CA	Vancouver, BC (Canada)
Chicago, IL	Omaha, NE	Washington, DC
Cranford, NJ	Pasadena, CA	
Dallas, TX	Phoenix, AZ	

Source: Scot Case, "Building a Better Future; Government LEEDs the Way," June 2006, www.govpro.com/ArchiveSearch/Article/27938, accessed March 30, 2007.

Figure 8.1. The Robert Redford Building, the Natural Resources Defense Council's office building in Santa Monica, California, earned a LEED Platinum rating. Photo by Grey Crawford, courtesy of Natural Resources Defense Council (NRDC).

Figure 8.2. The 47,000-square-foot transit maintenance facility in Santa Clarita, California, built by HOK, was the first LEED-certified straw-bale building in the world. Photos by John Edward Linden, courtesy of HOK.

straw-bale project ever.[14] Certified in 2006, the 47,000-square-foot facility (with 22,000 square feet of offices) exceeds State of California energy-efficiency requirements by 44 percent. The $20 million project includes a well-insulated cool roof, plenty of daylighting and high-performance glazing, and nighttime ventilation to flush warm air out of the building and replace it with cooler air. The underfloor air distribution system allows the building to utilize cooler outside air for a good portion of annual cooling.[15]

Austin City Hall is a dramatic example of a high-performance government project that combines energy efficiency with striking visual elegance. The City Hall and Public Plaza (and 750-car parking garage) are located in a 100-year-old building at the edge of the Warehouse District on the shores of Town Lake. The project is dominated by landscape features, the building form reflects the geology of the area, and the building materials include limestone, bronze, glass, water, and shade to create the city's "living room."

The 118,000-square-foot building contains several city departments, along with the offices of the mayor, city manager, and city council; the council chambers; and a supporting cafe and gallery. Designed by the firm

Figure 8.3. Designed by Antoine Predock Architect and Coltera+Reed, the LEED Gold-certified Austin City Hall is called the city's "living room." Courtesy of Antoine Predock Architect PC, design architect; Cotera+Reed, executive architect; and Timothy Hursley, photographer.

of Antoine Predock Architect, with Cotera+Reed Architects, the project contains four floors and cost an estimated $50 million when completed in 2004. The LEED Gold certification recognizes City Hall's achievements in reducing energy use by 55 percent compared to a conventional building, and eliminating landscape water use.

In Wisconsin, the Department of Natural Resources regional headquarters in Green Bay, completed in 2005, received a LEED-NC Gold certification, becoming only the seventh certified project in the state and the first green building built by the State of Wisconsin. The three-story, 34,500-square-foot building houses 156 employees and includes an additional 13,000-square-foot shop and storage area. The building provides daylighting and views to the outdoors for most employees.

For an incremental investment of $70,000 in the $4.7 million project (1.5 percent of the total), engineers estimate that the building will save 55 percent of the energy consumed by a conventional building, about $25,000 per year.[16] Recent calculations show that the building is easily achieving goals of meeting an Energy Star rating of 85 or better. The project arranged to purchase green power from Wisconsin Public Service's Nature Wise program for a minimum of two years. A large, south-facing roof on the main building was designed to accommodate photovoltaic solar panels in the future, as funds become available.

Government agencies and nonprofits are beginning to see that their stewardship role for public resources requires them to build green, to take a long-term owner's perspective on energy costs and green building benefits. You can expect to see more government agencies adopt green building policies with each passing year.

Chapter 9
The Revolution in Education

The educational construction market, estimated at $125 billion from 2006 to 2008, is the largest single market sector in the building industry. About 64 percent of all new-building and renovation construction spending on education goes to K–12 schools, with the balance going to colleges and universities[1]; about 17 percent of total educational construction goes to private schools and universities, with the balance going to public schools and colleges.[2]

The green building revolution is about to flood the education market like a tidal wave. Already, more than 500 LEED-registered projects are in the education sector: some 260 in higher education and 245 in the K–12 sector as of March 2007.[3] As of September 2006, 12 percent of all LEED-certified projects were in the education sector.[4] Sustainability is a very significant issue on college campuses and is destined to become a major issue for school districts nationwide as the case for green schools becomes better known.

In the education market, about 54 percent (by value) of all construction is for new buildings, 27 percent for additions, and 19 percent for alterations or remodels; thus, major construction accounts for more than 80 percent of the value of all education projects. For this reason, the greening of educational facilities is significant. A demographic reason for this preponderance is that the average age of school and college buildings in 1999 was 40 years, or near their estimated lifespan of 42 years; most of the buildings built in the 1950s through the 1970s to accommodate the rapid influx of baby boomers are now due for replacement.[5]

Green Buildings in Higher Education

The higher education market, at 7 percent of LEED project registrations, appears poised to increase in scope and importance in the next few years, as more campuses adopt sustainability as a paradigm for all their operations, including curricula, purchasing, facility operations, student housing, and new construction of all types.

A new higher education organization formed in January 2006, the Association for the Advancement of Sustainability in Higher Education (AASHE), had over 200 campus members a year later and continues to grow rapidly. AASHE serves as an umbrella group for the campus sustainability community.[6] According to Matthew St. Clair, an AASHE board member and sustainability manager for the University of California system, "The green building movement is growing rapidly in all sectors of the economy, especially in higher education. Green building in higher education may now have hit a critical mass given the reputation-driven nature of higher education. Enough universities have instituted green building practices that all others have to follow or suffer a potential competitive image disadvantage."[7]

AASHE's Director of Strategic Initiatives, Judy Walton, highlights four primary factors driving green buildings in higher education[8]:

1. Marketing benefits, including publicity for a showcase "green" building, assistance in recruiting new students, and help in creating a marketing niche for the institution in a highly competitive environment.
2. Concern about rising energy costs in the future, and desire to construct energy-efficient buildings as protection against such costs.
3. Desire to do the right thing—recognition that environmental stewardship and employee well-being, including concern for employee health and productivity, is central to the university's mission.
4. Student and faculty pressure, including strong desire to "walk the talk" of environmental and social responsibility.

In response to these driving forces and the compelling business case for green buildings in higher education, many college and university presidents are requiring that all new construction projects achieve at least a LEED Silver rating. In 2005, the Washington legislature mandated this achievement for all state-funded schools. Table 9.1 shows the driving forces and business case benefits for green buildings in higher education.

The University of Washington's new Benjamin Hall Interdisciplinary Research Building, designed by CollinsWoerman Architects, was procured through a "Design-Build-Operate-Maintain" contract with a private com-

Table 9.1

Drivers for Green Buildings in Higher Education

1. Savings on energy costs and utility infrastructure
2. Reputation enhancement or maintenance; public relations
3. State-level mandates (public institutions)
4. CEO-level leadership from university or college president
5. Student and faculty pressure for green buildings of all types
6. Recruitment of preferred students
7. Recruitment of preferred faculty (this is still speculative)
8. Attracting a new donor pool for campus buildings (this is still speculative)

pany. Under this process, the bid came as a complete package at the beginning of the project, and the designer-builder is obligated to operate and maintain the building at a guaranteed price. This meant that decisions regarding building materials and systems were made on the basis of life-cycle costs and benefits. Annual energy savings are expected to be $220,000. The building is more efficient and more flexible than typical university laboratory buildings, allowing for a wider variety of uses that complement one another under the same roof. The project received LEED-CS Gold certification in 2006, only the second LEED-CS achievement in the country at a higher education institution.[9]

A leading university architect, Nels Hall of Portland, Oregon's YGH Architecture, says:

> In recent years, sustainable buildings have become less of a novelty and more of an accepted response to issues of health, operating costs, and ecological stewardship. Buildings designed to meet LEED standards are now widely seen at college campuses. Colleges and universities are now expanding programs beyond individual building projects to comprehensive campus sustainability programs. For example, the University of California (UC) and the California State University (CSU) systems [with a combined 33 campuses] have institutionalized an annual sustainability conference that promotes innovative practices and recognizes successful programs. In 2005, Humboldt State University students overwhelmingly passed a campus ballot initiative that supported sustainable practices.[10]

Driving forces and demonstrated business case benefits are leading to a larger number of green buildings in higher education, according to the University of California's St. Clair:

Figure 9.1. Designed by CollinsWoerman, Benjamin Hall at the University of Washington was the second academic building in the country to receive a LEED-CS Gold rating. Courtesy of Karen Steichen, CollinsWoerman.

There are a number of drivers: environmental standards, environmental concerns (increasingly climate change), health concerns, energy costs. The latter may be the primary driver for most institutions, with the other drivers as ancillary benefits. The University of California, for example, has been suffering from rising energy costs at the same time that state funding has remained constant or decreased, so there is strong motivation and even necessity to reduce energy costs, with green building being one means to that end.

The University of California's new campus in Merced, its tenth, recently received a LEED Gold certification for its new central utility plant. (UC

Figure 9.2. As part of a strong campuswide LEED commitment, the University of California, Merced, received LEED Gold certification for its new central utility plant. Courtesy of Swinerton Builders.

Merced has committed to a minimum of LEED Silver certification for all new buildings on the campus.) The complex consists of three buildings: a three-story unit that houses most of the university's power and infrastructure operations, a telecommunications building, and a two-million-gallon water storage tank. Water is stored in the tank and chilled at night, when electricity demand is lowest, then circulated through the buildings to cool them during the day. The process helps the university beat California's strict energy-conservation guidelines by 12 to 14 percent for each building. Overall, in its first year of operation, the complex used 35 percent less energy than a building constructed to current state standards.[11]

The driving forces differ for large and small schools, public universities, and private colleges and universities. One large difference is that private schools can combine capital and operating budgets to consider the life-cycle costs of energy-efficiency investments, while most public institutions cannot. Most legislatures separate capital budgets from operating costs and don't provide an institutional mechanism for combining them, other than using third-party "energy services companies" that will make capital investments and share savings with the university.

A good example of a smaller private institution pushing the envelope on LEED-certified buildings is Pacific Lutheran University in Tacoma, Washington, which recently constructed the Morken Center for Learning and Technology, an integrated learning environment for math, computer science, and business. In addition to its abundant daylighting, designed by Zimmer Gunsul Frasca Architects, the Morken Center requires no fossil fuels to operate. Instead, the 55,000-square-foot, $21 million building is heated and cooled with a cutting-edge geothermal heat-pump system that regulates its temperature with water stored in 85 wells located 300 feet underground. To further reduce energy use, its light fixtures are 33 percent more efficient and provide 25 percent more light per fixture than a standard system.[12]

Higher education construction is a significant proportion of total school construction. Some representative projects that received LEED certification in 2006 include the following:

University of British Columbia Life Sciences Centre, LEED-NC Gold
Haverford College (Pennsylvania), Integrated Athletics Center, LEED-NC Gold
Central College (Iowa), residence hall, LEED-NC Gold
Grinnell College (Iowa), environmental research facility, LEED-NC Gold
Carnegie Mellon University (Pennsylvania), Collaborative Innovation Center, LEED-CS Gold
Warren Wilson College (North Carolina), Orr Cottage, LEED-NC Gold
University of Victoria (British Columbia), Medical Sciences Building, LEED-NC Gold
Pennsylvania State University, Architecture/Landscape Architecture, LEED-NC Gold
Oregon State University, Kelly Engineering Building, LEED-NC Gold
Yale University (Connecticut), Malone Engineering Center, LEED-NC Gold
University of Colorado, Boulder, Technology Learning Center, LEED-NC Gold

Judy Walton keeps close track of campus sustainability efforts.[13] In her view, "The past several years have witnessed explosive growth of campus sustainability initiatives, with green building and design a significant component."

Figure 9.3. Designed by Zimmer Gunsul Frasca, the Morken Center at Pacific Lutheran University in Tacoma, Washington, requires no fossil fuels to operate. Courtesy of Zimmer Gunsul Frasca Architects.

According to Walton, at least 40 higher education institutions have adopted a green building policy. In addition, Washington State has a LEED Silver requirement for all new state-funded buildings, including those at public colleges and universities, and the University of California system has a green building policy that affects all ten campuses. Arizona State University has a governor's executive order stipulating that all new state-funded building meet at least the LEED Silver standard.

By early 2007, at least 60 institutions had one or more LEED-certified buildings on campus, with more than 75 such buildings total. This represents less than 5 percent of all higher education buildings constructed in the past five years, but green buildings are likely to become the norm in higher education by 2010, as many local efforts to green individual campuses bear fruit. Table 9.2 shows colleges and universities that have mandated LEED certification for new buildings.

Leith Sharp has directed the Green Campus Initiative at Harvard University since 2000 and has seen Harvard's interest and commitment to sustainability evolve since then. "When I was first recruited to Harvard, there wasn't a strong commitment to this. It was sort of a fringe issue—a marginal issue. My role in coming here [from Australia] was really to bring it to the center of the institution, as an institutional priority. We spent the first four years building relationships, engaging people in conversation, so that they came to understand the relationship between their own decisions as university staff, students, or faculty and the net environmental impact of their decisions."[14]

Sharp's comments indicate the vital need at the university level to engage all parties in dialogue. Unlike most large institutions, universities have a long-standing commitment to a decentralized and democratic decision-making process. (The CEO of a 20,000-person workforce has a lot more power to get things done than the president of a 20,000-student university!) Her experience reflects dedication to getting the process right, and the result includes Harvard's first LEED Platinum-certified project at no added cost. This building at 46 Blackstone Street in Cambridge houses Harvard's University Operations Services group and the Harvard Green Campus Initiative. The 44,500-square-foot office building project connects two older buildings with a glass atrium. Energy performance is modeled to be over 40 percent more efficient than code; the project uses over 40 percent less potable water and includes a bioswale for treating stormwater on-site.

Table 9.2
Colleges and Universities with LEED Initiatives

Arizona State University	Rice University (TX)
Ball State University (IN)	Santa Clara University (CA)
Bowdoin College (ME)	State University of New York (various)
Brown University	University of California (systemwide)
California State University System (various)	University of Cincinnati
Carnegie Mellon University	University of Florida
Clemson University (SC)	University of North Carolina, Chapel Hill
Connecticut College	University of Oregon
Dartmouth College	University of South Carolina
Duke University	University of Vermont
Emory University (GA)	University of Washington
Georgia Institute of Technology	Washington (State) Community Colleges
Harvard University	
Lewis and Clark College (OR)	
Massachusetts Institute of Technology	
Northwestern University	
Omaha Metropolitan Community College	
Pitzer College (CA)	
Pomona College (CA)	
Princeton University	

Source: USGBC, *LEED Initiatives in Governments and Schools*, March 2007, available at https://www.usgbc.org/ShowFile.aspx?DocumentID=691, accessed April 1, 2007.

It purchases renewable energy to offset all of its remaining electricity use.[15]

The primary design challenge was to transform two historic structures into a single, state-of-the-art green building that would provide a collaborative workplace environment while ensuring occupant health and comfort. The design solution maximizes the principles of sustainability in a modern workspace facility. A new vertical light-slot connects two previously detached buildings, providing daylight into newly "discovered" interior space.[16] Harvard's Green Campus Initiative regards the sustainable design and construction practices established in this project as "the model for use in future Harvard projects."[17]

Sharp explains, "Over those four years we were able to build a critical mass of people who really started to get it—that they had a responsibility to address this stuff. Simultaneously we worked on developing services so that once they decided that they wanted to do a green building or wanted

Figure 9.4. Architect Bruner/Cott's renovation of Harvard's 100-year-old Blackstone Station earned a LEED Gold rating. Photo by Richard Mandelkorn, courtesy of Bruner/Cott & Associates.

to reduce their energy use, we then provided them with real services, support, technical expertise, and zero-interest loans to help them achieve it. Through the combination of effective advocacy and education, along with service provision and expert assistance, we've been able to move the university to a point where it's quite confident about tackling sustainability and is now becoming ambitious in what it believes it should do and can do."[18]

Greening Secondary Education

On a parallel with the higher education market, the K–12 schools market continues to grow, fueled in many states by population growth from immigration and also by the need to replace or renovate older schools. However, owing to the unique nature of funding for most K–12 projects, i.e., via school bonds, the rapid rise in construction costs in recent years has significantly affected the ability of schools to include extra-cost green building measures in their projects. Many projects have cut back on all added amenities just to be able to complete their basic program requirements and get a school open on time.

Many changes are under way in this environment. Anne Schopf is an architect in Seattle and the design partner for Mahlum Architects. In her experience designing education projects, she says: "Societal pressures are leading to more green schools, because school boards and staff are more often aware and educated about environmental issues. There is also pressure for improved indoor air quality. Concerns about student performance always gets us to great daylighting solutions."[19]

A survey of school facilities officers identified six major triggers for building green educational projects:[20]

- Desire to lower operating costs, cited by 92 percent of survey respondents
- Desire to increase health and well-being of students and staff, 88 percent
- Energy cost increases, 87 percent
- Emphasis on student productivity, 77 percent
- Emphasis on staff productivity, 64 percent
- Utility rebates and other incentives, 61 percent

The survey showed that school facilities directors thought hard benefits (such as reduced utility costs) were important, but they also cited soft benefits (such as improved health and productivity) quite frequently.

Since schools spend one-third of their operations and maintenance budget on energy and other utilities, it's easy to see why lower operating costs are cited so frequently.[21] What, then, are the barriers to more green school construction? The same survey said that 87 percent of the respondents believed that higher first costs were the main obstacle, while 60 percent cited the time and cost to get approval to do something different. Forty-five percent thought that different accounting for capital and operating costs was a barrier, since that made it harder to use life-cycle costing to justify extra energy-saving investments.[22]

An early 2000s example of green school design was Cesar Chavez Elementary School in Long Beach, California, a project of LPA Architects. Sustainable features include natural ventilation with operable windows, as well as abundant natural daylight derived from operable skylights, light shelves, sunscreens, and rooftop light monitors.[23] School planning responded to and incorporated LEED requirements. After the first year of operation, Chavez Elementary used 33 percent less energy than a standard school built to the state energy code and used 100,000 gallons less water, through low-water-use landscaping and a weather-controlled irrigation system.[24]

Seattle-based green building consultant Kathleen O'Brien discussed her experience with a green building mandate that hit Washington State schools in 2005.

There was an initiative [by the Washington State legislature in 2005] to make all state-funded buildings LEED silver. Schools resisted this. Our firm helped school districts create an appropriate set of guidelines called the Washington Sustainable Schools Protocol.[25] The guidelines were voluntary, but the school districts knew that they could potentially become required. We did a pilot project with five schools across the state using the guidelines to prove they worked, while identifying any problems applying the Protocol. As of July 1, 2007 all school districts with over 2,000 students are required to follow the protocol and, a year later, the rest of the schools will be required. In the meantime, we worked with the local USGBC Chapter and the State's Office of Superintendent of Public Instruction (OSPI) to put on

Figure 9.5. Designed by LPA Architects, Cesar Chavez Elementary School in Long Beach, California, uses 33 percent less energy and saves 100,000 gallons of water per year compared to a conventional school. Courtesy of LPA, Inc./Costea Photography.

workshops to introduce the protocol, the legislative requirements, funding. In recognizing that people are naturally made uncomfortable by change, the training and the phase-in of the requirements provided some breathing space so school districts could adopt and adapt.[26]

Beyond mandates, many schools have been experimenting with LEED and related green building guidelines. In California and three other states, the Collaborative for High Performance Schools (CHPS) guidelines are being followed, along with LEED.[27] The guidelines consist of a comprehensive system of benchmarks designed by the CHPS technical committee with the goal of designing high performance schools. The first green building rating system designed specifically for K–12 schools, CHPS seeks to facilitate environments that are not only energy-efficient but also healthy, comfortable, and well lit, with the amenities needed for a quality education. As of March 2007, 18 districts in California had adopted CHPS guidelines for new school construction.[28]

Already, more than 250 school projects have registered with the USGBC to pursue LEED certification with new building projects. A 2006 study found that schools were likely to be the next major market for green building construction. Other findings included the following:

- A concern for "improved health and well-being" was the most critical social factor driving education green building—a factor that had not been as highly rated in prior research on the commercial and residential green building markets.
- The fiscal advantages of green building, such as energy cost savings, are the major motivation behind the construction of green schools and universities.
- Higher first costs are the primary challenge to building green in this sector, though recent studies have found only minor first cost increases, which are more than recouped in a building's operational cost savings.
- The expectation of operational cost decreases resulting from green building is the most important trigger for faster adoption of green school building.
- There is a strong need for access to and information on green building products, particularly those that improve health, such as products that reduce mold and indoor air pollutants.[29]

Benefits of Green Schools

Researchers have known since the late 1990s that daylighting and views to the outdoors raise school performance by more than 20 percent. A study of the test performance of 21,000 schoolchildren in California, Colorado, and Washington statistically proved the case for greener school design.[30]

A 2002 project, the 58,000-square-foot Ash Creek Intermediate School in Monmouth, Oregon, designed by BOORA Architects, shows that daylighting, good design, and cost-effective school construction are quite compatible.[31] At a construction cost of $124 per square foot, the school was built for about $10 per square foot less than local costs for other middle schools. Energy use is estimated at 30 percent below Oregon energy code, saving the school $11,000 per year.

Passive solar design was the key architectural philosophy, according to Heinz Rudolf of BOORA. He used tours of other daylit schools he'd designed to convince the school's construction committee of the wisdom of the measures he was proposing. Having certified other schools at the LEED Silver and Gold levels, Rudolf was confident Ash Creek would receive a Silver rating if it applied for LEED certification.[32]

Figure 9.6. Designed by BOORA Architects, Ash Creek Intermediate School in Monmouth, Oregon, cost $10 less per square foot to build than other local middle schools. Photo by Sally Painter, courtesy of BOORA Architects.

Surveys also show that most seasoned observers believe greener schools have enormous benefits. For example, a 2005 survey of 665 construction industry executives by Turner Construction Company showed that they believed green K–12 schools had the following benefits:

- improved community image, 87 percent
- ability to attract and retain teachers, 74 percent
- reduced student absenteeism, 72 percent
- improved student performance, 71 percent
- lower 20-year operating costs, 73 percent[33]

The Green Schools Report

Late in 2006, well-known researcher Gregory Kats published a revolutionary study of the costs and benefits of green schools. This study was sup-

Table 9.3
Financial Benefits of Green Schools

Benefit Category	Benefit/(cost) per square foot*
Energy	$ 9
Emissions reduction	$ 1
Water and wastewater utility bills	$ 1
Increased lifetime earnings of students	$49
Asthma reduction from better air quality	$ 3
Cold and flu reduction from better air quality	$ 5
Teacher retention	$ 4
Employment impact from higher costs	$ 2
Total	$74
Cost of greening (2% assumed)	($3)
Net Financial Benefits	$71

*20-year net present value

Source: Gregory Kats, *Greening America's Schools Costs and Benefits,* October 2006, www
.cap-e.com/ewebeditpro/items/O59F11233.pdf, accessed April 3, 2007.

ported by the U.S. Green Building Council, the American Federation of
Teachers, the American Institute of Architects, the American Lung Association, and the Federation of American Scientists. Many of the study's conclusions apply equally well to higher education, but they are devastating for
the status quo in secondary education building design, renovation, and remodeling. The study examined the costs and benefits of green schools, assuming a cost increase of 2 percent, or $3 per square foot, to an average na-
tional school construction cost of $150 per square foot.[34]

The report, "Greening America's Schools," found that building green
would save an average school $100,000 each year, net of costs—enough to
pay for two additional teachers. The report broke new ground by demonstrating that green schools are extremely cost-effective. Total financial benefits from green schools outweigh costs by 20 to 1. Table 9.3 shows the cal-
culated benefits from green school construction and operations, based on a
study of 30 green schools built in 10 states between 2001 and 2006.

The bottom line is very simple. If you are a school board member, school
superintendent, or concerned parent, you should take this evidence to heart
and support building green schools in your school district. Even subtracting
the potential benefit of higher lifetime earnings resulting from higher test
scores, the net benefits of green schools outweigh the costs by eight to one,

an 800 percent gain; excluding the benefits from teacher retention and the extra jobs generated by the assumed higher costs of green schools, the benefits still outweigh the costs by six to one. For a return on investment of 600 percent, you'd be wise to go forward. Even counting just utility cost savings, the benefits outweigh the costs by three to one.

As the results of the study become better known, look for green school design and construction activity to accelerate in the 2007–2010 period. There are no longer any good reasons for school architects and administrators to provide anything but high-performance green design for future projects. The facts are in—now it's time for them to act.

Chapter 10
The Revolution in Housing

Green homes are taking the market by storm in 2007. Building on a base of 174,000 Energy Star–certified single-family homes in 2006, the LEED for Homes pilot rating system, and the National Association of Home Builders (NAHB) Model Green Home Building Guidelines, along with dozens of local green home rating programs, homebuilders are building and certifying thousands of new homes that go beyond just energy savings to create healthier and more resource-efficient living environments.[1]

A recent survey of homebuilders and green home buyers lends credence to this view. Harvey Bernstein of McGraw-Hill Construction said at a 2007 conference, "It's also powerful that people [we surveyed] are really starting to commit to building truly green homes, moving away from just adding energy-efficient appliances or one aspect that's green. They're paying attention to the holistic benefit of green."[2]

Just in time, too, because the slowdown in new home construction requires builders to create new points of differentiation in their product, and green building approaches are showing that they can help sell homes. The importance of residential construction to the green building market consists of one simple fact: even with a 15 percent slowdown in new housing starts in 2007 compared with 2006, the value of new residential construction is predicted to be roughly the same as all of commercial construction, about $400 billion each. Developers in 2007 will construct about 1.1 to 1.3 million new single-family homes and about 300,000 apartment and condominium units.[3] By 2030, 50 percent of the entire U.S. housing stock will have been created after 2007, meaning that this sector represents an unprecedented opportunity for green buildings.[4]

Consider the Grupe Company's Carsten Crossings development in Rocklin, California, part of Newland Communities' Whitney Ranch development.[5] Grupe is a production builder with a strong commitment to energy efficiency and sustainability. The company has a comprehensive buyer ed-

Figure 10.1. The Grupe Company's Carsten Crossings community in Rocklin, California, features new homes that come with energy-efficient features including a SunPower™ Sun Tile roof-integrated solar electric system. Courtesy of the Grupe Company.

ucation program that highlights energy efficiency. Each development's model home has a hands-on energy display featuring innovative energy technologies such as solar water heating panels, tankless water heaters, and radiant wall and roof barriers.[6]

Averaging 2,500 square feet, the homes also feature a 2.4-kilowatt photovoltaic system integrated with the building's roof tiles, taking advantage of major new federal and California incentives for solar electric power. In a testament to the marketing power of solar-powered and energy-efficient homes, by May 2006 the company had sold 23 of 30 green homes constructed. In 2006 and 2007 other large Northern California home builders, including Centex and Lennar, followed suit with sun-powered roof tiles.[7]

Even Realtors, who assist buyers in finding homes, are getting into the act. In February 2007, Oregon's Regional Multiple Listing Service launched a new web-site menu feature that will allow homebuyers to search under "home performance" to find homes certified under one or more of three programs: Energy Star, Oregon's Earth Advantage program, and LEED for Homes.[8]

Energy Star Homes

Homes that earn the Energy Star must meet guidelines for energy efficiency set by the U.S. Environmental Protection Agency and submit to on-site inspection. Energy Star–qualified homes are at least 15 percent more energy-efficient than homes built to the 2004 International Residential Code. In 2006, about 174,000 new single-family homes were built to the Energy Star standard, representing about 12 percent of all new homes.

Each Energy Star–rated home is estimated to save about 2,000 kilowatt-hours of electricity annually, worth about $200 in utility-bill reductions.[9] Energy Star–qualified homes include a variety of energy-efficient features such as higher levels of insulation, high-performance windows, tighter exterior construction, ducts that don't leak, more efficient heating and cooling equipment, and Energy Star–qualified lighting and appliances. These features contribute to improved home quality and homeowner comfort, lower energy demand, and reduced air pollution.

Homebuilders' Association Guidelines

The NAHB created its Model Green Home Building Guidelines earlier in this decade. Since then, many local and state homebuilders associations have adopted these guidelines as the basis for their own green building certification programs. The NAHB has also partnered with the Green Building Initiative (GBI) to assist with the certification of homes built using these guidelines.[10]

The NAHB guidelines provide three levels of certification: Bronze, Silver, and Gold. Projects must achieve a minimum score (varying by certification level) in seven guiding principles of builder and environmental concern, to ensure a balanced whole-systems approach[11] :

- Lot design, preparation, and development
- Resource (materials) efficiency
- Energy efficiency
- Water efficiency
- Indoor environmental quality
- Operation, maintenance, and homeowner education
- Global impact (e.g., low-VOC products)

Other homebuilder associations (HBAs) offer programs modeled after those of Built Green Colorado, a program of the HBA of Metropolitan Denver, which has certified more than 30,000 new homes over the past 10 years. The program claims a market share in the metro Denver area of 28 percent and has about 140 participating homebuilders. In 2006, the program's goal was to certify 6,000 new homes.[12] Most of the homebuilder programs are self-certified, an important difference from LEED for Homes and Energy Star, both of which require on-site inspection and some testing in order to receive third-party certification.

The GBI program is now available from 11 local homebuilders' associations in 10 states. More than 40 green-home rating programs exist throughout the country, some of them long-standing, such as those of Austin Energy in Austin, Texas, and the City of Scottsdale, Arizona.[13] Rating systems are also offered by nonprofits such as Build It Green in California (with its GreenPoint Rated system) and Earth Advantage in Oregon.[14]

The proliferation of rating systems and certification organizations can be confusing to both homebuilder and homebuyer. For that reason, I expect that one or two national green-home rating brands will emerge.

LEED for Homes

Following on the success of its other LEED programs, the USGBC launched the LEED for Homes (LEED-H) pilot program for evaluation in 2005, with the goal of evaluating the program over a two-year period. As of March 2007, LEED-H had nearly 300 participating builders, 1,000 registered projects, and 6,000 registered housing units. Among registered projects, 18 percent represented affordable housing units and a whopping 58 percent, or 2,484 projects, were in multifamily units. By April 2007, 63 projects had been certified, representing 159 housing units, an average of 2.5 units per project.

One early LEED-H pilot project is Mosier Creek Homes in Mosier, Oregon, a small town located along the Columbia River about 50 miles east of Portland. Built by Urban Fund, Inc., the project contains 22 townhomes and 12 flats and is certified at the LEED-H Silver level. Rooftop photovoltaic systems and solar thermal energy panels supply nearly 50 percent of the energy used.

To reduce the cost premium of the solar energy systems, the developer created a separate partnership to build, own, and operate them, taking advantage of state and federal tax credits and local utility incentives. Because Mosier Creek Solar LLC owns the systems, homeowners can share in incentives and financial benefits typically available only to commercial businesses. (Homeowner tax credits are limited to $2,000 for each type of solar energy system installed.)

Because of this commercial ownership arrangement, in five years Mosier Creek Solar will be able to save approximately $22,000 on the initial $28,000 unit cost of the system that produces the solar energy used in the project.[15] The residences will all be Energy Star certified, according to the developer.

Developer Peter Erickson says of his experience with the LEED-H program:

> My cost ended up being between $3,500 and $4,200 per residence more than if I hadn't gone for LEED certification. What I ended up with was a house that was pressurized and checked for leaks. Everything was monitored: electrical use for lighting, electrical use for energy, air changes per hour for ventilation. What came out of that is a house that uses 30 percent less energy than if I had built this house only to local codes. If you take the high side of that extra cost, say $4,200, it pays for itself in three years in reduced energy bills. . . . So it was a marketing edge that the other builders don't have.[16]

The green aspects also helped Erickson raise investment money for the project, as he explains: "I had an investor who was willing to take a slightly lower return in exchange for doing this in a green and solar fashion. It turns out that he may not have to take a lower return, because our sales are not tanking [as everyone else's are] and our presales have been excellent."

Multifamily Homes

The green multifamily home market is just developing, reflecting developers' belief in urban residents' interest in environmental issues. As a result, 10 apartment and condo projects had been LEED-NC certified as of summer 2007. In addition, about 5 percent of all currently registered projects, or another 200, are multifamily projects.

"Multifamily development is an environmental home run, even before consideration of the type or quality of construction or whether either meets

Figure 10.2. One of the LEED for Homes pilot projects, the Urban Fund's Mosier Creek Homes in Mosier, Oregon, incorporates solar water heating and electricity. Photo by Richard Hallman, Freelance Imaging, courtesy of Urban Fund, Inc.

special green standards," says urban development expert John McIlwain. "Even environmentally sound single-family development has a far greater adverse environmental impact than the average apartment or condominium building."[17]

I had the opportunity to live in a LEED-certified apartment building in Portland, Oregon, for six months in 2005 and 2006. Completed in 2005, The

Louisa is a 285,000-square-foot, 242-unit, 16-story apartment tower. It was built on top of a one-square-block retail podium as part of Gerding Edlen's Brewery Blocks development, described in Chapter 7, and is LEED Gold-certified.

I liked numerous features of this project: the bamboo floors, the dual-flush toilets, the tight building envelope that made the units very quiet, and the low-VOC cabinets, carpets, and finishes that meant the absence of "new home smell" when I moved in as the first tenant. Best of all, the apartment was nonsmoking, a requirement for LEED residences. Occupying 50 percent of the second floor was a green roof that provided a parklike setting above the city streets. Energy savings are projected at 40 percent over comparable local projects, and the apartment balconies are designed specifically to provide summer shading for the windows of the units below. The project was fully leased within the first year, and the owners got the highest rents in town—I can personally attest to that!

Another exemplary multifamily green project is Acqua + Vento in Calgary, Alberta, developed by Windmill Development Group and completed in 2006. Designed by architects Busby Perkins+Will for two sites in a downtown redevelopment area, the two three-story condominium buildings, each with 22 townhomes, take an aggressive approach to meeting environmental objectives. Aiming for LEED Platinum certification, a first for Canadian residential developments, the project's sustainable design initiatives include an enhanced building-envelope design, stormwater collection, graywater recycling, dual-flush toilets, and photovoltaics. The buildings are designed to reduce energy use by 50 percent and water use by 60 percent compared to a conventional building.[18]

In New York City, two LEED Gold-certified apartment buildings, the Solaire and the Helena, led the way for further green development. Completed in 2005 and designed by FXFOWLE Architects, the 600,000-square-foot Helena comprises 580 apartments in 37 stories. Located on the Hudson River at West 57th Street, the project contains an in-house sewage treatment plant, efficient microturbines for on-site power production, and a 12,000-square-foot green roof. Energy costs are estimated to be 33 percent below comparable nearby properties. Potable water savings are close to 1.5 million gallons per year. A 13-kilowatt building-integrated photovoltaic system is located in the building's canopy, and the project purchases green power from offsite to supply 50 percent of its power requirements.[19]

Figure 10.3. The Louisa, a 16-story apartment building in Portland, Oregon's Brewery Blocks development, designed by GBD Architects, has a second-floor green roof over a ground-floor retail podium. Photo by Gregg Galbraith, Red Studio, Inc., courtesy of Gerding Edlen.

Affordable Green Housing

There is considerable activity in the architecture and development community to design and build affordable green housing, typically in multiple-unit buildings. Some of the significant activity and support is coming from the Green Communities program of Enterprise Community Partners,[20] Global Green USA, and the Home Depot Foundation, to name a few. Why shouldn't people in subsidized housing have access to lower utility bills, healthier indoor air, and the other benefits of green buildings? Why shouldn't the average apartment be water-conserving, comfortable, and cheaper to operate?

The Green Communities program has committed $555 million to building 8,500 affordable green housing units across the country over the next five years. Green Communities says that it "incorporates many innovations from the 'mainstream' green building movement, including the use of environmentally sustainable materials, reduction of environmental impact,

Figure 10.4. Windmill Development Group's Acqua + Vento in Calgary, Alberta, designed by Busby Perkins+Will, features 44 condominiums and is aiming for LEED Platinum. Courtesy of Busby Perkins+Will.

and increased energy efficiency. Green Communities takes the idea of green several steps further, emphasizing design and materials that safeguard the health of residents, and locations that provide close, easy access to public transportation, schools, and services."[21]

Modular Green Homes

About 100,000 manufactured homes will be sold in 2007.[22] Many of these could be green homes, with a little effort. In 2006, the first "super green" modular homes hit the market. The LivingHome®, designed by Ray Kappe and built by Steve Glenn in Santa Monica, California, was certified LEED-H Platinum, with 91 of 108 possible points.[23] The cost of a 2,500-square-foot LivingHome is estimated at $200 to $250 per square foot from the factory and about $350 when completed on a building site. The home won the 2007 NAHB EnergyValue Housing Award.[24]

Michelle Kaufmann Designs produces the Glidehouse™ and the Sunset®

Breezehouse™. The signature feature of the Sunset Breezehouse is the Breeze-Space at the center, under a distinctive butterfly-shaped roof. Costs range from $150 to $250 per square foot, excluding site development expenses. Key sustainable design features include lighting, materials, and layout.[25]

Low-energy lighting design features include the following:

- window placement designed to minimize need for artificial lighting
- energy-efficient fluorescent lighting

Eco-friendly materials include the following:

- renewable, recyclable materials such as bamboo flooring and Richlite countertops made from recycled paper
- water-saving fixtures in the bathrooms, such as dual-flush toilets
- formaldehyde-free cabinets and energy-smart appliances in the kitchen
- nontoxic paints used for the walls of the house
- on-demand (tankless) water heater
- radiant heating system

Sustainable design layout features include the following:

- cross-ventilation in all major rooms
- large, operable doors in BreezeSpace designed to maximize breezes for cooling
- stone floor in BreezeSpace for efficient thermal mass heating
- sloped roof for solar panels using the butterfly roof configuration
- spray-in insulation in roofs for energy-efficient envelope

Looking over this list, it's easy to see that all of these modular home elements can be combined into production housing, apartments, and condominiums as well, to create energy-efficient, water-conserving, healthier homes. But is there enough market demand for them to get builders and developers to change their current housing styles and market offerings?

The Green Home Revolution

A 2007 McGraw-Hill survey of 341 green home purchasers revealed some interesting patterns. For the survey, a green home was defined as one that of-

Figure 10.5. The Sunset Breezehouse, by Michelle Kaufmann Designs, is a modular home that blurs the boundary between interior and exterior space. Photo by James Watts, courtesy of Michelle Kaufmann Designs.

fered energy efficiency and at least two other green features. As reported at the NAHB's 2007 National Green Building Conference, the results showed that green homeowners tend to be wealthier and better educated than average and that they reside disproportionately in the South and West. Seventy-one percent are women, 65 percent are married, and their average age is 45. At an average premium of $18,500 on top of a home price of $292,000, the estimated 18,000 green homes bought each year from 2004 to 2006 represented a value of $3.3 billion.[26] By 2010, McGraw-Hill estimates that the green home market will range from $7 billion to $20 billion, a span that reflects a considerable uncertainty about how fast the market will grow from the 2006 base.

The most intriguing finding of the survey was that the highest percentage of buyers who bought a green home (28 percent) did so because they learned about it from a friend, indicating that green home owners have a high level of satisfaction with their purchase. Some 20 percent had learned about green buildings from TV and 14 percent from the Internet. Lastly, 85 percent would recommend a green home to others.

Table 10.1
Barriers to Growth of Green Homes, 2007 to 2010

1. Extra costs for green features, especially solar energy systems, water-conserving fixtures, and higher levels of home energy efficiency
2. Higher costs for home certification (builders don't want to pay more than $300 to $400 per unit for third-party certification)
3. Lack of expressed buyer demand for green homes
4. Cost and difficulty of marketing green homes to a small percentage of total buyers
5. Legal issues revolving around express or implied warranties for home performance (third-party certification is the best way to handle this)
6. Training and education required for builders' sales and marketing teams
7. Internal changes needed in purchasing, home design, and construction practices

What motivated the green home buyers? The top factor (cited by 90 percent of respondents) was a desire to save money on energy. Eighty-five percent wanted superior performance (comfort, acoustics, drafts), while 80 percent had been encouraged to buy by some sort of cash incentive. Some 69 percent were worried about increasing energy costs, while 52 percent cited third-party certification as a reason for buying. Influencing factors were high utility costs (84 percent), environmental concerns (84 percent), health reasons (81 percent), and the prospect of having a more highly valued home (73 percent).[27]

More than 60 percent of survey respondents said that limited consumer awareness, additional costs, and limited availability of homes were obstacles to green homes' gaining a bigger market share, with the need for consumer education the biggest hurdle to overcome. Nonetheless, consider the positive survey results, the increasing number of green-home rating programs, and the clearly expressed builder interest all over the country. Based on this information, it seems likely that green homes will experience major growth from 2007 to 2010. Given that there are already hundreds of thousands of Energy Star homes, and figuring that more than 5 million homes will be built over those four years, there may easily be a million homes with some type of green certification by the end of 2010, representing about 20 percent of all homes built during that period.

There are still significant barriers, however, primarily those of cost and poorly expressed demand; other barriers are shown in Table 10.1. To tackle these barriers, we can expect to see all levels of government—federal, state, and local—offering incentives to spur the growth of green homes. Local governments that are especially concerned about global warming and the impacts of growth on utility systems will just require them, but in most areas incentives will be used more frequently, at least for the next five years. These incentives may include tax credits and rebates, sales tax and property tax exemptions (full or partial), accelerated permit processing, and expedited land use approvals.

Chapter 11
The Revolution in Neighborhood Design and Mixed-Use Development

In these early years of the 21st century, Americans are beginning to realize that the post–World War II model of suburban sprawl is unhealthy and damaging to the natural environment. Several studies have linked suburban sprawl and increased dependence on the automobile to an increase in health problems, particularly because we spend more time in cars and less time walking from place to place.[1] A 2006 report summarizing this research concluded that "greater proximity [between residential and commercial uses] increases individuals' perception that walking or bicycling is a viable alternative to driving. Furthermore, living in a mixed-use environment, within walking distance to shops and services, reduces the risk of obesity."[2]

Many of us in suburbs or sprawling metropolitan areas have to use a car for the most basic necessities of life: getting food, taking the kids to school, seeing a doctor, or going shopping for just about anything. One reaction that began in the 1980s was a trend toward transit-oriented development and a "new urbanism," exemplified in the work of such planning luminaries as Peter Calthorpe in California and the team of Andrés Duany and Elizabeth Plater-Zyberk in Florida.[3] Organizationally, these reactions found a home in the Congress for the New Urbanism and the Smart Growth movement.[4]

As a result, a mixed-use revolution is well under way. Baby boomers and young "creatives" are moving back into the cities, both to find a simpler and richer life and to associate with a critical mass of like-minded people. With this reawakening of the desire for closer ties with neighbors and the local community comes a host of interesting design challenges, most notably this one: How do we put all these uses together in a coherent framework that meets social needs and reduces energy use and environmental impact? The answer has been an explosion in mixed-use development, often combining office, retail, hospitality, and residential activities in the same building, with one use stacked on top of another, or in the same neighborhood in a multi-block development.

The New World of Mixed-Use Development

A 2006 survey of four large national real estate development organizations found that more than 25 percent of members' business was already in mixed-use projects, with 35 percent saying that it accounted for more than half their business.[5] Clearly, multiple-use projects are an important component of today's business environment. Thirty percent of the survey respondents agreed on the definition of mixed-use projects as "development of a real estate project with planned integration of some combination of retail, office, residential, hotel, recreation, or other functions." For developers, mixed-use development is pedestrian-oriented, combines elements of a live-work-play environment, and maximizes space utilization. It often features such amenities as parks and other forms of open space, includes significant architectural expression, and reduces traffic congestion.

Of the survey respondents, 93 percent thought that mixed-use development would grow in importance in the next five years, primarily because cities are encouraging such development and assisting private developers with planning and zoning decisions, incentive programs, and in some cases the assembling of land. Rising urban land prices and a growing desire to integrate home, work, and leisure also play a key role, respondents said. Two major downsides they cited are the extended time it may take to put all the pieces together and the greater financial risk of a phased development of disparate project elements. Respondents also thought that mixed-use projects cost more and took longer to complete.

Examples of Green Mixed-Use Projects

Given these uncertainties among developers, more green mixed-use projects in cities are under way than one might suspect. Here we profile two of the more significant projects in North America: Dockside Green in Victoria,

British Columbia, and the Noisette Community in North Charleston, South Carolina.

Dockside Green is a 15-acre, $500 million mixed-use development in a joint venture between Vancity Enterprises of Vancouver, British Columbia, and the local Windmill Development Group (also the developers of Acqua + Vento, discussed in the previous chapter). It will be situated in the heart of Victoria, adjacent to the Inner Harbour, along an abandoned and contaminated former industrial waterfront. With a planned total of 1.3 million square feet of mixed-use residential, office, retail, and industrial space, Dockside Green represents the biggest development of city land in Victoria's history. Upon completion, it expects to house 2,500 new residents in 1,100 housing units, each averaging about 1,000 square feet.[6]

By pledging to build only LEED Platinum project elements, the development team won a spirited public competition in 2004 against a better-funded competitor. Developer Joe Van Belleghem believes that his commitment to sustainability was a deciding factor, augmented by the practical experience he had garnered in developing the first LEED-NC Gold project in Canada, nearby Vancouver Island Technology Park.[7] The developers' commitment to a "triple bottom line" approach—integrating environment, economy, and ecology (sustainability)—is incorporated into every element of the project, including a recent commitment to be "greenhouse gas neutral." The project will use a biomass gasification system that will convert locally produced wood waste into clean-burning natural gas.[8] Building energy use will be reduced about 50 percent, water use will be reduced by 66 percent, and all sewage will be treated on-site and recycled or sent to a "bioswale filter" before it goes into the harbor.[9]

The Noisette Community in North Charleston, South Carolina, is the dream of one man, developer John Knott.[10] Noisette Company is transforming 3,000 acres into a "city within a city." In the late 1990s, the city and the developer agreed on a public-private partnership to transform 400 acres of an abandoned Naval Complex (closed in 1996) into a vibrant mixed-use community, using an unprecedented master planning effort. In addition to the project area, the master plan includes continuing efforts at redevelopment of the adjacent 2,600 acres.

In 2004, the city accepted the plan and gave the developer the green light to begin transforming Navy Yard. The Noisette plan encourages increased density, walking-distance access between neighborhoods and public and

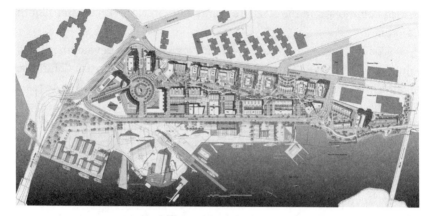

Figure 11.1. Developers of Dockside Green, a 15-acre mixed-use Canadian development, aim to build each building to LEED Platinum standards. Courtesy of Windmill/Vancity and Busby Perkins+Will.

commercial resources, improved and integrated transit options, reduced and slower traffic flow, expanded open space and recreational options, and reestablishment of community links to major environmental assets such as the Cooper River, which empties into Charleston Harbor. The state's first LEED-certified elementary school is part of the redevelopment effort. Noisette is directly responsible for developing about 3,000 new housing units and two million square feet of new commercial space.[11]

The first Noisette neighborhood, the 55-acre Oak Terrace Preserve, illustrates a variety of sustainable planning and building measures. Under construction in 2007, it will be an exemplary green community, one of a number of environmentally focused enclaves that have sprung up across the nation. What makes Oak Terrace Preserve special, certainly for the Southeast, is that the development, located in the formerly blighted Century Oaks neighborhood, will be a thoroughly green neighborhood in an urban area. Each of the 303 single-family houses and 74 townhouses will be built with recyclable, energy-efficient, sustainable materials and will be certified to EarthCraft House™ green-home standards by the Atlanta-based Southface Energy Institute.[12]

Another type of "green" mixed-use urban development is rising in Las Vegas, Nevada. MGM Mirage's Project CityCenter is a huge, 76-acre city-within-a-city on the Las Vegas Strip. CityCenter anticipates opening in 2009 with a 60-story, 4,000-room hotel and casino along with two 400-room boutique hotels (non-gaming) and 500,000 square feet of premier retail shops, entertainment venues, and fine dining. In addition, the project will include 2,800 residential units for those who would like to live in this new urban metropolis. It will be the country's largest new mixed-use development, with some 18 million square feet of space—an investment valued at $7 billion.[13] All buildings except the casino are expected to receive at least LEED Silver certification, owing in part to some generous property tax abatements enacted into law in 2005 by the State of Nevada.[14]

Another large urban project is the redevelopment of Stapleton Field, a former airport in Denver, Colorado, into a large mixed-use community. In December 2006, Forest City Commercial Group opened Northfield Stapleton, a 1.2-million-square-foot open-air "town center" in Denver, Colorado. According to the developer, the center is the first "Main Street"–style retail property to receive the LEED-CS Silver certification.[15]

LEED for Neighborhood Development

The USGBC, along with the Congress for the New Urbanism and the Natural Resources Defense Council, launched the LEED-ND pilot program in 2007. Enrolling and evaluating about 240 projects like Noisette and Dockside Green, LEED-ND will define what constitutes "green development" on a broader scale than just one building.

LEED-ND integrates the principles of green buildings, smart growth, and the new urbanism into the first national rating system for neighborhood design. The system focuses on best practices in four key areas affecting residential, commercial, and mixed-use development:

- smart location and links to transportation systems
- environmental preservation and restoration
- compact, complete, walkable, and connected neighborhoods
- high-performance green technologies and buildings

Appendix 2.6 lists all of the elements of the LEED-ND rating system.

The ultimate goal of LEED-ND is to develop and redevelop cities and communities that are healthier, use far less energy and water, and have a much

Figure 11.2. Located in Savannah, Georgia, Abercorn Common is a LEED Silver shopping center that includes solar hot water heaters, a cool roof, porous pavement, and water-efficient plumbing fixtures. Photo by David A. Arnold, The Partnership, courtesy of Ozell Stankus Associates Architects, Inc.

lower impact on natural habitats. Within the next five years, I expect LEED-ND to be used worldwide to define and create the first generation of zero-net-energy communities. Recalling our discussions of the planning for Dongtan Eco-City in China and Dockside Green in Canada, we can see that this trend is already beginning. Look for it to become a small wave by 2012 and a much larger flood by 2015.

Green Retail and Hospitality Design

Each element of green neighborhood design needs to come together to create the full picture. Two elements that have been lagging are the retail and hospitality industries, yet even there we can see some promising trends and exemplary developments. As of March 2007, about 75 retail projects were registered for LEED certification.

Abercorn Common in Savannah, Georgia, is a green retail development that boasts the nation's first LEED-certified McDonald's. In 2006, the project

Figure 11.3. Constructed by Swinerton Builders, the Orchard Garden Hotel in San Francisco is one of the first LEED-certified hotels. Courtesy of Swinerton Builders.

became the first retail LEED for Core and Shell certified project in the country, achieving the Silver level of performance.[16] According to developer Martin Melaver, there was no extra cost for building the second phase of the project, Shops 600, to meet LEED-CS standards. The 16,500 square feet of leasable retail space includes solar water heaters and a green roof. Harvested rainwater provides 5.5 million gallons a year of irrigation water, the project's entire consumption. A highly insulated building envelope and a reflective white roof reduce electricity consumption by more than 30 percent. Porous pavement in the parking lots reduces stormwater runoff by 30 percent, and water-efficient plumbing units reduce projected water use by 50 percent.[17]

Green hotels are beginning to be accredited under the LEED standard as well. As of March 2007, 22 hotels were registered under the LEED-NC system for future certification.[18] A 226-room Hilton Hotel in Vancouver, Washington, owned by the city, received LEED Silver certification in 2006. In this case, the cost premium was less than $1,000 per room, easily recouped in the first year from energy savings. According to the hotel, the free publicity was worth 10 times the initial cost premium.[19]

More recently, San Francisco's Orchard Garden Hotel, which opened in December 2006 adjacent to Chinatown, received the first LEED certification for a hotel in California. Constructed by Swinerton Builders, the 10-story, 55,000-square-foot, 86-room boutique hotel has a key-card system to control energy use; each time guests enter the room, they must insert a card to turn on lights and heating or air conditioning. When they leave, the reverse is true, ensuring that energy is not used unnecessarily in their absence.[20]

By 2020, I expect neighborhood and mixed-use designs to be quite different from those in 2000, as the trend toward transit-oriented, walkable neighborhoods becomes fully established. This trend will have a marked effect on reducing energy use and increasing the livability of our cities and suburbs.

Chapter 12
The Revolution in Health Care

The health care industry accounts for 13 percent of annual expenditures on nonresidential construction in the United States. For the green building revolution to realize its full potential, the health care industry needs to be a major participant. But the green health care market has developed far more slowly than other sectors, for a number of reasons, most of them related to the internal dynamics of the industry. Robin Guenther, a New York City architect who has been instrumental in greening health care, says:

> The health care industry has only really been engaged in controlling pollution from operations since around 1996, and so the health care organizations that you see as early adopters of sustainable buildings are those organizations that have been doing pollution prevention—things like waste reduction and mercury elimination. They finally felt like they had their operations in order, enough to take on green building. For many of them, also, getting their operations in order meant that they had directors of operational stewardship or people in job positions who would think about green buildings. Organizations that were a little slower about controlling pollution also weren't organized to consider green buildings.[1]

The first LEED-certified hospital, Boulder Community Foothills Hospital in Boulder, Colorado, was completed only in 2003, a full three years after the LEED rating system was introduced. The $53 million, 200,000-square-foot, 60-bed hospital received a LEED Silver rating. Projected energy savings were 35 percent compared to a prevailing 1999 standard.[2]

Green Guide for Health Care

Since the early 2000s, Guenther, along with a working group of architects and health industry professionals, has been addressing the issue of sustainability in health care with an alternative evaluation system based on LEED, called the Green Guide for Health Care. Guenther explains:

> The Green Guide for Health Care was a result of recognizing [that] health care was a little slow [to embrace green buildings] because the [LEED] tool wasn't customized. A group of people got together and attempted to modify LEED credits, based on the unique needs of health care facilities. It made a big difference because people began to get underneath the differences and found ways to approach them.

The GGHC has two sections. One part covers design and construction practices for new facilities, remodels, and major renovations, and the other part deals with operations and maintenance at existing facilities. The GGHC is a more complex (and comprehensive) rating system than LEED; it includes 12 prerequisites (vs. LEED-NC's 7) and 97 total points (vs. LEED-NC's 69). Except for water conservation, each of the major LEED credit categories—sustainable sites, energy and atmosphere, materials and resources, and indoor environmental quality—receive roughly equal emphasis.

Unlike LEED certification, GGHC is individually self-assessed but not third party–verified. Even though GGHC is a self-assessment, however, it introduces elements into design and operations that over time will change how health care projects are designed, because it gives designers and facilities managers a recognized checklist that they can apply to their projects, with each item based on a sound health care principle.

Participants in GGHC's pilot program included 115 facilities with more than 30 million square feet of space, located across the United States, Canada, and other countries. A new version, GGHC version 2.2, was released in January 2007[3]; Appendix 2.7 offers the complete text of these guidelines.

Early Green Health Care Facilities

At the present time, 16 LEED-certified health care projects have been constructed, including three buildings at a psychiatric hospital in Madison, Indiana, a project that was completed in 2005 and is shown in Figure 12.1.[4] With a strong emphasis on daylighting and views to the outdoors, the buildings also follow a well-known healing model for mental illness: reintegra-

Figure 12.1. At the Southeast Regional Treatment Center in Madison, Indiana, designers incorporated lots of daylighting. Photo by Hedrich Blessing, courtesy of HOK.

tion of people with nature. The focus on green operations involves the residents; for instance, patients are taught how to recycle everything—a prelude to reentering the outer world, where some find work in recycling facilities.[5] Other LEED-NC certified health care facilities include the Jewish Hospital Medical Center South in Hillview, Kentucky (LEED Silver), and the Providence Newberg Medical Center in Oregon (LEED Gold).[6]

Guenther's own project at the Dollard Discovery Health Center in Harris, New York, shown in Figure 12.2, illustrates many of the design principles at work in greening health care facilities. For this two-story, 28,000-square-foot diagnostic and treatment facility in rural upstate New York, completed in 2004 and LEED-certified, energy use was reduced by 27 percent compared with prevailing standards, using a ground-source heat pump system and a high-efficiency building envelope. The building is designed to use solar energy gain through the windows to help with winter heating; it also

Figure 12.2. Designed by Guenther 5 Architects, the Dollard Discovery Health Center in Harris, New York, uses 27 percent less energy than similar health care buildings. © David Allee, courtesy of Guenther 5 Architects.

maximizes daylighting, reducing lighting demand. Low-toxic finishes and minimal carpet use were also specified. The resilient flooring requires no waxing or stripping, and the green housekeeping program minimizes the use of chemicals for maintenance. Overall, the building is healthy, light, and cheaper to operate than a conventional building.[7]

LEED is catching on: the new $575 million, 10-acre campus for Children's Hospital of Pittsburgh hopes to achieve LEED Gold status for its research center and LEED Silver for the hospital when it's completed in 2009. Guenther discusses this trend:

> Now that there is a critical mass of projects out there, hospitals see that it makes business sense to go green, and they are seeing the fabulous PR that the innovator hospitals are getting. What we're beginning to get now is the "fast follower" group that is following on the success of the innovators.

The Business Case for Green Buildings in Health Care

The business case for health care is different than that for other projects. For one thing, about 76 percent of private, or nongovernmental, hospitals (employing 83 percent of health care workers) are nonprofit organizations, which means that the profit motive is less imperative and that access to capital for new projects is more difficult. Many hospitals are affiliated with universities and serve teaching and research functions that require accommodation in each project. Of the total number of hospitals, government hospitals represent about 20 percent, private nonprofits 60 percent, and private for-profits 20 percent.[8]

Table 12.1 shows some of the business case drivers for green buildings (and green operations) in health care. The primary driver for health care, as for most large institutions, is money—specifically, the return on energy-savings investments. Favorable community public relations come in second. The rest of the business-case benefits are slowly gaining acceptance, particularly among the more progressive institutions. Some of the possible business-case benefits, such as recruiting and retaining nurses and other key staff, while more accepted in other building types, are still seen as speculative advantages of green health care facilities.

What will it take to get green buildings into the health care design and operations system? First of all, CEOs must push sustainability to the top of the agenda. The opportunities for cost savings and positive community relations are often the primary drivers from a top executive's point of view. Second, the facilities staff and project management staff need to be fully educated about green design and operations. Third, the organization must contain an internal champion for sustainability, preferably reporting directly to the CEO or chief operations or finance officer. Fourth, each project must start with a vision for sustainability, something that the design, construction, and operations team can keep returning to when the project starts to devolve into something more "familiar."[9]

The world of health care design changes slowly, but it is changing. Robin Guenther says, "I think there's a huge driver in the mission connection. People can talk about having to make the economic argument for which strategies they do or don't do. But what really brings them in the door is getting the connection between the built environment and human health, and rec-

Table 12.1

Drivers for Green Buildings and Operations in Health Care

1. Economic return on energy- and water-efficiency investments; protection against future increases in energy prices through peak-shaving and other demand-reduction measures
2. Consistency with the health and healing mission of health care institutions—for example, locating new facilities on remediated urban brownfields
3. Economic gain from faster healing (and quicker discharge) of patients who have views of the outdoors and healing gardens on premises
4. Public relations benefits, considering the many stakeholders in the hospital and health care universe
5. Health benefits to the workforce from use of less-toxic chemicals in facility management
6. Recruitment and retention of key employees (nurses and other skilled practitioners)
7. Evidence-based health care should be in evidence-based green buildings!

ognizing that they can't go on being part of the problem, that they have to reconceptualize around this connection between mission and health. Over and over again, that's what the CEOs of the innovators say: 'It's the right thing to do. As soon as we heard about it we had to do it, because we are the health care industry.'"[10]

Accelerating the Revolution in Health Care Design

This transformation of attitudes among CEOs and boards of directors is critical to promoting green buildings in the health care industry. When top management makes the connection between the hospital's or clinic's mission and the healing power of green buildings, they often become the most effective advocates for sustainable design and operations. Kim Shinn, a mechanical engineer who works on a lot of health care projects in the Southeast, echoes this sentiment: "A couple of our health care system clients are getting enthused about green construction, having us do projects that are both Green Guide for Health Care–compliant and LEED-compliant. We have even had a couple of our projects that were well into design go green as a result of boardroom directives—health care systems are realizing and committing to green building as a part of their mission of 'First, do no harm.'"[11]

Walter Vernon leads an engineering firm in San Francisco focused on health care design. He thinks the time may be right for the health care industry to apply green principles. He argues for use of the term "greener" design, recognizing that the real task is to improve what we already have in health care rather than to replace it outright. He argues that "good green design has to support the goals of the organization."[12]

One of his recommendations is to take advantage of utility rebates and transferable tax credits, as well as third-party financing options for cogeneration, solar, and microturbine systems. Because hospitals are round-the-clock operations with a fairly predictable demand for electricity and hot water or steam, they are attractive to third-party "energy service companies," which invest in energy-saving measures and on-site generation, sharing the savings with the hospitals. Vernon concludes that in the end, "resistance to green design approaches may be more about culture than technology."

"I think evidence-based design is the most significant design trend that has happened in the hospital design business in my career—in the past 30 years," says Kim Shinn. "It is truly a watershed opportunity to change the way that health care facilities are designed. Green design is very much a part of evidence-based design, because many of the design practices that we think of as green design are associated with healthy indoor environmental quality. That's exactly the question asked by evidence-based design: How much can the building environment positively affect health care outcomes?"

Barriers to Green Buildings in Health Care

Table 12.2 presents some of the barriers to green health care design, construction, and operations. The restrictive environment of health care design is certainly a major factor: the need to prevent and control disease and to meet stringent building code requirements drives a lot of design decisions. But the primary barrier is still cost. In 2005, green building activists at a major Midwestern university called me asking for help in advising their new $500 million hospital on the benefits of green building and LEED certification. The design team had already quoted a price increase of 10 percent ($50 million!) to green the building. I knew this was way out of line, and I also knew that the design team was saying to the activists and the university, "Don't bother me with this green stuff; I've got enough on my plate just trying to build a hospital."

Table 12.2
Barriers to Green Buildings in Health Care

1. The LEED rating system is difficult to apply in health care because it was designed primarily for office buildings.
2. The health care industry is highly regulated and risk-averse; as a result, innovations must meet many tests before being adopted.
3. Initial cost is the driving force for all decisions; it is difficult to make a case for investing extra money in operations vs. patient treatment and staff compensation, for example.
4. LEED is perceived to add significant costs to projects.
5. Evidence of benefits such as productivity and healthier working conditions is inadequate.
6. Health care building codes restrict options such as natural ventilation and under-floor air distribution systems because of their focus on disease prevention.
7. Long lead times for project design and construction, together with cost escalations in materials and labor, make it difficult to keep a focus on green design decisions.

This attitude was prevalent just two years ago, but I doubt you'll see a design team responding that way in the future. It is very important to document the actual costs of greening health care as well as to document the list of benefits. This may take another two or three years, because it can take three to five years or more from initial decision to first occupancy for a major health care project, so many projects that were conceived, for example, in 2005, won't have conclusive operating data until 2009 or 2010.

Despite significant barriers of cost and codes, the green building revolution is spreading to health care. The result will be more-efficient, healthier hospitals, clinics, and outpatient surgery centers.

Chapter 13
The Revolution in Workplace Design

If you're like most office workers, you know that the standard "cube farm" layout, stale air, and lack of views leave a lot to be desired. No matter how much your company tells you they value and respect your efforts, you may suspect that the real goal of most firms is to minimize the cost of space for their workforce, cramming as many people into as small a space as possible, reducing the size of cubicles year by year, and leaving just enough room for a computer and one wall space for family pictures to remind you why you're putting up with all this.

Here's a mantra and a memory aid: 300 – 30 – 3. It costs $300 (or more) per square foot for the average employee's salary and benefits; $30 per square foot (or less) for rent; and $3 per square foot for energy. To maximize corporate gain, we should focus on improving the output from the $300 person, not hampering that output to save a fraction of $30 on space or a much smaller fraction of $3 on energy.

What Is a Healthy and Productive Workplace?

Sadly, an outmoded view of the worker still prevails, one who is just a cog in a vast production machine, placidly laboring in cube farms spreading out as far as the eye can see. Companies pretend to value collaboration, yet most offices provide no "free space" where that could happen, because it would mean reserving valuable real estate for people to just sit around and talk. Even most company conference rooms are fully booked all day, so collaboration must take place over lunch or in the break room.

Many companies replicate this old-fashioned design philosophy each time they get new space—mostly out of inertia, one suspects, and fear of change. As a result, green design sits astride a fault line between old and new views of how a productive and healthy workplace should be structured and should operate.

A recent survey by Gensler, the largest architecture firm in the United States, lends credence to these claims. Gensler's 2006 Workplace Survey was conducted online among a sample of more than 2,000 American office workers representing eight industry groups: accounting, banking, legal, financial services and insurance, consulting, energy, retail, and manufacturing. These are the "knowledge workers" that any company needs to recruit and retain to remain profitable. Of those surveyed, 89 percent said the quality of the work environment is important to job satisfaction. Does their current workplace design encourage innovation and creativity? Half said no, it does not.[1]

Survey respondents thought their companies would be able to perform 22 percent more work, on average, with a better-designed physical working environment. Nine in 10 workers believed that better office design leads to better overall employee performance. Forty-six percent thought that their companies did not place a priority on creating a productive workplace. More than 54 percent would not want to show their offices to potential recruits.

Penny Bonda is an interior designer and a recognized expert on green commercial interiors.[2] "New attention is being paid to the health and well-being of the people inside the building," she says. "It used to be that when you built out an office you paid attention to the space and function needs, the traditional things we used to plan for in designing workspaces. Now there is focused attention being paid to how the space makes occupants feel and how it is affecting productivity. This shift comes from the research that says people are healthier and feel better in green offices, and so they do a better job."[3]

The green building revolution has landed smack in the middle of the healthy workplace debate, and workplace design will never be the same. As the statistics on productivity and health presented in Chapter 4 dramatically show, views to the outdoors, daylighting, underfloor air systems, lighting quality, and improved fresh-air ventilation have huge impacts on productivity and health. One can postulate that if people are healthier and more productive, if they see positive evidence that their employer cares for them because of visible green building measures, they are more likely to stay at the company and to recommend that their friends work at the company. Perhaps the slogan for green workplace design should be:

Office workers of the world, unite!
You have nothing to lose but your cubicles!

Green Workplace Design

Green design measures are fairly easy to include in most new building projects, but the building-remodeling market has more constraints. First, daylighting is difficult to retrofit, because it is so dependent on building depth and window geometry. The obvious solution is for firms to seek out tenant spaces where there is already good daylighting. As more green buildings come online, this will become progressively easier. But for firms needing multiple floors in an existing building, the daylighting choices are still somewhat limited.

Firms can, however, choose furniture, partitions, and office layouts that provide a view to the outdoors from most of the workstations; it's mostly a matter of design. They can also make sure that only finishes, furnishings, and furniture low in volatile organic compounds (VOCs) are used. According to Penny Bonda, "The manufacturing community has really responded to the interest in green interiors and is continually introducing new products that are getting better and reaching higher. Benjamin Moore is a really good example of that—they've been a leader in low-VOC paints for a long time and have recently introduced a product, Aura, which has improved performance while maintaining its low emission levels. Also, many companies that have had good products in terms of recycled content and recyclability keep innovating to go one step further."[4]

For improved fresh-air ventilation, it's often difficult to change a building's HVAC systems, so the alternative might be to look for a building with operable windows. Many sections of large cities have a surprising number of older office buildings with such windows. Essentially any building constructed before World War II will have operable windows unless they've been nailed shut, painted over, or boarded up.

In Portland, Oregon, I worked for nearly four years in a 1920s-era four-story office building with operable windows. It was a delight on a nice spring, summer, or fall day to open the window a crack and let the fresh air in. Because the building had a small floor area, about 13,000-square feet, it was fairly easy to give most of the workstations a view to the outdoors. We couldn't change the HVAC system, but we did change the lighting controls to take advantage of the daylight coming through the very large windows, so that we didn't have to use electric lighting all the time. The building was originally the first department store in town; our adaptations illustrate how building uses change over time, and why future flexibility is an important feature of sustainable design.

Another constraint on including green features in tenant improvements is the short duration of most projects. Ninety to 120 days is a typical project length, for two reasons: tenants usually wait until their need to move is overwhelming, so they want to be in a space quickly; and landlords don't like to see leasable space stay vacant for long, so they often impose fairly rapid timetables on the duration of tenant build-outs. As a result, decisions about green measures must be made much more quickly, with less time for second thoughts and redesign than in new construction projects.

While we have been making the case for the business benefits of sustainable interior design, it is true that such efforts are likely to cost more than most green measures in new building design, because there are fewer opportunities for cost savings from integrated design. (Sometimes lower-cost purchasing makes ecological sense, however. For example, the dot-com crash of 2000 put most of the fancy new office furniture of technology firms on the used furniture market, there was little reason in most major cities to buy new furniture, so many companies picked up perfectly good "salvaged" furniture for a fraction of its original cost.) To cut the overall costs of sustainable design in your next office move, investigate the local market for used office furniture and partitions to see if it's better (and cheaper) to buy what's used but still usable. Not only is that a sustainable thing to do, but it could save you considerable money that can be invested, for example, to reduce energy use by upgrading lighting, office equipment, and computers.

LEED for Commercial Interiors

Holley Henderson is a sustainable design consultant in Atlanta who's been active in the LEED-CI program. She echoes the points made above, saying, "I find [significant] reluctance to going green in projects that are extremely fast, to the point that there is barely enough time to get the building or the space done before move-in. Or from those organizations or people that won't see the numbers [on productivity and health benefits]—not only people who don't have the data but those who refuse to look at it. I also find reluctance in projects that only care about first costs. And there are still some people who don't care about design or function and only want to meet code and move into a building."[5]

Nevertheless, Henderson's overall experience demonstrates that getting high levels of sustainability into tenant improvements can be done for most projects. In fact, more than 460 projects nationwide had registered under the LEED-CI program by the end of 2006, and 105 had been certified by the end of February 2007.[6]

So, what are some green design measures that you can include in your next "revolutionary" tenant move? Here are a few easy suggestions:

- Pick a building that has good daylighting and views to the outdoors from most or all of the work spaces; rearrange the standard (or previous) office layout to make this feasible.
- Specify zero- or low-toxicity paints, adhesives, carpets, and furnishings, including furniture, cabinetry, and furnishings with no urea-formaldehyde particleboard or composite wood.
- Change out the lighting to dimmable fluorescents or compact fluorescent bulbs wherever possible, to cut heat gain in summer and lighting bills all year long.
- Install lighting controls that allow you to use daylighting whenever possible and occupancy sensors that turn off lighting when you leave.
- Look for opportunities to provide individual control of temperature, lighting, and ventilation, including operable windows.
- Choose Energy Star–rated office equipment to minimize energy use and heat gain, since you'll be paying for air-conditioning.
- Agree with the landlord to submeter the premises, so that you can encourage energy conservation in your organization and reap the benefits.

Keeping these opportunities and constraints in mind, consider one exemplary green tenant improvement.

In Toronto, international design firm HOK decided to upgrade its new 20,700-square-foot space with a LEED-CI Gold-certified renovation. In this case, offices and studio were designed to make use of the building attributes: sealed concrete floors, open ceilings, and exposed columns. The project's sustainable design measures included daylighting; occupancy/daylight sensors; recycled-content, renewable, local, and low-emitting materials; construction waste recycling; and flexible workstations. Operable windows were part of the energy conservation measures, with overall savings estimated at 30 percent. Purchased green power supplied 75 percent of the remaining electricity use. The project also included extensive education of occupants in the operation of all building systems, an essential move to realize the anticipated energy savings.[7]

All of these approaches and more are codified in the LEED for Commercial Interiors standard. Recognizing that there are fewer ways to green a tenant build-out than a new building or major renovation, the LEED-CI standard contains only 52 core points instead of the 64 in LEED-NC.

Since LEED-CI doesn't deal with site improvements, it uses surrogate measures to reflect good site selection and design by asking that prospective tenants choose buildings that meet LEED site design criteria or, better yet, that are LEED-certified already. For example, you can choose to locate near transit stops, provide bicycle lockers and showers, provide preferred parking for carpools and vans, and subsidize mass transit use by employees. You can also design the lighting in your space to turn off at night and, in some situations, to provide more lighting control zones so that janitors don't have to light up an entire floor to clean each section of it.

In terms of water conservation, since you probably won't be irrigating your space, why not persuade the landlord to install water-free urinals, dual-flush toilets, and low-flow faucets and showerheads? For energy conservation, why not put an Energy Star refrigerator and dishwasher in the kitchen on each floor? Look for every conservation opportunity, and you may be amazed at how many you'll find. To save energy, trade in your older copiers, computers, and printers for the most energy-efficient units on the market. Make sure that all of your energy-using basic systems, such as lighting, heating, cooling, fans, and water heating, are commissioned before occupancy. When you're all done, work with the landlord to buy green power from an outside vendor to offset the balance of your projected or actual electricity use.

Figure 13.1. HOK's LEED-CI Gold-certified design office in Toronto boasts daylighting and operable windows. Photo by Richard Johnson, courtesy of HOK.

During construction, be sure to require the contractor to use best practices to preserve indoor air quality, including sealing all ductwork, carpet, and surfaces that may absorb or adsorb dust, moisture, mold, and other pollutants.

For materials and resource conservation, look at how much of an older building you can preserve. Examine whether there are good-quality salvaged materials on the market, such as doors, partitions, office furniture, and cabinets that you can buy and install in your new location. Be sure to take quality furnishings with you into the new space. Look at buying high-recycled-content materials wherever possible, including any new furniture. Consider using furniture, flooring, and other materials made with agricultural fiberboards, cork, bamboo, or linoleum. Lastly, whenever possible, specify lumber or composite wood products certified by the Forestry Stewardship Council (FSC). For an office remodel, an engineering firm in Portland hired a local contractor to install formaldehyde-free, FSC-certified particleboard for specially designed workstations throughout a 20,000-square-foot office.

In some situations, firms use a LEED-CI tenant improvement certification to assist their internal and external branding as a sustainable design firm. But any firm can reap the benefits of better health and a more productive work environment by taking time to consider these measures in project planning and then incorporating them into specifications for the remodeling

Figure 13.2. The InterfaceFLOR showroom in Shanghai was the first LEED-CI certified project in China. Courtesy of InterfaceFLOR Asia-Pacific.

contractor. InterfaceFLOR created a LEED-CI Platinum-certified showroom in
Atlanta and a Gold-certified showroom in Shanghai as part of its continuing efforts to create a brand image as the most sustainable manufacturer in
the floor coverings industry. The Shanghai showroom, located on the second
floor of Raffles City in the heart of the historic district, is a 4,500-square-foot
facility that received 33 credit points from the USGBC, most notably for water conservation, energy efficiency, and use of reclaimed materials. Low-
flow fixtures reduce its expected water use by more than 40 percent, and 60
percent of the furniture is reclaimed or reused, including wooden arches
that were constructed from antique timbers reclaimed from nearby buildings scheduled for demolition.[8]

Chapter 14
The Revolution in
Property Management

Green building advocates realized early on that existing developments represent a major opportunity for achieving energy and water savings and reducing the overall environmental impacts of building operations. After all, in any five-year period, new construction and major renovations affect only a small fraction of the existing building stock. As a result, the USGBC created the LEED for Existing Buildings (LEED-EB) standard in 2004, as a means to benchmark building operations against a variety of sustainability criteria. By the end of 2006, nearly 250 projects had registered to participate in LEED-EB, and about 40 had been certified. Compared with the success of the LEED-NC program, this program has had a slow start. Nevertheless, there is considerable evidence that the LEED-EB program is poised to take off, as more organizations begin to track their carbon footprint and attempt to reduce it.

Of course, building owners have long been renovating and improving their buildings' energy use, using as a benchmark the federal Energy Star program for commercial buildings. Energy Star evaluates energy use, in terms of BTUs per year per square foot, for buildings of a similar type within the same climatic region. By the end of 2006, Energy Star had awarded ratings to about 3,200 buildings, representing 575 million square feet, in all 50 states.[1] An Energy Star designation indicates that a building is in the top 25 percent of all similar buildings for lowest annual energy use per square foot.[2] Overall, Energy Star–rated buildings use about 35 percent less energy than similar buildings.

At the federal government level, the Federal Energy Management Program has been in place since 1973. At present, federal agencies are tasked to reduce their energy use 35 percent by 2010 compared to 1985 levels.[3] Many state and local governments have had similar programs. Reducing energy use is a clear payoff for most government agencies as well as many private businesses, because the return on investment is very high, especially at the beginning, when programs can capture the easiest retrofits.

In recent years, there has been a strong effort by government and business to reduce lighting energy use and associated cooling demands by replacing incandescent with fluorescent bulbs, especially compact fluorescents and, more recently, with LED lights. And, of course, many people are familiar with the demand-reduction programs of most electric utilities throughout the United States, which offer incentive payments and technical assistance to both businesses and consumers for cutting energy use.

The commercial office building industry spends approximately $24 billion annually on energy and contributes 18 percent of U.S. carbon dioxide emissions. Energy represents the single-largest operating expense for office buildings, typically a third of variable expenses.[4] In 2006, recognizing the need to help building owners and managers reduce energy use, Building Owners and Managers Association (BOMA) International, a trade group representing 16,500 members of this sector, launched the BOMA Energy Efficiency Program (BEEP) to educate its members about energy-efficiency upgrades. According to BOMA International, if only 2,000 buildings adopt BEEP's no- and low-cost best practices over the next three years, energy consumption and carbon emissions in those buildings will be reduced by 10 percent, resulting in $400 million in energy savings and 6.6 billion pounds less carbon dioxide released into the atmosphere.[5]

For energy-efficiency upgrades in new or existing commercial buildings, the federal government offers a tax deduction of $1.80 per square foot for measures that save at least 50 percent of heating and cooling energy, using a 2001 performance standard referenced in the 2005 Energy Policy Act. Separate partial deductions of 60 cents per square foot are available for measures treating only one of these three systems: lighting, HVAC, and building envelope (insulation and glazing) upgrades. For public buildings, the law allows the design team to take the deduction, since governments don't pay taxes.[6] As an example, energy-savings renovations in a 500,000-square-foot commercial structure that met the requirements of the law could create a $900,000 tax deduction for the building owner. At a 30 percent marginal tax rate, that amount could be worth $270,000, or about 54 cents per square foot.

LEED for Existing Buildings

But energy savings alone don't make for green operations. The LEED-EB standard encourages facility managers and building owners to broaden their horizons to include other issues:

- improved air quality, which betters the health of building occupants
- lower water use, with savings on utility bills
- greater recycling efforts, with reduced waste disposal costs
- reduced use of toxic materials, both inside and outside buildings, to improve worker health and productivity
- lower overall operations and maintenance costs

What sort of measures are part of LEED-EB certification? Some of the most prevalent include the following:

- Change site management practices to reduce the use of chemical fertilizers and pesticides in favor of integrated pest management, and to use native and adapted plants instead of ornamentals, to create better habitat.
- If the building is not close to transit, provide a shuttle link for employees to encourage use of available public transit.
- Provide bicycle lockers and changing rooms to encourage bicycle commuting.
- Provide hybrid vehicles for the organization's fleet or incentives for employees to purchase them; give employees preferred parking for low-emission, high-mileage vehicles to encourage their purchase and use.
- Promote carpools and telecommuting for employees to reduce single-occupant vehicle use.
- If there is enough area around the building, restore open space and mitigate stormwater runoff. (Installing a green roof also helps to meet these requirements.)
- If the roof needs replacing, install an Energy Star–compliant roofing material.
- Shield outdoor lighting to prevent light trespass and night-sky light pollution.

- Change landscaping practices to reduce or eliminate potable water use for irrigation.
- Reduce water use in the building by replacing older fixtures with more efficient units, including water-free urinals, low-flow sinks, and low-flush toilets.
- Recommission the building to ensure that all energy-using equipment is performing according to design intent, and replace older equipment with more efficient systems. As a minimum, achieve an Energy Star rating of 60 (meaning that the structure ranks in the top 40 percent among all similar buildings).
- Replace all HVAC equipment that is still using CFC refrigerants banned under the Montreal Protocol. (This was done by the National Geographic Society in its LEED-EB upgrade, described below.)
- Install energy-saving retrofits of HVAC, lighting, and water heating systems to improve energy performance by 20 percent or more over current baseline usage.
- Install on-site renewable energy systems such as photovoltaics, or purchase green power from a recognized provider of wind and solar energy.
- Educate the building staff on appropriate operations and maintenance best practices to reduce energy use.
- Meter energy use in greater detail, so that areas of improvement can be easily found.
- Measure and promote waste recycling by occupants to achieve 50 percent reduction of the waste stream.
- Adopt environmentally preferable purchasing policies to promote the use of salvaged and recycled-content materials, locally produced materials, bio-based materials such as agricultural fiberboard, and sustainably harvested (certified) wood products.
- Use only paints, adhesives, carpets, and other products that have low or zero emissions of volatile organic compounds.
- Adopt green cleaning practices for building maintenance.
- Install carbon dioxide sensors to control building ventilation systems.
- Improve energy use with lighting and occupancy controls.
- For construction projects, adopt high standards for waste recycling and indoor air quality maintenance.

- Where possible, redesign office and workspace layouts to promote views to the outdoors and improved daylighting for occupants.

Clearly, there are a large number of actions that any facility, office, or factory can take to create a healthier and more resource-efficient place to work. LEED-EB can be used as a benchmarking and rating system to assess both current performance and annual improvements. The most difficult part of the journey is just getting started, because most of these changes cut across departmental lines and require coordination among many levels of an organization.

Successful LEED-EB Projects

One good example of a successful LEED-EB project is the 2006 Platinum certification of three buildings at the headquarters of Adobe Systems, a software maker in San Jose, California, shown in Figure 14.1. These projects represent the largest such effort in the world to date. To demonstrate its commitment to environmental stewardship, an important public issue in northern California, Adobe decided to invest $1.1 million over five years to turn its three existing towers downtown—ranging in age from three to ten years and totaling almost one million square feet of offices and 940,000 square feet of garage space—into an environmentally friendly campus, and it chose to do it under the LEED-EB program.

In that five-year period, Adobe reduced electricity use by 35 percent, natural gas use by 41 percent, building water use by 22 percent, and irrigation water use by 75 percent. Adobe now recycles 85 percent of its solid waste. Through saving energy and buying green power, Adobe reduced pollutant emissions by 26 percent. By the company's own reckoning, the projects they've undertaken have resulted in an overall 114 percent return on investment. Retrofit and upgrade projects include reduced lighting energy use, the addition of motion sensors to turn off lights and HVAC equipment when spaces are unoccupied, installation of variable-speed drives on pumps and fans to match supply to demand, real-time metering to reduce electricity bills by cutting power use during peak periods, upgraded building automation and control systems, and recommissioning of major energy-using systems.[7]

Figure 14.1. Adobe Systems demonstrated its commitment to environmental stewardship with three LEED-EB Platinum-certified buildings on their San Jose campus. Photo by William A. Porter, courtesy of A&R Edelman.

An early LEED-EB Platinum project was the California Environmental Protection Agency headquarters building in Sacramento, shown in Figure 14.2. Owned and managed by Thomas Properties Group LLC, this 25-story, 950,000-square-foot building completed its Platinum certification in 2003 with a series of projects that reduced energy use by 34 percent (compared with the then-prevailing 1998 state energy code), diverted 200 tons of waste from landfills per year, and increased the building's asset value by about $12 million. Total investment was about $500,000, with annual energy and water savings of $610,000. The building received an Energy Star rating of 96, putting it in the top 4 percent of all energy-efficient operations.[8]

Another state-owned building in Sacramento, the six-story, 336,000-square-foot Department of Education building, received LEED-EB Platinum certification in 2006. Completed in 2003, this building received LEED-NC Gold certification as a newly constructed project, and was the first major project in the world to receive both high-level designations. It also has an Energy Star rating of 95, with energy use about 40 percent less than re-

Figure 14.2. The LEED-EB Platinum-certified California Environmental Protection Agency building uses 34 percent less energy than a comparable building. John Swain Photography, courtesy of Thomas Properties Group, Inc.

quired by state code. The building features more than 100 different sustainable solutions to improve energy efficiency, indoor air quality, water conservation, and resource conservation.[9]

The National Geographic Society operates a four-building headquarters complex in Washington, D.C., whose buildings range from 20 to 100 years old. With a $6 million retrofit, the organization added $24 million to property value, receiving LEED-EB Silver certification in 2003.[10]

The JohnsonDiversey Corporation headquarters in Sturtevant, Wisconsin, was certified LEED-EB Gold in 2004. The three-story, 277,000-square-foot building contains 70 percent offices and 30 percent labs. Because it was built in 1997 with sustainability in mind, it was fairly easy to fine-tune existing systems to receive the LEED-EB designation.[11] With a $74,000 LEED-EB project cost, JohnsonDiversey saved about $90,000 in annual energy costs, reduced water use by more than two million gallons, and documented employee recycling rates above 50 percent.

One recent institutional commitment to LEED-EB deserves note. In December 2006, the University of California, Santa Barbara campus agreed to use LEED-EB to assess 25 buildings over the next five years. Jon Cook, acting director of physical facilities, said, "We believe that performance under the LEED system is a key indication that we are achieving our goals" of taking care of the environment and of the health of employees and building occupants.[12]

Barriers and Incentives to Greener Building Operations

These case studies demonstrate substantial savings and other benefits from a comprehensive evaluation and retrofit program at large facilities. So what's holding everyone else back? The most significant factor, of course, is money. It's hard to get money for operations upgrades in most companies, compared with investing in marketing to increase revenues, developing new products, and implementing cost-reduction projects. In public agencies, the split between capital and operating budgets means that facility managers and building operators need to argue the case every year for enough money just to operate their buildings, making it even more difficult to get money for longer-term savings programs.

Private building ownership is often similarly fractured, with a split between ownership and operations. Specialized property management firms typically get a percentage of rents to operate and maintain buildings. Any investment funds need to be secured from the owners. According to BOMA International, 41 percent of all building owners operate fewer than six buildings, making discretionary investment money more difficult to obtain. Only 17 percent of all properties are owned by firms with more than 50 holdings; these are the firms most likely to have ready access to capital and to see the broader benefits of green upgrades and operations.[13]

Table 14.1 lists the benefits of green upgrades and some of the major barriers. Basically, without a comprehensive corporate or institutional commitment to sustainability, it's difficult for the facility manager or sustainability director, someone lower on the corporate "food chain," to get the funds required for a good LEED-EB certification effort, which can cost $50,000 to $100,000, not counting the costs of upgrades necessary to meet the stan-

Table 14.1a
Benefits of Greening Existing Operations

1. Saving energy and water costs can often return the initial investment in less than one year, as well as creating eligibility for federal and state tax incentives and utility rebate payments.
2. Reducing exposure to toxic chemicals used in cleaning can improve health and productivity.
3. Lighting and ventilation upgrades and retrofits can improve health and productivity.
4. Positive public relations can help attract new tenants and keep existing ones.
5. Improved morale among occupants and better working conditions may lead to greater retention of key employees.
6. Greening is a positive and productive response to corporate sustainability initiatives.

Table 14.1b
Barriers to Greening Existing Operations

1. There may be resistance to the cost of doing something that's discretionary. In private business, it's hard to get money for investments that don't go toward new products or sales; in public agencies and institutions, there is typically a need for a legislative appropriation.
2. Greening may require coordinating across a number of departments and gathering data that no one had thought to assemble before.
3. Management may question the value of incurring certification costs just to "prove" what the organization is already doing.
4. Facilities and maintenance staff may not have the time or knowledge to implement a new program.

dard. In commercial real estate, the divided responsibilities between owners and tenants make it difficult to have the dialogue necessary for a LEED-EB upgrade. For the California EPA building, a long-term lease with a single tenant made it easier for the property owner to realize the financial returns from certification.

Chapter 15

The Revolution in Building Design and Construction Practice

Green building is revolutionizing the practice of architecture and engineering, forcing all design professions to look at the broader effects of their project work. Just as the green building revolution has spurred designers and builders to incorporate sustainable design into many types of buildings, it has also affected the professional practices of architects, interior designers, engineers, and contractors. For example, by the end of 2006, more than 35,000 design and construction professionals, along with thousands of building officials, financiers, brokers, and other industry participants, had become recognized as LEED Accredited Professionals (LEED APs) by taking a national exam in the LEED system. This number will undoubtedly exceed 50,000 by the end of 2008. By mid-2007, several large architectural firms had more than 400 LEED APs.[1]

The Challenge of Integrated Design

By learning to use the LEED system for building evaluation, these professionals are committing themselves to a new approach to building design and construction. Yet it is a painful process for many, because the skill sets for participating in an integrated design process and for actually designing green buildings are still not widespread in the architecture and engineering fields.

In my experience, engineers are particularly reluctant to be full participants in the early stages of project design, for several reasons. Many have told me, "We only get paid to design the building once," yet architects go through many iterations to arrive at a final design concept. For this reason, engineers typically wait until the architect's design is firmly established before beginning serious design efforts. Yet integrated design requires their involvement from the earliest stages. Building engineers also have become narrowly focused on heating, cooling, and lighting buildings using mechanical and electrical systems, rather than approaching projects with full consideration of building envelope (glazing and insulation) measures, renewable energy systems, natural ventilation, and other techniques that don't rely on equipment alone.

Professional education is also a factor. Mechanical and electrical engineers tend to know far less about architecture than architects know about engineering design, for two reasons. First, architects have to take courses in building engineering, and many architecture schools have been teaching passive solar design and bioclimatic design for decades. Second, architects have complete responsibility for project budget and construction, so they have to integrate every aspect of building design into a final product, whereas engineers tend to focus on their own narrow specialties.

These are broad generalizations, of course; even as more experienced engineers struggle to learn sustainable design approaches, there is a new generation coming out of school that knows how to integrate considerations of health, comfort, and productivity into engineered systems while fully appreciating architectural concerns.

For example, proper daylighting design requires electrical engineers and lighting designers to integrate electric lighting controls with daylighting. This may mean that less electric lighting is required, which in turn reduces the need for air-conditioning (the province of the mechanical engineer), since all electric light eventually becomes heat that must be removed from a building. Reducing the size of an air-conditioning system reduces costs; these savings can then be applied to exterior shading devices, skylights, rooftop monitors, and other means to create effective daylighting. Yet most engineers design buildings using handbooks and "rules of thumb," and are reluctant to reduce HVAC system sizes from established norms. In design-build projects, mechanical contractors typically design HVAC systems, and they are even more risk-averse; moreover, they have little incentive to downsize HVAC systems, since the more money the project spends on HVAC, the more they make.

Green buildings present other professional challenges. For example, plumbing designers have traditionally taken water into a building from a municipal utility and sent out wastewater to the public sewer. One pass through the building has been all they were required to think about. Now, many projects want not only to conserve water via efficient fixtures, but also to capture and reuse rainwater, which requires a dual piping system, on-site water treatment, and use of "less than potable" water in toilets. (Some projects even want water-free urinals in public restrooms.) So plumbing engineers have had to add all these systems to their repertory, and have had to learn how to deal with local plumbing officials not well versed in these new systems and technologies.

Electrical engineers have traditionally brought power into a building from the local electrical utility; now they are being asked to design on-site power systems using solar power, microturbines, or cogeneration systems, on a scale and with an importance to the client that they have not previously experienced. Figure 15.1 shows the 40,000-square-foot Chicago Center for Green Technology, which supplies 72 kilowatts from photovoltaics, in three different configurations, to produce 136,000 kilowatt-hours of electricity per year. The Center was completed in 2003 at a building cost of $5.4 million and certified as a LEED-NC pilot Platinum project.[2]

Mary Ann Lazarus is director of sustainable design for HOK, the largest architectural and engineering firm in the United States.[3] She is also the coauthor of a standard textbook on sustainable design.[4] Lazarus says,

> From what I can tell, the architectural profession and our standard design process is behind the times. Integrated design is not something that naturally happens—because of the way that contracts work, because of traditional relationships between contractors, engineering consultants, design teams, and the architects. We need to be willing to work at making integration happen and adjust contract, schedule, and fees appropriately. In five years, I think that things that we now consider sustainable design, such as basic LEED certification, will be considered fundamental requirements for buildings. They will become expected components, and if you don't do them, you're going to be behind in the market and you're not going to design buildings that have long-term value.[5]

Practiced properly, integrated design requires major changes in the current system for designing and delivering projects, in order to realize high-performance goals on conventional budgets. Table 15.1 shows the major

Figure 15.1. Farr Associates' Chicago Center for Green Technology has a rooftop photovoltaic system. © Farr Associates Architecture | Planning | Preservation, Chicago, Illinois. Photo by Chris Kelly.

components of an integrated design approach that addresses the challenges of energy conservation.

The "Slow Building" Revolution

Think of the sustainable design revolution as similar to the Slow Food movement, which began in Italy as a way to combat the American "fast food

Table 15.1

Integrated Design Approaches for Energy Savings

Component	Approach and Benefit
1. Always ask, "Why are we doing this?"	Sometimes a building can be reused rather than torn down; asking "why?" several times may bring out underlying motives and change designs.
2. Study the site.	The actual building site should inform design decisions; there may be resources available that haven't been noticed before.
3. Use free and renewable resources.	Sun, wind, rainfall, groundwater, and geothermal heat and coolness are free resources; how can they be used to avoid costs?
4. Reduce demand through effective conservation measures.	Demand reduction is almost always cheaper than adding supply; for instance, the value of additional insulation is cheaper than adding size to an HVAC system.
5. Switch demand to off-peak periods.	Thermal energy storage systems make chilled water or ice when power is cheap, allowing a project to avoid buying expensive power during summer peak cooling periods.
6. Use radiant heating and cooling approaches to reduce the size of HVAC systems.	We are comfortable in higher summer temperatures if there are cool surfaces nearby, and we are comfortable in winter when there are warm surfaces close to us.
7. Make sure the building's energy-using systems are "right-sized" and made as efficient as possible.	There are trade-offs between the higher cost of conventional larger systems and smaller, higher-efficiency systems that can reduce overall project cost; most engineered systems are overdesigned.
8. Commission the project and train . the users in effective operation of the building systems.	Nothing will work right unless people understand the intent of the design and can operate the building systems.

invasion," the use of hundreds of chemicals in processed foods, and the lack of harmony and community in the basic cultural process of eating. The Slow Food movement aims to preserve the culturally significant nature of local cuisines, along with associated food plants and seeds, domestic animals, and farming within an ecoregion.[6]

In the same way, the "slow building" movement focuses on creating designs that are appropriate for a given bioregion, taking into account climate, natural resources, local economies, indigenous building styles, and cultural values. It is opposed to the widespread "internationalization" of buildings, which makes it impossible to tell what climate or country a building represents because most office buildings tend to look (and function) alike, anywhere in the world. The slow building revolution looks to slow down the design process in favor of a sustainable design approach that takes more into account than just design program objectives, budget, and schedule.

The slow building revolution looks for local and regional materials, sustainably harvested wood products, and nontoxic finishes. It aims to maximize the use of available solar resources at a building site, to recycle and reuse rainwater, and to use earth energies for heating and cooling. The slow building revolution recognizes that natural ventilation and abundant daylighting are desirable building measures for climates such as Seattle and Portland, but won't work in Miami, where the abundant sunlight and high humidity dictate different design approaches. Similarly, solar power systems and abundant shading are more appropriate for the Arizona desert than for the rocky coast of Maine, where the cold winters argue for earth-sheltering the north-side of buildings and letting the southern sun reflect off the snow and into buildings in winter.

This type of whole-systems thinking is just the opposite of the one-size-fits-all design you might get from typical architecture or engineering firms, particularly those that are commercially successful. The pressure to grow, to put more people to work, to satisfy every client demand is very strong and often in conflict with a firm's basic commitment to green design principles. Having worked in the world of commercial architecture and engineering for the past decade, I can tell you that these pressures are very real and that most firms don't encourage clients to incorporate green building measures into projects, even when they know they should.

The slow building movement regards reducing the environmental impact of buildings and restoring habitat not as another "check box" for a development project, but as an essential element in maintaining the long-term sustainability of our modern urban culture. It looks at toxic chemicals as something to get out and keep out of a building, not as things that are useful because they are cheap. It looks to buy locally harvested and extracted building materials, salvaged materials, and recycled-content materials not because they give "LEED points" to a project, but because investing in the local economy is an intelligent and vital element of sustainable design.

The Business of Sustainable Design

We've talked at length about the business case for green buildings. What about the design and construction firms themselves? Do they see a business benefit in a focus on green design? In a 2006 survey of nearly 900 industry participants, 39 percent said that acquiring sustainable building expertise had helped them attract new clients or projects, with 11 percent saying it had resulted in a "significant" amount of new business (up from only 6 percent in a similar 2003 survey) and 53 percent saying it had resulted in "some" new business. Fully 77 percent of the respondents expected significantly more green building activity over the next two to three years.[7]

It's clear from these survey results that sustainable design is a business benefit to design and construction firms. Here are some of the ways in which a focus on sustainable design benefits these companies:

- Differentiates the company in the marketplace, helping it stand out from competitors
- Adds to the company's "skill set" in a way that brings value to clients
- Builds employee morale by integrating a company's values with its practice
- Assists in recruiting new employees who value sustainable design
- Helps keep experienced employees with the firm (because of the current shortage of experienced green designers, many other firms will be trying to hire them)
- Attracts new business and helps retain current business from clients who want the benefits of green buildings without paying to help a firm learn about them.

Does this create competitive advantage? In late 2005, architect Russell Perry became director of sustainable design at SmithGroup, the country's seventh-largest architecture and engineering firm, with more than 800 employees in the United States.[8] On the importance of sustainable design to such a large firm, he says, "Everything depends on leadership. Our board of directors strongly endorses the idea that sustainable design will be an essential part of competitiveness for any large design firm in the future." The goal at SmithGroup is to be in the top five of all design firms in terms of the percentage of professionals who are LEED Accredited Professionals. Of the marketing advantages, Perry says:

I'm pretty sure we've gained some advantage. When sustainability is an item in a Request for Qualifications, and certainly when it has an assigned score in the assessment of various teams, we want to meet or beat any of our competitors' qualifications. I think we're at that place now.

Secondly, we want to get to a place where sustainability as a firm focus and our experience with completed projects will give us an advantage among our current and prospective clients. My assessment is that we're there right now when we're judged against most of our key competitors.

As a further benefit, we find we're being "short-listed" more regularly and even sole-sourced because of our distinct focus on sustainable design and cost-effective, high-performance outcomes.[9]

Revolutionizing a Design Firm

Many architecture and engineering firms are discovering that sustainable design is more than an "add-on" to their conventional design practice; it has to permeate the firm's activities at every level. Figure 15.2 shows the five key areas in which firms need to change their "DNA": leadership, education and training, operations, communications, and knowledge management.

Leadership is the first requirement. At SmithGroup, according to Perry, each principal (there are more than 140) has committed to become a LEED Accredited Professional by the end of 2007. This helps the rest of the firm to understand management's priorities and tells employees what the firm values and what is likely to be rewarded. (What may be difficult for outsiders to understand is that most architects and engineers haven't taken a serious "test" of their credentials since they acquired a professional license; taking the LEED AP exam, with its 50 to 60 percent passing rate, is a major personal and professional commitment for most senior management.) At Lionakis Beaumont Design Group, a 200-person architecture firm in Sacramento, California, the journey to sustainability began more than seven years ago. Early in the process, each of the firm's principals became a LEED AP.[10] This achievement tells both staff and clients that sustainable design is important to the firm.

In the area of education and training, in addition to standard continuing professional education, most design and construction firms send some of their staff to an all-day LEED workshop, typically as preparation for

Figure 15.2. Elements of sustainable design success.

taking the LEED AP exam. Through the end of 2006, more than 45,000 people had taken one of these workshops. By learning the LEED system and process, these professionals become better equipped to participate in integrated design and to achieve high-performance results on subsequent design projects.

Most professional firms have found that it's not enough to design good projects; they need to "walk the talk" to keep the respect of their employees and clients. They are internalizing their commitment to sustainability: buying hybrids if they operate cars, recycling a greater percentage of office waste, using less paper, buying carbon offsets for their travel, and purchasing environmentally beneficial products. Many firms set up internal sustainability committees and train their staff in various environmental assessment methods. If they move, firms that are serious about sustainability even make sure they locate in a LEED-certified building or tenant space.

Communications plays a large role in professional firms, both internal and external. When firms make a strong commitment to sustainability, they find that it needs to be reinforced through both external (marketing and public relations) and internal communications. Many firms use their employee newsletters and intranet to continually remind all staff to focus on how to "green" their projects. Very large design and construction firms have a particular challenge in communicating management's commitment to sustainability and often find it necessary to have one or more senior-level "roving green ambassadors" visiting the various offices on a regular basis and communicating about sustainable design through teleconferences and video conferences.

Knowledge management is also a critical component of changing a firm's "DNA." At SmithGroup, according to Perry, a major goal for 2007 is to assess each project—beginning in the Washington, D.C. office—according to the LEED rating system, whether or not the client is paying for a formal LEED certification. "At the end of schematic design, we intend to have each team prepare a LEED scorecard—as a checklist for how many opportunities we've uncovered for including sustainable design measures in the project, and as an exercise that forces the design team to think about these things early enough in design to get them into the project."

"Lessons learned" are gleaned from each project and put into a central, accessible database, so that future projects for the same client or of the same type (hospitals or sports facilities, for instance) can immediately benefit from the knowledge gained through the previous project.

Revolutionizing Sustainability: Restorative Design

Many of the leading-edge thinkers in sustainable design believe that green buildings are only a palliative measure until we can develop a wholly different approach to development, one that seeks to restore the functioning of ecosystems and dramatically improve people's health through a fundamental redesign of buildings, neighborhoods, and communities. They call this new approach "regenerative" or "restorative" design. While sustainable design says, "Let's not make this place any worse," restorative design seeks to return a place to its original condition. Going beyond that goal, regenerative design aims to improve a place by making it healthier and more vital over many generations.[11] According to architect William Reed, one of its more energetic proponents, regenerative design involves three steps: "understand the master pattern of place, translate the patterns into design guidelines and conceptual design, and provide ongoing feedback, a conscious process of learning and participation through action, reflection, and dialogue."[12]

As one group of proponents has put it, "Regenerative development conceptualizes projects as engines of positive or evolutionary change for the systems into which they are built. Rather than looking at how to minimize the impact on wildlife habitat and corridors, for example, regenerative designs look at how to increase habitat quality."[13] As with green design, an integrated design process begins to unlock the secrets of a place.

Architect Gail Lindsey says there are three components to making integrated design simple:

- Find exemplary models—people doing it a lot more easily and with a much different focus.
- Change the process. Cultivate mutually enriching relationships between the design team, the people of the project, and the place being worked with.
- Change the performance metrics. "We have metrics of energy efficiency and air quality, but we're missing the other metrics that I think are quintessential to determining the health of the land," Lindsey says.

"Design is based on relationships and the interconnections of things," she continues. "We're starting to see those connections, but we can take them so much further and quicker than we do now. I like to think of what we do in terms of conscious evolutionary design."

There are still only a few examples of such a radical approach to building design, site dynamics, and neighborhood revitalization. Yet it remains a long-term and strategic goal for the green building revolution. Why not use our time, money, and talent to heal the earth and create beautiful, healthy environments for people?

One of the most detailed explorations of what a regenerative approach to urban design would look like is the "Lloyd Crossing Sustainable Urban Design Master Plan," created in 2004 for the Portland, Oregon, Development Commission by the Seattle architecture firm Mithun. This plan aims to restore a 35-block, 10-million-square-foot urban district just east of downtown Portland to its original "predevelopment" functioning. Imagine, the plan asks, that by 2050 the habitat and net carbon dioxide production in this place had decreased to 1850 levels. What would it take to get from here (2005) to there (2050) without sacrificing economic benefit or environmental quality? How could a large urban area subsist solely on solar energy (income) without using any fossil fuels (capital)? How could we supply all the water needs and wastewater treatment from rainfall (income) on the project area, without having to rely on importing water and exporting sewage (capital)? After all, a sensible personal financial strategy is to subsist solely on income and not eat up your capital; shouldn't we approach sustainable urban design with the same end in mind? With these extraordinary project goals, the plan developed an economically viable strategic approach to transforming the district into an environmentally and financially sustainable enterprise.[14]

Chapter 16
Join the Revolution!

By now, you're probably convinced that the green building revolution is real, important, sustainable, and happening all around you. You may be asking yourself, where do I sign up? This chapter briefly outlines some of the opportunities available to each one of us to "join the revolution." No one knows how this revolution will proceed, but one thing is certain: it won't happen without your efforts!

What You Can Do at Home

You've probably read dozens of articles about becoming more environmentally conscious around the home. At my house we recycle everything we can, even the inner cardboard rolls from paper towels and toilet paper! But there are all kinds of new opportunities to consider.

1. You probably travel a lot, so you can buy carbon offsets from one of the many organizations that have sprung up to offer them. With your offset money, these groups buy wind power capacity, plant trees, and invest in solar power. When I took a trip to Australia in 2007, I bought Green Tags from the Bonneville Environmental Foundation to cover the carbon dioxide emissions from 15,000 miles of air travel.[1] Some major travel web sites, such as Travelocity.com and Expedia.com, now offer an option to offset your carbon load when you book your air travel.[2]

2. Buy a photovoltaic or solar water heating system in 2007 and 2008; you can take advantage of the (maximum) $2,000 federal tax credit for each system (based on 30 percent of cost) and begin harvesting clean, renewable energy. There are also many state tax credits, sales tax abatements, utility incentives, and other potential benefits.[3]

3. Buy a dual-flush toilet; there are plenty on the market and, no, you don't have to flush twice to get the "stuff" to disappear. I lived in a LEED Gold-certified building in Portland, Oregon, with a dual-flush toilet, and it worked just fine. These toilets have a big button for a big flush and a little button for a little flush, so just about anyone can figure out how they work, and you'll save about 35 percent of the water use of a standard toilet. Of course, if you're in an older home with a toilet bought before 1992—one that uses 3.5 gallons per flush—you should change it out immediately; even a standard 1.6-gallons-per-flush, water-conserving toilet will be a big improvement.

4. If your old clunker is ready to give out, consider buying a hybrid car. Models with lots of federal tax credits are still available, and you'll amaze yourself and your friends as you see the gas gauge hovering around 40 miles per gallon for most of your travel. If you typically buy 500 gallons of gas per year, you'll now be buying about 300, and you'll be not only saving money but beginning to reduce your ecological footprint.

What You Can Do at Work

In the previous chapter, we discussed how firms are changing their operations to have less impact on the environment. But most of the changes don't begin at the top. They occur because concerned individuals got together, came up with an action plan, and sold it to top management. As Alexis de Tocqueville observed in the 1830s, a defining characteristic of Americans is that they don't wait for someone in authority to tell them what to do, they just organize a group and do it.[4] If your company doesn't use hybrids or support employees' public transit use, start lobbying the leaders to get on board. If your firm is moving to new quarters, insist that they choose a LEED-NC registered (and certified) building and pursue a LEED-CI rating for the tenant improvements.

Through an arrangement with a plumbing-fixture manufacturer, a building engineering firm with about 100 employees in Portland, Oregon (and a former employer of mine), now offers a program to subsidize the installation of dual-flush toilets in employees' homes, each saving about 6,000 gallons of water per year.[5] The same firm has bought four hybrid cars

Figure 16.1. Kohler's water-free urinals. Courtesy of Kohler Co.

for travel to client meetings and job sites and subsidizes 60 percent of the cost of public transportation for employees, which has led to 80 percent transit use. It's also testing very-low-flush urinals in the two office washrooms, saving 85 percent of the water use of a typical one-gallon-per flush fixture.

If you work for a large corporation, you might be surprised at how many incentives will be offered in the coming years for you to "go green." For example, early in 2007, Bank of America offered a $3,000 cash rebate to any of its 185,000 employees who bought a hybrid car.[6] Many companies are offering transit subsidies, participation in local "car sharing" programs (so you can get home in the event of a family emergency), showers and bicycle lockers for bicycle commuters, and similar measures to keep you from having to drive to work.

If you work at a government agency or school district, see what you can do to affect its design, construction, remodeling, and purchasing policies. There's nothing an elected official, planning commission member, or senior civil servant likes more right now than a way to look good by instituting a sustainability policy. With the mayors of most of America's large cities pledged to taking action to slow climate change, they're going to be looking to their staffs to come up with practical proposals to meet this commitment. You can start by getting a green building policy passed for your jurisdiction's own buildings. Make sure that all new construction has long-term sustainability built into it. Then tackle the harder stuff, such as purchasing policies and building operations. Try to get the organization to certify one building to the LEED-EB standard, to create a benchmark for measuring the sustainability of its operations across the board.

If you work at a college or university, you probably already know that sustainability is a huge issue on most campuses, and you are probably already being asked to suggest actions that the institution can take. In the past six years, Leith Sharp of Harvard's Green Campus Initiative has managed to register 20 projects for LEED certification and certify eight of them. Harvard has specified LEED Gold as the minimum standard for its new campus in Allston, Massachusetts, which will total more than 4 million square feet of buildings. If one motivated and talented woman can accomplish so much at a major institution, surely we can all find ways to move our own school board or college toward sustainability.

Many college and university student bodies are taxing themselves to pay for the extra costs of running the student union on renewable energy or of building a new student recreation center or student union as a green building. If you're a student, why not start a similar movement on your campus?

With a colleague, Dr. Tom Buckholtz, I developed a method for streamlining these types of changes in higher education, called "Gain Impact. Save Time," or GIST. The "gist" of our advice is to take a systematic approach to change initiatives, doing first things first and second things second, which will make success easier. It's tempting to jump right into a program, such as campuswide recycling or food waste composting, because students have a bias toward action. Yet without building strong staff support and participation, many student-led initiatives die on the vine. You can download a copy of our white paper and get started at your own institution.[7]

Greening Your Local Government

The United States comprises about 3,000 counties and more than 30,000 incorporated cities. Counting special districts, it contains nearly 75,000 political subdivisions, including about 14,000 school districts. There are plenty of opportunities to make your voice heard. Dozens of cities and a few counties have already adopted green building policies of one type or another. Portland, Oregon, a city of about 530,000 residents, has had an Office of Sustainable Development (OSD) since 2000, initiated by Dan Saltzman, one of the five City Commissioners (council members), and funded largely by garbage collection fees. With just a handful of staff, the OSD created a strong public education campaign about green buildings and promoted a series of green technology innovations in residential and small commercial projects through a modest grants program called the Green Investment Fund.[8]

What can you do to encourage your city or county government to create a focus on green buildings? As Margaret Mead famously remarked, "Never doubt that a small group of thoughtful, committed citizens can change the world; indeed, it's the only thing that ever has."[9] Even small towns are crafting green building ordinances. Early in 2007, the town of Babylon, New York, on Long Island, with a population of 211,000,[10] became the 10th city in the United States to require LEED certification for all future privately owned developments larger than 4,000 square feet.

Why not go to the U.S. Green Building Council web site and see what other cities and counties are doing?[11] By early February 2007, according to the USGBC, more than 70 local jurisdictions had adopted green building resolutions, policies, or action plans. Local governments can take many actions, including the following:

- Adopt faster permit processing for green buildings.
- Allow developers that commit to green buildings to build taller structures.
- Commit to LEED Silver (or better) certification for all future municipal buildings and major renovations.
- Commit to LEED-CI certification of all tenant improvements in city or county offices.
- Commit to at least one LEED-EB certification of an existing building each year.
- Institute environmentally preferable purchasing for all municipal departments.
- Partner with private developers and nonprofits to make all affordable housing projects models of cost-effective sustainable design and operations.

- Join the U.S. Green Building Council and begin participating and learning more about green buildings.

Investing in the Revolution

Ordinary citizens have many opportunities to "put their money where their mouth is." You may want to look at each investment (and each purchase) you make with the thought that your money can help fuel the green building revolution. (Please note that I am not necessarily recommending particular investments.)

Over the last 15 years, socially responsible mutual funds have done very well. According to Amy Domini, who created the Domini 400 Social Index, from its inception in May 1990 through the end of 2005, this socially screened index outperformed the S&P 500 by 493 percent to 427 percent,[12] proving once again what your mother (ideally) taught you, that it's possible to do well by doing good.

A number of publicly traded real estate investment trusts, some mentioned earlier, have committed to investing in LEED-certified buildings. Venture capital investors have also gotten into the act, spotting the immense opportunities that exist in renewable energy and green building technologies. In 2006, venture capital investments in clean energy totaled $2.4 billion, about 9.4 percent of all venture investments in energy technologies, up more than 250 percent from 2005. The annual "Clean Energy Trends" report predicts that revenues from just four clean energy technologies (biofuels, wind power, solar power, and fuel cells) will grow fourfold, from $55 billion in 2006 to $226 billion in 2016.[13] Companies making and selling these technologies may also represent good investments.

You may even want to start a company to manufacture, distribute, sell, or install a green building product, service, or technology. Many business schools have started sustainable entrepreneurship programs, and many graduates are coming out of these programs each year with MBA degrees and business plans to make the world a better place through their own actions. Who will be the first to develop a successful national retail concept, like Starbucks, to sell sustainable home improvements? Who will develop the next line of recycled-content furniture from plastic bottles, or a paint that gives off only healthy odors, or a fabric so environmentally benign that you can compost it in your garden when its useful life is over? Who will create a successful financing concept to get solar power systems on one million rooftops? Perhaps you have that combination of tough-mindedness and blissful idealism that characterizes successful entrepreneurs!

The green building revolution has just begun, but it's quickly becoming mainstream. It is one of the great social and political revolutions of our time. We can all play a part, and each one of us should. If you've read this far, you've probably come up with dozens of ideas how you can help this amazing, positive paradigm shift to happen faster. So let's all get to work!

appendix 1
Resources for Revolutionaries

Conferences

Greenbuild, www.greenbuildexpo.com

Organized by the U.S. Green Building Council

    Held every fall; Boston is scheduled to host in 2008

The world's largest green building conference, this international exposition is a "must" for those in the commercial development world. Mostly an industry show, it is open to the public and is especially valuable for the exhibits and the educational programs.

West Coast Green, www.westcoastgreen.com

    Typically held every September in San Francisco

Covers both residential and commercial green buildings; includes a few hundred exhibit booths. Open to the public.

LOHAS (Lifestyles of Health and Sustainability), www.lohas.com

Organized by the Natural Marketing Institute

    Typically held every spring

Covers a broad range of consumer sustainability issues, including green building. Open to the public.

American Solar Energy Society conference, www.ases.org

    Typically held every summer

This conference can provide you with an annual update on solar energy. Open to the public.

Greening the Campus Conference, www.bsu.edu/provost/ceres/greening

Ball State University (Muncie, Indiana)

This biennial conference has been held since 1996 and focuses on a broad range of campus topics. Ideal for students and faculty. The 2007 conference was held in September.

Books

In this fast-changing field, most books are outdated shortly after they are published. Nevertheless, a few have good shelf life, even now. You might find them interesting, perhaps even life-changing.

Ray Anderson, *Mid-Course Correction* (Atlanta, GA: Peregrinzilla Press, 1998)
This classic book tells how a corporate paradigm shift began with a personal transformation by the CEO. Ray Anderson speaks from the heart, with experience, passion, and eloquence.

Al Gore, *An Inconvenient Truth* (Emmaus, PA: Rodale Press, 2006)
The by-now classic book on why we need to make a wholesale change in our energy-wasting habits. Though long on analysis and short on prescription, Gore's book has had a revolutionary impact.

David Gottfried, *Greed to Green* (Berkeley, CA: WorldBuild Publishing, 2004)
If you want an insider's perspective on the formation and early years of the U.S. Green Building Council, Gottfried's amazing story of personal and organizational transformation pulls no punches.

Paul Hawken, Amory Lovins, and L. Hunter Lovins, *Natural Capitalism: Creating the Next Industrial Revolution* (Boston: Little Brown, 1999)
This book is a classic treatment of a wide variety of topics, all related to how much we can learn from natural systems and how little we are applying what we already know. It will reward anyone who wants to understand how to take the next leap in green building design.

Stephen R. Kellert, *Building for Life: Understanding the Human-Nature Connection* (Washington, DC: Island Press, 2006)
Inspired by the work of architects like Frank Lloyd Wright, Eero Saarinen, and Norman Foster, Kellert proposes a new architectural model to reinvigorate our daily lives. His ideas are a bridge back to the natural world.

Tachi Kiuchi and Bill Shireman, *What We Learned in the Rain Forest: Business Lessons from Nature* (San Francisco: Berrett-Koehler, 2002)
An excellent guide to how using sustainability principles can help any organization ensure its evolutionary success.

Bruce Mau, *Massive Change* (London and New York: Phaidon Press, 2004)
This book is not about the world of design, it's about the design of the world for long-term success.

William McDonough and Michael Braungart, *Cradle to Cradle: Changing the Way We Make Things* (New York: North Point Press, 2002)
This book "walks the talk," as it's not even printed on ordinary paper! The authors take us step by step through their advocacy of a new industrial paradigm and include great case studies showing how they've begun the process for a number of companies.

Andrea Putman and Michael Philips, *The Business Case for Renewable Energy: A Guide for Colleges and Universities* (Washington, DC: National Association of College and University Business Officers, 2006)
This is the best one-volume summary of the current business case for solar and wind power. Written for campuses, it is broadly applicable to government agencies, nonprofits, and corporate users. Available from www.nacubo.org.

Alex Steffen, ed., *World Changing: A User's Guide for the 21st Century* (New York: Harry N. Abrams, 2006)
It's hard to know what to say about this nearly six-hundred-page compendium of everything we know about green solutions, except that you need a copy in your library for reference.

Jerry Yudelson, *Developing Green: Strategies for Success* (Herndon, VA: National Association of Industrial and Office Properties, 2006)
Written for developers, this book is the best introduction available to the business case for green buildings. Includes case studies of green developments submitted for the NAIOP Green Development of the Year award in 2005. Comes with a CD of case studies. Available from www.naiop.org.

Periodicals
It's hard to keep up with the proliferation of green building magazines and related publications. Here are a few I read on a regular basis. Most are available in both hard copy and electronic versions, so if you're averse to having too much paper around, you can keep up with the news online.

Building Design & Construction, www.bdcmag.com
BD&C's editor, Rob Cassidy, is an authoritative voice in the industry. Written primarily for "Building Team" practitioners, the magazine is eminently accessible to anyone.

Buildings, www.buildings.com
Buildings *magazine provides a good introduction to the practical side of building design, construction, and operations, as well as good coverage of specialty topics in the industry.*

Dwell: At Home in the Modern World, www.Dwell.com
Primarily a consumer magazine, Dwell *provides excellent coverage of green homes on a regular basis.*

Eco-Structure, www.eco-structure.com
Eco-Structure *is the most-illustrated trade magazine covering the green building industry. Well-written case studies and a broad selection of topics make it a good way to keep up.*

Environmental Design & Construction, www.edcmag.com
Now ten years old, ED&C *provides first-class editorial coverage of issues relevant to green building, along with well-written case studies of leading projects.*

Green Source, www.construction.com/greensource
Started in 2006 by the publishers of Engineering News-Record *and* Architectural Record, *the most authoritative publications in their field, the quarterly* Green Source *is edited by the team at* Environmental Building News. *The case studies are the best written you will find anywhere.*

Metropolis, www.metropolismag.com
If you want to know what's going on in the broader world of sustainable design, Metropolis *is a "must read." Featuring outstanding coverage of all aspects of design, the monthly has sharpened its focus on green building in recent years.*

Natural Home and Garden, www.naturalhomemagazine.com
This monthly is a consumer magazine focused on the product and design issues facing the average person trying to live a more sustainable lifestyle.

Solar Today, www.solartoday.org
This is the official publication of the American Solar Energy Society, but it's written for a general audience; you can even find it at the checkout counter of natural foods stores.

Sustainable Industries Journal, www.sijournal.com
This monthly provides extensive coverage of West Coast developments across a wide range of sustainable industries, including green building. It's more of a digest, with articles that are short and easy to read, making it a good choice for busy decision-makers.

Web Sites
Clean Edge, www.cleanedge.com
The self-described "clean tech" market authority, this newsletter keeps you up to date on renewable energy and related companies and venture capital activity in this fast-paced industry.

Green Building Initiative, www.thegbi.org
This is the official web site for the Green Globes rating system. At this site, you may register and download a trial version of the system for use in one of your projects.

GreenBuzz, www.greenbiz.com
Visit GreenBuzz for a read on the sustainable-business movement.

IGreenBuild, www.igreenbuild.com
For a good overview of the business and product side of the green building movement, visit this site.

U.S. Green Building Council, www.usgbc.org
This is the premier web site not only for the organization but for news and happenings in the broader field of green building. If a trend has "legs," you'll find it here. You can download copies of all the LEED rating systems and also search for LEED-registered and LEED-certified projects.

World Changing, www.worldchanging.com
Featuring emerging innovations and solutions for building a brighter green future, this is an essential site if you want to know what's going to be a mainstream concern in short order.

appendix 2
Green Building Rating Systems

This appendix provides details on each of the USGBC's six major LEED rating systems, including the main residential evaluation system, as well as the Green Guide for Health Care, a health care best practices guidance document. All systems are presented in their March 2007 version. Readers should note that these systems change on a periodic basis; to make sure you have the most current version available, visit the sponsoring organization's web site, www.usgbc.org/leed or www.gghc.org.

In addition to these seven systems, there are many others, which are mentioned in the text but not presented here in detail. These include the National Association of Home Builders' Model Green Building Guidelines; the EPA's Energy Star program for commercial and residential buildings (which focuses only on energy savings); Green Globes for commercial applications and Green Globes for residential applications (similar to the NAHB guidelines); the Collaborative for High Performance Schools system (adopted in four states); and about sixty individual residential programs from local and state home-builder associations, local electrical utilities such as Texas's Austin Energy and Arizona's Tucson Electric Power, and nonprofits such as Build It Green, which created the GreenPoint Rated system in California.

LEED for New Construction
LEED for Commercial Interiors
LEED for Existing Buildings
LEED for Core and Shell Buildings
LEED for Homes Pilot
LEED for Neighborhood Development
Green Guide for Health Care

appendix 2.1
LEED for New Construction
version 2.2

PROJECT CERTIFICATION CHECKLIST

Sustainable Sites		14 Points
Prereq 1	Prevent pollution from construction activity	Required
Credit 1	Choose a site that doesn't affect sensitive habitats or valuable lands	1
Credit 2	Choose a site in a dense urban area	1
Credit 3	Develop project on a brownfield	1
Credit 4.1	Provide access to public transportation	1
Credit 4.2	Provide bicycle storage and changing rooms	1
Credit 4.3	Provide for low-emitting and fuel-efficient vehicles	1
Credit 4.4	Provide no extra parking capacity	1
Credit 5.1	Protect or restore habitat in site development	1
Credit 5.2	Maximize open space in site development	1
Credit 6.1	Do not increase rate or quantity of stormwater runoff	1
Credit 6.2	Do not decrease water quality from stormwater runoff	1
Credit 7.1	Reduce urban heat island effect with landscaping	1
Credit 7.2	Reduce heat island effect with reflective roofing	1
Credit 8	Minimize light pollution from site lighting	1

Water Efficiency		5 Points
Credit 1.1	Reduce landscaping water use by 50%	1
Credit 1.2	Use no potable water for irrigation	1
Credit 2	Employ innovative wastewater technologies	1
Credit 3.1	Reduce building water use by 20%	1
Credit 3.2	Reduce building water use by 30%	1

Energy and Atmosphere		17 Points
Prereq 1	Commission all new building energy systems	Required
Prereq 2	Achieve minimum energy performance	Required
Prereq 3	Use no CFC refrigerants	Required
Credit 1	Reduce energy use by 10.5% to 42% compared with a baseline	1 to 10
Credit 2	Use on-site renewable energy for 2.5% to 12.5% of all energy use	1 to 3
Credit 3	Employ enhanced commissioning methods	1
Credit 4	Use less harmful refrigerants	1

| Credit 5 | Plan for measurement and verification of energy use | 1 |
| Credit 6 | Purchase green power for 35% or more of total electricity use | 1 |

Materials and Resources   13 Points

Prereq 1	Provide space for storage and collection of recyclables	Required
Credit 1.1	Reuse existing buildings/maintain 75% of walls, floors, and roof	1
Credit 1.2	Reuse existing buildings/maintain 95% of walls, floors, and roof	1
Credit 1.3	During reuse, maintain 50% of interior nonstructural elements	1
Credit 2.1	Divert 50% of construction waste from disposal	1
Credit 2.2	Divert 75% of construction waste from disposal	1
Credit 3.1	Reuse salvaged materials for 5% of building materials	1
Credit 3.2	Reuse salvaged materials for 10% of building materials	1
Credit 4.1	Use recycled-content materials for 10% of building materials	1
Credit 4.2	Use recycled-content materials for 20% of building materials	1
Credit 5.1	Use regionally sourced materials for 10% of building value	1
Credit 5.2	Use regionally sourced materials for 20% of building value	1
Credit 6	Use rapidly renewable materials for 2.5% of building value	1
Credit 7	Use certified wood for 50% of value of all new wood products	1

Indoor Environmental Quality   15 Points

Prereq 1	Meet minimum indoor air-quality performance levels	Required
Prereq 2	Control or eliminate environmental tobacco smoke	Required
Credit 1	Monitor carbon dioxide/provide outdoor air delivery to meet standards	1
Credit 2	Increase outdoor air ventilation rate by 30%	1
Credit 3.1	Manage indoor air quality during construction	1
Credit 3.2	Manage indoor air quality just before occupancy	1
Credit 4.1	Use low-VOC adhesives and sealants	1
Credit 4.2	Use low-VOC paints and coatings	1
Credit 4.3	Use low-emitting carpets and backing	1
Credit 4.4	Use zero urea-formaldehyde in composite wood and agrifiber products	1
Credit 5	Control indoor chemical use and pollutant sources	1
Credit 6.1	Provide lighting controls for 90% of occupants	1
Credit 6.2	Provide means to control thermal comfort for 50% of occupants	1
Credit 7.1	Design thermal comfort to meet standards at all times	1
Credit 7.2	Design and administer a thermal comfort survey after occupancy	1
Credit 8.1	Provide daylight to 75% of occupied spaces	1
Credit 8.2	Provide views for 90% of occupied spaces	1

Innovation and Design Process   5 Points

Credit 1.1–1.2	Innovation in design: exemplary performance above LEED standards	2
Credit 1.3–1.4	Innovation in design: provide measures not included in LEED	2
Credit 2	Use a LEED Accredited Professional on project team	1

Total Points   **69**

Certified: 26–32 points Silver: 33–38 points Gold: 39–51 points Platinum: 52–69 points

appendix 2.2
LEED for Commercial Interiors
Version 2.0

PROJECT CERTIFICATION CHECKLIST

Sustainable Sites		7 points
Credit 1	Site selection: select a LEED-certified building - OR -	3
	Locate the tenant space in a building with the following characteristics (up to 3 points from 6 measures):	
	Brownfield redevelopment	1/2
	Stormwater management: no increase	1/2
	Stormwater management: maintain water quality	1/2
	Heat island reduction, landscape and hardscape	1/2
	Heat island reduction, reflective roof	1/2
	Visual pollution reduction from site lighting	1/2
	Reduce irrigation water use by 50%	1/2
	Eliminate irrigation water use	1/2
	Employ innovative wastewater technologies	1/2
	Reduce fixture water use by 20%	1/2
	Use on-site renewable energy	1/2 to 1
	Demonstrate other quantifiable environmental performance	1/2 to 3
Credit 2	Choose a site in a dense urban area	1
Credit 3.1	Provide access to public transportation	1
Credit 3.2	Provide bicycle storage and changing rooms	1
Credit 3.3	Alternative transportation, parking availability	1
Water Efficiency		2 points
Credit 1.1	Reduce fixture water use by 20%	1
Credit 1.2	Reduce fixture water use by 30%	1
Energy and Atmosphere		12 points
Prereq 1	Commission all building energy systems	Required
Prereq 2	Achieve minimum energy performance	Required
Prereq 3	Use no CFC refrigerants	Required
Credit 1.1	Reduce lighting power density	3
Credit 1.2	Employ lighting controls	1
Credit 1.3	Optimize HVAC system performance	2

Credit 1.4	Reduce energy use from equipment and appliances	2
Credit 2	Employ enhanced commissioning methods	1
Credit 3	Energy use, measurement, and payment accountability—submetering	2
Credit 4	Purchase green power for 50% or more of total electricity use	1

Materials and Resources   14 points

Prereq 1	Provide space for storage and collection of recyclables	Required
Credit 1.1	10-year lease of space	1
Credit 1.2	Building reuse, maintain 40% of interior nonstructural components	1
Credit 1.3	Building reuse, maintain 60% of interior nonstructural components	1
Credit 2.1	Divert 50% of construction waste from disposal	1
Credit 2.2	Divert 75% of construction waste from disposal	1
Credit 3.1	Reuse salvaged materials for 5% of building materials	1
Credit 3.2	Reuse salvaged materials for 10% of building materials	1
Credit 3.3	Reuse salvaged materials for 30% of furniture and furnishings	1
Credit 4.1	Use recycled-content materials for 10% of building materials	1
Credit 4.2	Use recycled-content materials for 20% of building materials	1
Credit 5.1	Use 20% of total materials that are manufactured regionally	1
Credit 5.2	At least 10% of total materials extracted/manufactured regionally	1
Credit 6	At least 5% of total materials from rapidly renewable sources	1
Credit 7	Use certified wood for 50% of value of all new wood products	1

Indoor Environmental Quality   17 points

Prereq 1	Meet minimum indoor air-quality performance levels	Required
Prereq 2	Control or eliminate environmental tobacco smoke	Required
Credit 1	Monitor carbon dioxide and provide outside air to meet standards	1
Credit 2	Increase outdoor air ventilation rate by 30%	1
Credit 3.1	Manage indoor air quality during construction	1
Credit 3.2	Manage indoor air quality just before occupancy	1
Credit 4.1	Use low-VOC adhesives and sealants	1
Credit 4.2	Use low-VOC paints and coatings	1
Credit 4.3	Use low-emitting carpets and backing	1
Credit 4.4	No urea-formaldehyde in composite wood and agrifiber products	1
Credit 4.5	Use low-emitting materials for systems furniture and seating	1
Credit 5	Control indoor chemical use and pollutant sources	1
Credit 6.1	Provide lighting controls for 90% of occupants	1
Credit 6.2	Provide means to control thermal comfort for 50% of occupants	1
Credit 7.1	Design thermal comfort to meet standards at all times	1
Credit 7.2	Provide permanent monitoring system for thermal comfort	1
Credit 8.1	Provide daylight for 75% of occupied spaces	1
Credit 8.2	Provide daylight for 90% of occupied spaces	1
Credit 8.3	Provide views for 90% of seated spaces	1

Innovation and Design Process   5 points

Credit 1.1–1.2 Exemplary performance above LEED standards   2

Credit 1.3–1.4 Innovation in design: provide measures not included in LEED 2

Credit 2   Use a LEED Accredited Professional on project team   1

Total Points   **57**

Certified: 21–26 points Silver: 27–31 points Gold: 32–41 points Platinum: 42–57 points

appendix 2.3
LEED for Existing Buildings
Version 2.0

PROJECT CERTIFICATION CHECKLIST

Sustainable Sites		14 Points
Prereq. 1	Prevent pollution from construction activity	Required
Prereq. 2	Building at least two years old	Required
Credit 1.1	Green site and building exterior management plan with 4 specific actions	1
Credit 1.2	Green site and building exterior management plan with 4 more specific actions	1
Credit 2	Occupy at least a two-story building in a high-density area	1
Credit 3.1	Provide access to public transportation	1
Credit 3.2	Provide bicycle storage and changing rooms	1
Credit 3.3	Provide for low-emitting and fuel-efficient vehicles	1
Credit 3.4	Promote carpooling and telecommuting	1
Credit 4.1	Protect or restore open space on 50% of site area	1
Credit 4.2	Protect or restore open space on 75% of site area	1
Credit 5.1	Reduce stormwater rate and quantity by 25%	1
Credit 5.2	Reduce stormwater rate and quantity by 50%	1
Credit 6.1	Reduce urban heat island effect with landscaping measures	1
Credit 6.2	Reduce heat island effect with reflective roofing	1
Credit 7	Minimize light pollution from site lighting	1

Water Efficiency		5 Points
Prereq 1	Reduce fixture water use to within 20% of current standards	Required
Prereq 2	All water quality permits are in compliance	Required
Credit 1.1	Reduce potable water use for landscaping by 50%	1
Credit 1.2	Reduce potable water use for landscaping by 95%	1
Credit 2	Employ innovative wastewater technologies	1
Credit 3.1	Reduce building water use by 10%	1
Credit 3.2	Reduce building water use by 20%	1

Energy and Atmosphere		23 Points
Prereq 1	Commission all existing building energy systems	Required
Prereq 2	Demonstrate an Energy Star rating of at least 60	Required

Prereq 3	Use no CFC refrigerants	Required
Credit 1	Improve energy performance, secure Energy Star rating of 63 to 99	1 to 10
Credit 2	Use renewable energy: on-site 3% to 12% / off-site 15% to 60%	1 to 4
Credit 3.1	24 hours of annual staff education	1
Credit 3.2	Best practices preventive maintenance program	1
Credit 3.3	Continuous monitoring of building systems	1
Credit 4	Use less harmful refrigerants	1
Credit 5.1	Performance measurement: enhanced metering (4 specific actions)	1
Credit 5.2	Performance measurement: enhanced metering (8 specific actions)	1
Credit 5.3	Performance measurement: enhanced metering (12 specific actions)	1
Credit 5.4	Track report on emission reductions	1
Credit 6	Document overall building operating costs	1

Materials and Resources — 16 Points

Prereq 1.1	Conduct a waste stream audit	Required
Prereq 1.2	Provide space for storage and collection of recyclables	Required
Prereq 2	Reduce use of light bulbs with high mercury content	Required
Credit 1.1	Divert 50% of construction waste from disposal	1
Credit 1.2	Divert 75% of construction waste from disposal	1
Credit 2.1–2.5	Sustainable product purchasing: 10% to 50% of total purchases	1 to 5
Credit 3.1–3.2	Optimize use of low-VOC products: 45% to 90% of annual purchases	1 to 2
Credit 4.1–4.3	Make sustainable cleaning products 30% to 90% of annual purchases	1 to 3
Credit 5.1–5.3	Occupant recycling: recycle 30% to 50% of total waste stream	1 to 3
Credit 6	Reduce average mercury content in light bulbs	1

Indoor Environmental Quality — 22 Points

Prereq 1	Outside air introduction and exhaust systems	Required
Prereq 2	Control or eliminate environmental tobacco smoke	Required
Prereq 3	Asbestos removal or encapsulation	Required
Prereq 4	PCB removal	Required
Credit 1	Outside air delivery monitoring	1
Credit 2	Increase outside air ventilation by 30%	1
Credit 3	Construction IAQ management plan	1
Credit 4.1	Documenting absenteeism and health care cost impacts	1
Credit 4.2	Document other productivity impacts	1
Credit 5.1	Use MERV-13 filters for outside air intakes	1
Credit 5.2	Isolate high-volume copy/print room/fax stations	1
Credit 6.1	Provide individual lighting controls for 50% of occupants	1
Credit 6.2	Provide individual temperature/ventilation controls for 50% of occupants	1
Credit 7.1	Comply with ASHRAE standard 55-2004	1

Credit 7.2	Provide a permanent monitoring system to assure comfort	1
Credit 8.1– 8.2	Daylight and views: daylight for 50% to 75% of spaces	1 to 2
Credit 8.3– 8.4	Provide outdoor views for 45% to 90% of spaces	1 to 2
Credit 9	Develop and implement an ongoing IAQ maintenance plan	1
Credit 10.1– 10.6	Green cleaning: up to 6 credit points	1 to 6

Innovation in Upgrades, Operations, and Maintenance   **5 Points**

Credit 1.1–1.2	Innovation in design: exemplary performance above LEED standards	2
Credit 1.3–1.4	Innovation in design: provide measures not included in LEED	2
Credit 2	Use a LEED Accredited Professional on project team	1

Total Points   **85**

Certified: 32–39 points Silver: 40–47 points Gold: 48–63 points Platinum: 64–85 points

appendix 2.4
LEED for Core and Shell Buildings
Version 2.0

PROJECT CERTIFICATION CHECKLIST

Sustainable Sites		15 Points
Prereq 1	Prevent pollution from construction activity	Required
Credit 1	Choose a site that doesn't affect sensitive habitats or valuable lands	1
Credit 2	Choose a site in a dense urban area	1
Credit 3	Develop project on a brownfield	1
Credit 4.1	Provide access to public transportation	1
Credit 4.2	Provide bicycle storage and changing rooms	1
Credit 4.3	Provide low-emitting and fuel-efficient vehicles	1
Credit 4.4	Provide no extra parking capacity	1
Credit 5.1	Protect or restore habitat in site development	1
Credit 5.2	Maximize open space in site development	1
Credit 6.1	Do not increase rate or quantity of stormwater runoff	1
Credit 6.2	Do not decrease water quality from stormwater runoff	1
Credit 7.1	Reduce urban heat island effect with landscape	1
Credit 7.2	Reduce heat island effect with reflective roofing	1
Credit 8	Minimize light pollution from site lighting	1
Credit 9	Provide tenant design and construction guidelines	1

Water Efficiency		5 Points
Credit 1.1	Reduce landscaping water use by 50%	1
Credit 1.2	Use no potable water for irrigation	1
Credit 2	Employ innovative wastewater technologies	1
Credit 3.1	Reduce building water use by 20%	1
Credit 3.2	Reduce building water use by 30%	1

Energy and Atmosphere		14 Points
Prereq 1	Commission all building energy systems	Required
Prereq 2	Achieve minimum energy performance	Required
Prereq 3	Use no CFC refrigerants	Required

Credit 1	Reduce energy use by 10.5% to 35% compared with a baseline	1 to 8
Credit 2	Use on-site renewable energy for 1% of all energy use	1
Credit 3	Employ enhanced commissioning methods	1
Credit 4	Use less harmful refrigerants	1
Credit 5.1	Plan for measurement and verification of energy use of base building	1
Credit 5.2	Plan for measurement and verification of tenant energy use with submetering	1
Credit 6	Purchase green power for 35% or more of total electricity use	1

Materials and Resource   11 Points

Prereq 1	Provide space for storage and collection of recyclables	Required
Credit 1.1	Reuse existing buildings; maintain 25% of existing walls, floors, and roof	1
Credit 1.2	Reuse existing buildings; maintain 50% of existing walls, floors, and roof	1
Credit 1.3	During reuse, maintain 75% of interior nonstructural elements	1
Credit 2.1	Divert 50% of construction waste from disposal	1
Credit 2.2	Divert 75% of construction waste from disposal	1
Credit 3	Reuse salvaged materials for 1% of building materials	1
Credit 4.1	Use recycled-content materials for 10% of building materials	1
Credit 4.2	Use recycled-content materials for 20% of building materials	1
Credit 5.1	Use regionally sourced materials for 10% of building value	1
Credit 5.2	Use regionally sourced materials for 20% of building value	1
Credit 6	Use certified wood for 50% of value of all wood products in building	1

Indoor Environmental Quality   11 Points

Prereq 1	Meet minimum indoor air-quality performance levels	Required
Prereq 2	Control or eliminate environmental tobacco smoke	Required
Credit 1	Monitor carbon dioxide and provide outdoor air delivery to meet standards	1
Credit 2	Increase outdoor air ventilation rate by 30%	1
Credit 3	Manage indoor air quality during construction	1
Credit 4.1	Use low-VOC adhesives and sealants	1
Credit 4.2	Use low-VOC paints and coatings	1
Credit 4.3	Use low-emitting carpets and backing	1
Credit 4.4	Use zero urea-formaldehyde in composite wood and agrifiber products	1
Credit 5	Control indoor chemical use and pollutant sources	1
Credit 6	Provide individual comfort controls for 50% of occupants	1
Credit 7	Design thermal comfort to meet standards at all times	1
Credit 8.1	Provide daylight to 75% of occupied spaces	1
Credit 8.2	Provide views to 90% of occupied spaces	1

Innovation and Design Process   5 Points

Credit 1.1–1.2 Innovation in design: exemplary performance above LEED
                standards   2
Credit 1.3–1.4 Innovation in design: provide measures not included in LEED   2
Credit 2   Use a LEED Accredited Professional on project team   1

Total Points   **61**

Certified: 23–27 points Silver: 28–33 points Gold: 34–44 points Platinum: 45–61 points

LEED for Homes Pilot

Version 1.11a, February 1, 2007

PROJECT CHECKLIST
Minimum no. of points required:

Certified:	45
Silver:	60
Gold:	75
Platinum	90

		Available
Innovation and Design Process (ID)	*(Minimum of 0 ID points required)*	*9*

Integrated Project Planning

1.1	Preliminary rating	Prerequisite
1.2	Integrated project team	1
1.3	Design charrette	1

Quality Management for Durability

2.1	Durability planning (preconstruction)	Prerequisite
2.2	Wet room measures	Prerequisite
2.3	Quality management	Prerequisite
2.4	Third-party durability inspection	3

Innovative / Regional Design

3.1	Provide description and justification for specific measure	1
3.2	Provide description and justification for specific measure	1
3.3	Provide description and justification for specific measure	1
3.4	Provide description and justification for specific measure	1

Location and Linkages (LL)	*(Minimum of 0 LL points required)*	*10*

Site Selection

1	LEED-ND Neighborhood	10
2	Avoid environmentally sensitive sites and farmland	2

Preferred Locations

3.1	Select an edge development site	1
3.2	OR Select an infill site	2
3.3	Select a previously developed site	1

Infrastructure

4	Site within 1/2 mile of existing water and sewer	1

Community Resources and Public Transit

5.1	Basic community resources / public transportation	1
5.2	OR Extensive community resources / public transportation	2
5.3	OR Outstanding community resources / public transportation	3

Access to Open Space

6	Publicly accessible green spaces	1

Sustainable Sites (SS)	*(Minimum of 5 SS points required)*	*21*

Site Stewardship

1.1	Erosion controls (during construction)	Prerequisite
1.2	Minimize disturbed area of site	1

Landscaping

2.1	No invasive plants	Prerequisite
2.2	Basic landscaping design	2
2.3	Limit turf	3
2.4	Use drought-tolerant plants	2

Shading of Hardscapes

3	Locate and plant trees to shade hardscapes	1

Surface Water Management

4.1	Design permeable site	4
4.2	Design and install permanent erosion controls	2

Nontoxic Pest Control

5	Select insect and pest control alternatives from list	2

Compact Development

6.1	Average housing density $\geq$ 7 units / acre	2
6.1	OR Average housing density $\geq$ 10 units / acre	3
6.3	OR Average housing density $\geq$ 20 units / acre	4

Water Efficiency (WE)	*(Minimum of 3 WE points required)*	*15*

Water Reuse

1.1	Rainwater harvesting system	4
1.2	Gray water reuse system	1

Irrigation System

2.1	Select high-efficiency measures from list	3
2.2	Third-party verification	1
2.3	OR Install landscape designed by licensed or certified professional	4

Indoor Water Use

3.1	High-efficiency fixtures (toilets, showers, and faucets)	3
3.2	OR Very high efficiency fixtures (toilets, showers, and faucets)	6

Energy and Atmosphere (EA)   (Minimum of 2 EA points required)   *38*

Energy Star Home

1.1	Meets Energy Star for homes with third-party testing	Prerequisite
1.2	Exceeds Energy Star for homes	34

Insulation

2.1	Third-party inspection of insulation, at least HERS Grade II	Prerequisite
2.2	Third-party inspection of insulation, HERS Grade 1 and 5% above code	2

Air Infiltration

3.1	Third-party envelope air leakage tested $\leq$ 7.0 air changes/hour	Prerequisite
3.2	Third-party envelope air leakage tested $\leq$ 5.0 air changes/hour	2
3.3	Third-party envelope air leakage tested $\leq$ 3.0 air changes/hour	3

Windows

4.1	Windows meet Energy Star for windows	Prerequisite
4.2	Windows exceed Energy Star for windows (Table)	2
4.3	Windows exceed Energy Star for windows (Table	3

Duct Tightness

5.1	Third-party duct leakage tested $\leq$ 4.0 CFM per 100-sq.ft. to outside	Prerequisite
5.2	Third-party duct leakage tested $\leq$ 3.0 CFM per 100-sq.ft. to outside	2
5.3	Third-party duct leakage tested $\leq$ 1.0 CFM per 100-sq.ft. to outside	3

Space Heating and Cooling

6.1	Meets Energy Star for HVAC with Manual J and refrigerant charge test	Prerequisite
6.2	HVAC is better than Energy Star	2
6.3	HVAC substantially exceeds Energy Star	2

Water Heating

7.1	Improved hot water distribution system	2
7.2	Pipe insulation	1
7.3	Improved water heating equipment	3

Lighting

8.1	Install at least three Energy Star-labeled light fixtures (or CFLs)	Prerequisite
8.2	Energy-efficient fixtures and controls	2
8.3	OR Energy Star Advanced Lighting Package	3

Appliances

9.1	Select appliances from list	2
9.2	Very-efficient clothes washer (MEF > 1.8; WF < 5.5)	1

Renewable Energy

10	Improved hot water distribution system	10

Refrigerant Management

11   Minimize ozone depletion and global warming contributions   1

Materials and Resources (MR) (Minimum of 2 MR points required)   *14*

Material-Efficient Framing

1.1   Overall waste factor for framing order shall be no more than 10%   Prerequisite

1.2   Advanced framing techniques   3

1.3   OR Structurally insulated panels   2

Environmentally Preferable Products

2.1   Tropical woods, if used, must be certified by Forest Stewardship Council   Prerequisite

2.2   Select environmentally preferable products from list   8

Waste Management

3.1   Document overall rate of diversion   Prerequisite

3.2   Reduce waste sent to landfill by 25% to 100%   3

Indoor Environmental Quality (IEQ) (Minimum of 6 IEQ points required)   *20*

Energy Star with IAP

1   Meets Energy Star w/Indoor Air Package (IAP)   11

Combustion Venting

2.1   Space heating and domestic hot water equipment OR w/closed power-exhaust   Prerequisite

2.2   Install high-performance fireplace   2

Moisture Control

3   Analyze moisture loads and install central system (if needed)   1

Outdoor Air Ventilation

4.1   Meets ASHRAE Standard 62.2   Prerequisite

4.2   Dedicated outdoor air system (w/heat recovery)   2

4.3   Third-party testing of outdoor air flow rate into home   1

Local Exhaust

5.1   Meets ASHRAE Standard 62.2   Prerequisite

5.2   Timer / automatic controls for bathroom exhaust fans   1

5.3   Third-party testing of exhaust air flow rate out of home   1

Supply Air Distribution

6.1   Meets ACCA Manual D   Prerequisite

6.2   Third-party testing of supply air flow into each room in home   2

Supply Air Filtering

7.1 $\geq$ 8 MERV filters, w/adequate system air flow   Prerequisite

| 7.2 | OR $\geq$ 10 MERV filters, w/adequate system air flow | 1 |
| 7.3 | OR $\geq$ 13 MERV filters, w/adequate system air flow | 2 |

Contaminant Control

8.1	Seal ducts during construction	1
8.2	Permanent walk-off mats OR shoe storage OR central vacuum	2
8.3	Flush home continuously for 1 week with windows open	1

Radon Protection

| 9.1 | Install radon-resistant construction if home is in EPA Zone 1 | Prerequisite |
| 9.2 | Install radon-resistant construction if home is not in EPA Zone 1 | 1 |

Garage Pollutant Protection

10.1	No air handling equipment OR return ducts in garage	Prerequisite
10.2	Tightly seal shared surfaces between garage and home	2
10.3	Exhaust fan in garage	1
10.4	OR Detached garage OR no garage	3

| *Awareness and Education (AE)*   *(Minimum of 0 AE points required)* | *3* |

Education for Homeowner and/or Tenants

1.1	Basic occupant's manual and walk-through of LEED home	Prerequisite
1.2	Comprehensive occupant's manual and multiple walk-throughs / trainings	1
1.3	Increase public awareness of LEED home	1

Education for Building Managers

| 2.1 | Basic building manager's manual and walk-through of LEED home | 1 |
| **Total Points** | | **130** |

appendix 2.6
LEED for Neighborhood Development Pilot

Project Checklist

Smart Location and Linkage		30 Points
Prereq 1	Smart location	Required
Prereq 2	Proximity to water and wastewater infrastructure	Required
Prereq 3	Preservation of imperiled species and ecological communities	Required
Prereq 4	Wetland and water body conservation	Required
Prereq 5	Farmland conservation	Required
Prereq 6	Floodplain avoidance	Required
Credit 1	Brownfield redevelopment	2
Credit 2	High-priority brownfield redevelopment	1
Credit 3	Preferred location	10
Credit 4	Reduced automobile dependence	8
Credit 5	Bicycle network	1
Credit 6	Housing and jobs proximity	3
Credit 7	School proximity	1
Credit 8	Steep slope protection	1
Credit 9	Site design for habitat or wetlands conservation	1
Credit 10	Restoration of habitat or wetlands	1
Credit 11	Conservation management of habitat or wetlands	1

Neighborhood Pattern and Design		39 Points
Prereq 1	Open community	Required
Prereq 2	Compact development	Required
Credit 1	Compact development	7
Credit 2	Diversity of uses	4
Credit 3	Diversity of housing types	3
Credit 4	Affordable rental housing	2
Credit 5	Affordable for-sale housing	2
Credit 6	Reduced parking footprint	2
Credit 7	Walkable streets	8
Credit 8	Street network	2
Credit 9	Transit facilities	1
Credit 10	Transportation demand management	2

Credit 11	Access to surrounding vicinity	1
Credit 12	Access to public spaces	1
Credit 13	Access to active public spaces	1
Credit 14	Universal accessibility	1
Credit 15	Community outreach and involvement	1
Credit 16	Local food production	1

Green Construction and Technology		**31 Points**
Prereq 1	Construction activity pollution prevention	Required
Credit 1	LEED-certified green buildings	3
Credit 2	Energy efficiency in buildings	3
Credit 3	Reduced water use	3
Credit 4	Building reuse and adaptive reuse	2
Credit 5	Reuse of historic buildings	1
Credit 6	Minimize site disturbance through site design	1
Credit 7	Minimize site disturbance during construction	1
Credit 8	Contaminant reduction in brownfields remediation	1
Credit 9	Stormwater management	5
Credit 10	Heat island reduction	1
Credit 11	Solar orientation	1
Credit 12	On-site energy generation	1
Credit 13	On-site renewable energy sources	1
Credit 14	District heating and cooling	1
Credit 15	Infrastructure energy efficiency	1
Credit 16	Wastewater management	1
Credit 17	Recycled content for infrastructure	1
Credit 18	Construction waste management	1
Credit 19	Comprehensive waste management	1
Credit 20	Light-pollution reduction	1

Innovation and Design Process		**6 Points**
Credit 1.1–1.2	Innovation in design: exemplary performance above LEED standards	2
Credit 1.3–1.4	Innovation in design: green measures not in LEED	2
Credit 1.5	Innovation in design: other measures	1
Credit 2	Use a LEED Accredited Professional on project team	1
Total Points		**106 Points**

Certified: 40–49 points Silver: 50–59 points Gold: 60–79 points Platinum: 80–106 points

Green Guide for Health Care

Version 2.2

DESIGN AND CONSTRUCTION PROJECT CHECKLIST

Prereq 1	Pursue an integrated design process	Required
Prereq 2	Develop a health mission statement and program	Required

Sustainable Sites — 21 Points

Prereq 1	Prevent off-site pollution from construction activities	Required
Credit 1	Select sites in nonsensitive habitats	1
Credit 2	Locate in built-up urban areas	1
Credit 3.1	Brownfield redevelopment: basic remediation level	1
Credit 3.2	Brownfield redevelopment: residential remediation level	1
Credit 3.3	Brownfield redevelopment: minimizing future hazards	1
Credit 4.1	Locate facilities to provide public transportation access	1
Credit 4.2	Provide bicycle storage and changing rooms	1
Credit 4.3	Provide for low-emitting and fuel-efficient vehicles	1
Credit 4.4	Do not increase parking capacity beyond code minimums	1
Credit 5.1	Site development: protect or restore open space or habitat	1
Credit 5.2	Site development: reduce development footprint	1
Credit 5.3	Site development: 50% or more spaces in structured parking	1
Credit 6.1	Do not increase rate or quantity of stormwater runoff	1
Credit 6.2	Do not decrease stormwater runoff quality	1
Credit 7.1	Heat island effect: non-roof	1
Credit 7.2	Heat island effect: roof	1
Credit 8	Reduce light pollution	1
Credit 9.1	Connection to the natural world: outdoor places of respite	1
Credit 9.2	Connection to the natural world: exterior access for patients	1
Credit 10.1	Community contaminant prevention: airborne releases	1
Credit 10.2	Community contaminant prevention: leaks and spills	1

Water Efficiency — 6 Points

Prereq 1	Potable water use for medical equipment cooling	Required
Credit 1	Water-efficient landscaping: no potable water use or no irrigation	1
Credit 2.1	Potable water use reduction: measurement and verification	1
Credit 2.2	Potable water use reduction: domestic water: equip urinals and handwash sinks with sensor operators	1
Credit 2.3	Potable water use reduction: domestic water: use low-flow fixtures	1
Credit 2.4	Potable water use reduction: 20% of cooling tower use	1
Credit 2.5	Potable water use reduction: recycle condensate	1

Energy and Atmosphere — 21 Points

Prereq 1	Commission all new building energy systems	Required
Prereq 2	Achieve minimum energy performance	Required

Prereq 3	Use no CFI refrigerants	Required
Credit 1	Optimize energy performance: 10.5% to 42% savings vs. a standard building	1 to 10
Credit 2	Use on-site renewable energy: 50 to 150 watts per 1,000 square feet	1 to 3
Credit 3	Employ enhanced commissioning methods	1
Credit 4	Enhanced refrigerant management	1
Credit 5	Measurement and verification	1
Credit 6	Purchase green power for 20% to 100% of total electricity use	1 to 4
Credit 7	Equipment efficiency	1

Materials and Resources   21 Points

Prereq 1	Provide space for storage and collection of recyclables	Required
Prereq 2	Eliminate mercury	Required
Credit 1.1–1.2	Building reuse: maintain 40% or 80% of existing walls, floors, and roof	1 to 2
Credit 1.3	Building reuse: maintain 50% of interior nonstructural elements	1
Credit 2.1	Construction waste management: divert 50% from disposal	1
Credit 2.2	Construction waste management: divert 75% from disposal	1
Credit 2.3	Construction practices: site and materials management	1
Credit 2.4	Construction practices: utility and emissions control	1
Credit 3	Use sustainably sourced materials: 10% to 50%	1 to 5
Credit 4	Eliminate persistent, bioaccumulative, and toxic compounds: dioxins, mercury, lead, and cadmium	1 to 3
Credit 5.1	Furniture and medical furnishings: resource reuse	1
Credit 5.2	Furniture and medical furnishings: materials	1
Credit 5.3	Furniture and medical furnishings: manufacturing, transportation, and recycling	1
Credit 6	Copper reduction	1
Credit 7.1	Resource use: design for flexibility	1
Credit 7.2	Resource use: design for durability	1

Indoor Environmental Quality (EQ)   24 Points

Prereq 1	Minimum IAQ performance	Required
Prereq 2	Environmental tobacco smoke control	Required
Prereq 3	Hazardous material removal or encapsulation	Required
Credit 1	Outdoor air delivery monitoring	1
Credit 2	Natural ventilation	1
Credit 3.1	Construction EQ management plan: during construction	1
Credit 3.2	Construction EQ management plan: before occupancy	1
Credit 4.1	Low-emitting materials: interior adhesives and sealants	1
Credit 4.2	Low-emitting materials: wall and ceiling finishes	1
Credit 4.3	Low-emitting materials: flooring systems	1
Credit 4.4	Low-emitting materials: composite wood and insulation	1
Credit 4.5	Low-emitting materials: furniture and medical furnishings	1
Credit 4.6	Low-emitting materials: exterior applied products	1
Credit 5.1	Chemical and pollutant source control: outdoor	1
Credit 5.2	Chemical and pollutant source control: indoor	1
Credit 6.1	Controllability of systems: lighting	1
Credit 6.2	Controllability of systems: thermal comfort	1
Credit 7	Thermal comfort	1
Credit 8.1a–c	Daylight for occupied spaces: 6% to 18% above "square-root-base" daylit area	1 to 3
Credit 8.1d–e	Daylight for occupied spaces: 75% to 90% of regularly occupied spaces	1 to 2

Credit 8.2	Connection to the natural world: indoor places of respite	1
Credit 8.3	Lighting and circadian rhythm	1
Credit 9.1	Acoustic environment: exterior noise, acoustical finishes, and room noise levels	1
Credit 9.2	Acoustic environment: sound isolation, paging and call system, and building vibration	1

Innovation and Research   4 Points

Credit 1	Innovation in design: exemplary performance above GGHC levels or in categories of importance not addressed by GGHC	1 to 2
Credit 2	Documenting health, quality of care, and productivity performance impacts: research initiatives	1 to 2
Construction Total		97 Points

OPERATIONS PROJECT CHECKLIST

Building Operations   5 Points

Prereq 1	Ongoing self-certification	Required
Prereq 2	Integrated operations and maintenance process	Required
Prereq 3	Environmental tobacco smoke control	Required
Prereq 4	Outside air introduction and exhaust systems	Required
Credit 1.1	Building operations and maintenance: staff education	1
Credit 1.2	Building operations and maintenance: building systems maintenance	1
Credit 1.3	Building operations and maintenance: building systems monitoring	1
Credit 2.1	IAQ management: maintain indoor air quality	1
Credit 2.2	IAQ management: reduce particulates in air distribution	1

Transportation   3 Points

Credit 1.1	Alternative transportation: public transportation access	1
Credit 1.2	Alternative transportation: low-emitting and fuel-efficient vehicles	1
Credit 1.3	Alternative transportation: carpool programs	1

Energy and Atmosphere   18 Points

Prereq 1	Existing building commissioning	Required
Prereq 2	Minimum building energy performance	Required
Prereq 3	Ozone protection	Required
Credit 1	Optimize energy performance: Energy Star score of 63 to 99	1 to 10
Credit 2.1	On-site and off-site renewable energy: 1% of total use from on-site power or 5% of total use purchased from off-site sources	1
Credit 2.2	On-site and off-site renewable energy: 2% or 10%	1
Credit 2.3	On-site and off-site renewable energy: 5% or 25%	1
Credit 2.4	On-site and off-site renewable energy: 10% or 50%	1
Credit 3	Energy-efficient equipment	1
Credit 4	Refrigerant selection	1
Credit 5.1	Performance measurement: enhanced metering	1
Credit 5.2	Performance measurement: emission reduction reporting	1

Water Efficiency   8 Points

Prereq 1	Minimum water efficiency	Required
Credit 1	Water-efficient landscaping: reduce potable water use by 50% to 100%	1 to 2
Credit 2	Building water use: reduce 10% to 50%	1 to 5
Credit 3	Performance measurement: enhanced metering	1

Indoor Environmental Quality   5 Points

Prereq 1	Polychlorinated biphenyl (PCB) removal	Required
Credit 1.1	Community contaminant prevention: airborne releases	1
Credit 1.2	Community contaminant prevention: leaks and spills	1
Credit 2.1	Indoor pollutant source control and other occupational exposures: chemical management and minimization	1
Credit 2.2	Indoor pollutant source control and other occupational exposures: high-hazard chemicals	1
Credit 3	Chemical discharge: pharmaceutical management and disposal	1

Waste Management   6 Points

Prereq 1	Waste stream audit	Required
Credit 1	Total waste reduction: 15% to 35%	1 to 3
Credit 2.1	Regulated medical waste reduction: <10%	1
Credit 2.2	Regulated medical waste reduction: minimize incineration	1
Credit 3	Food waste reduction	1

Maintenance Practices   9 Points

Credit 1.1	Outdoor grounds and building exterior management: implement 4 strategies	1
Credit 1.2	Outdoor grounds and building exterior management: implement 8 strategies	1
Credit 2	Indoor integrated pest management	1
Credit 3	Environmentally preferable cleaning policy	1
Credit 4	Sustainable cleaning products and materials: 30% to 90% of annual purchases	1 to 4
Credit 5	Environmentally preferable janitorial equipment	1

Environmentally Preferable Purchasing   11 Points

Credit 1.1	Food: organic or sustainable	1
Credit 1.2	Food: antibiotics	1
Credit 1.3	Food: local production / food security	1
Credit 2	Janitorial paper and other disposable products	1
Credit 3	Electronics purchasing and end-of-life management	1
Credit 4.1	Toxic reduction: mercury	1
Credit 4.2	Toxic reduction: Di-Ethyl Hexyl Phthalate	1
Credit 4.3	Toxic reduction: natural rubber latex	1
Credit 5	Furniture and medical furnishings	1
Credit 6	Indoor Air Quality-compliant products: 45% to 90% of annual purchases	1 to 2

Innovation and Documentation   7 Points

Credit 1.1–1.2	Exemplary performance above GGHC standards	1 to 2
Credit 1.3–1.4	High performance in categories not addressed by GGHC	1 to 2
Credit 2	Documenting sustainable operations: business case impacts	1
Credit 3.1	Documenting productivity impacts: absenteeism and health care cost impacts	1
Credit 3.2	Documenting productivity impacts: research initiatives	1
Operations Total		72 Points

Endnotes

Foreword

1. The Fourth Report of the Intergovernmental Panel on Climate Change, released in February 2007, stated that the probability that global climate change is human-caused is 90 percent. Accessed at www.ipcc.ch, June 3, 2007.

Preface

1. U.S. Green Building Council unpublished data, furnished to the author, March 2007.
2. See, for example, Hansen's review article "The Threat to the Planet," *New York Review of Books*, July 13, 2006, www.nybooks.com/articles/19131, accessed April 2, 2007.

Chapter 1

1. Architecture 2030, www.architecture2030.com/current_situation/building _sector.html, accessed May 30, 2007.
2. Per-Anders Enkvist, Tomas Naucler, and Jerker Rosander, "A Cost Curve for Greenhouse Gas Reduction," *McKinsey Quarterly*, March 2007, p. 35, www.mckinsey quarterly.com/article_page.aspx?ar=1911, accessed March 22, 2007.
3. David Gottfried, *Greed to Green*, (Berkeley, CA: WorldBuild Publishing, 2004).
4. United Nations Framework Convention on Climate Change, Kyoto Protocol, http://unfccc.int/kyoto_protocol/items/2830.php, accessed June 5, 2007.
5. U.S. Green Building Council unpublished data furnished to the author, March 2007.
6. www.energystar.gov/index.cfm?fuseaction=qhmi.showHomesMarketIndex, accessed April 2, 2007.
7. U.S. Green Building Council unpublished data furnished to the author, March 2007.
8. U.S. Census Bureau: Construction Spending: Public Construction, http://www .census.gov/const/www/totpage.html, accessed June 5, 2007.
9. U.S. Green Building Council, www.usgbc.org/ShowFile.aspx?DocumentID=742#8, accessed March 21, 2007.
10. U.S. Green Building Council, www.usgbc.org/ShowFile.aspx?DocumentID=742#9 and #10, accessed March 21, 2007.
11. Shefali Ranganathan, "Energy in Buildings," September 11, 2006, www.eesi .org/publications/Fact%20Sheets/Buildings_energy_9.11.06.PDF, accessed March 21, 2007.

12. California Department of General Services, "Green California," www.green
.ca.gov, accessed March 21, 2007.

13. USGBC case study, www.usgbc.org/ShowFile.aspx?DocumentID=2061, accessed
April 1, 2007.

14. Energy Information Administration, "Petroleum Navigator," http://tonto.eia
.doe.gov/dnav/pet/hist/wtotworldw.htm, accessed March 21, 2007.

15. U.S. Environmental Protection Agency and U.S. Department of Energy, "Are You
Ready to Take Advantage of the New Commercial Tax Incentives?" www.energy
star.gov/ia/business/comm_bldg_tax_incentives.pdf, accessed April 2, 2007.

16. U.S. Department of Energy, "Nevada Law Promotes Green Building, Alters Renewable Mandate," www.eere.energy.gov/states/news_detail.cfm/news_id=9149,
accessed April 2, 2007.

17. Deborah Snoonian, "AIA Board of Directors Sets Ambitious Agenda for Sustainability," *Architectural Record*, December 27, 2005, http://archrecord.construction
.com/news/daily/archives/051227aia.asp, accessed April 2, 2007.

Chapter 2

1. Author's analysis, based on reported certifications for new construction projects
at the end of 2006. By 2007, LEED had certified about 513 systems and Green
Globes about 10, or 2 percent of the total.

2. GSA Report to Congress, www.usgbc.org/ShowFile.aspx?DocumentID=1916, accessed March 6, 2007.

3. Author's analysis of USGBC LEED-project registration and certification data,
March 30, 2007.

4. Laura Case and David Payne, Emory University, interview, March 2007.

5. Nancy Carlisle, "Laboratories for the 21st Century: Case Studies," www.labs21cen
tury.gov/pdf/cs_emory_508.pdf, accessed March 20, 2007.

6. Hines, "1180 Peachtree," www.hines.com/property/detail.aspx?id=507, accessed
March 20, 2007.

7. Jerry Lea, Hines, March 2006.

8. Ibid.

9. Amanda Sturgeon, "Achieving LEED-CI Platinum: Perkins+Will's New Platinum
Digs in Seattle," in www.aia.org/cote_a_0703_walktalk, accessed March 20, 2007.

10. Ibid.

11. Heidi Schwartz, "Moss Landing Laboratories Fulfills One Man's Crusade," April 1,
2004, www.mlml.calstate.edu/news/newsdetail.php?id=35, accessed March 20,
2007.

12. Green Building Initiative, www.thegbi.org.

13. "Green Buildings and the Bottom Line," *Building Design+Construction,* supplement, November 2006, pp. 56–57, www.bdcnetwork.com. Reprinted with permission from Building Design+Construction. Copyright 2006 Reed Business Information. All rights reserved.

14. Lurita Doan, letter to Hon. Christopher Bond, Chairman, Subcommittee on Trans-

portation, Treasury, the Judiciary, HUD, and Related Agencies, September 15, 2006, www.usgbc.org/ShowFile.aspx?DocumentID=1916, accessed April 3, 2007.

15. Ibid.

16. U.S. Green Building Council, "GSA Says LEED Most Credible Green Building Rating System," September 17, 2006, www.usgbc.org/News/USGBCInTheNewsDetails .aspx?ID=2628, accessed April 3, 2007.

Chapter 3

1. Some buildings may have green elements but do not pursue formal certification. My estimate is that these represent less than half of the green building market at present and will decline rapidly over the next three years as a share of all green buildings. The case for certification of buildings is made elsewhere; the fact is that most people who claim to be doing green design but don't bother to certify the project through an independent third party are practicing self-deception, since without certification as a goal, many of the green elements are cut from most projects for budget reasons.

2. Charles Lockwood, "As Green as the Grass Outside," *Barron's*, December 25, 2006, http://online.barrons.com/article/SB116683352907658186.html?mod=9_0031_b _this_weeks_magazine_main, accessed March 6, 2007.

3. Peter Verwer, CEO, Australian Property Council, presentation at the Green Cities '07 conference, Sydney, Australia, February 13, 2007, www.gbcaus.org.au.

4. Jerry Lea, Hines, interview, March 2007.

5. Richard Cook, Cook+Fox Architects, New York City, interview, March 2007.

6. 2005 Survey of Green Building Plus Green Building in K-12 and Higher Education, www.turnerconstruction.com/greensurvey05.pdf, accessed March 6, 2007.

7. ecologic3, www.ecologic3.com, accessed June 2007.

8. Paul Shahriari, GreenMind, Inc., interview, March 2007.

9. U.S. Green Building Council, *Making the Business Case for High-Performance Green Buildings* (Washington, DC: U.S. Green Building Council, 2002), available at www.usgbc.org/resources/usbgc_brochures.asp, accessed March 6, 2007. See also *Environmental Building News* 14, no. 4 (April 2005), available at www.building-green.com, accessed March 6, 2007.

10. See www.eia.doe.gov/oiaf/aeo/key.html, accessed March 6, 2007, for the November 2006 forecast.

11. See the recent meta-study by Lawrence Berkeley National Laboratory, *The Cost-Effectiveness of Commercial-Buildings Commissioning*, available at http://eetd.lbl .gov/emills/PUBS/Cx-Costs-Benefits.html. This research reviewed 224 studies of the benefits of building commissioning and concluded that based on energy savings alone, such investments have a payback within five years.

12. Oregon Business Energy Tax Credit, "Application for Preliminary Certification Sustainable Buildings," www.oregon.gov/ENERGY/CONS/BUS/docs/Sustain-ableAp.doc, accessed March 6, 2007.

13. Oregon Department of Energy, "Business Energy Tax Credits," www.oregon.gov/ENERGY/CONS/BUS/BETC.shtml, accessed March 6, 2007.

14. Natural Resources Defense Council, "New York's Green Building Tax Credit," September 19, 2002, www.nrdc.org/cities/building/nnytax.asp, accessed March 6, 2007.

15. Lynn Simon, Simon & Associates, personal communication, February 2, 2007. See also www.eere.energy.gov/states/news_detail.cfm/news_id=9149, accessed March 6, 2007, and www.leg.state.nv.us/22ndSpecial/bills/AB/AB3_EN.pdf, accessed March 6, 2007. The Nevada Legislature in 2007 is considering repealing this law because of its high cost in terms of lost revenues.

16. U.S. Department of Energy, The Energy Policy Act of 2005, www.energy.gov/taxbreaks.htm, accessed March 6, 2007.

17. Eleven case studies have shown that innovative daylighting systems can pay for themselves in less than one year due to energy and productivity benefits. Vivian Loftness et al., *Building Investment Decision Support (BIDS)* (Pittsburgh: Center for Building Performance and Diagnostics, Carnegie Mellon University, n.d.), available at http://cbpd.arc.cmu.edu/ebids, accessed March 6, 2007.

18. Carnegie Mellon University, http://cbpd.arc.cmu.edu/ebids/images/group/cases/lighting.pdf, accessed March 6, 2007.

19. Greg Kats, "The Costs and Financial Benefits of Green Buildings," www.cap-e.com/ewebeditpro/items/O59F3303.ppt#2, accessed March 6, 2007.

20. "Speedy Permitting Has Developers Turning Green in Chicago," *Building Design+Construction,* November 2005, p. 28; www.bdcnetwork.com, accessed March 6, 2007.

21. S. Richard Fedrizzi, CEO, U.S. Green Building Council, personal communication, October 2006.

22. *Building Online,* "Fireman's Fund First to Introduce Green Building Coverage," October 12, 2006, www.buildingonline.com/news/viewnews.pl?id=5514, accessed March 6, 2007.

23. U.S. Green Building Council. "Adobe Headquarters Awarded Highest Honors from U.S. Green Building Council," December 5, 2006, www.usgbc.org/News/PressReleaseDetails.aspx?ID=2783, accessed March 6, 2007.

24. "The Business Case for Green Building," *Urban Land,* June 2005, p. 71, available at www.uli.org.

25. U.S. Green Building Council, "New York Announces Energy and Environmental Package World Trade Center Complex Will Go for LEED Certification," September 14, 2006, www.usgbc.org/News/PressReleaseDetails.aspx?ID=2590, accessed March 6, 2007.

26. National Association of Industrial and Office Properties, www.naiop.org.

27. Gerding Edlen Development, www.gerdingedlen.com; Justin Stranzi, *Daily Journal of Commerce,* (Portland, OR), February 26, 2007, p. 4.

28. Urban Land Institute, www.uli.org/AM/Template.cfm?Section=GreenTech1&Template=/MembersOnly.cfm&ContentID=37654, accessed December 31, 2006.

29. Corporate Office Properties Trust, www.copt.com/?id=162, accessed March 6, 2007.

30. Lisa Chamberlain, "Square Feet; Finding the Green In Building Renovation," *New York Times*, January 10, 2007.

31. Rose Companies, www.rose-network.com/projects/index.html, accessed March 6, 2007.

32. Sydney Mead, "EcoTrust Toolkit: Jean Vollum National Capital Center," www.ecotrust.org/ncc/index.html, accessed March 6, 2007.

33. The Kresge Foundation, "Green Building Initiative," www.kresge.org/content/displaycontent.aspx?CID=7, accessed March 6, 2007.

Chapter 4

1. Jim Goldman, Turner Construction, interview, March 2007.

2. Gregory Kats et al., "The Costs and Financial Benefits of Green Buildings," 2003, www.cap-e.com/ewebeditpro/items/O59F3303.ppt#1, accessed March 6, 2007.

3. Dennis Wilde, Gerding Edlen Development, personal communication, 2006.

4. A case study of this project may be ordered at no cost from the engineering firm, Interface Engineering, at www.ieice.com. See also Andy Frichtl and Jerry Yudelson, "Platinum on a Budget," *Consulting-Specifying Engineer,* October 2005, www.csemag.com/article/CA6271678.html?text=Platinum, accessed March 6, 2007.

5. Lisa Fay Matthiessen and Peter Morris, "Costing Green: A Comprehensive Database," Davis Langdon, 2004, www.davislangdon.com/USA/research.

6. Lisa Fay Matthiessen, Todd See, and Peter Morris, "Building on Bren: Putting a Price on Green Lab Design," 2006, www.davislangdon.us.

7. Leith Sharp, Harvard Green Campus Initiative, interview, March 2007.

8. Steven Winter Associates, "GSA LEED Cost Study," downloadable (578 pp.) from the Whole Building Design Guide web site, www.wbdg.org/ccb/GSAMAN/gsaleed.pdf, accessed March 18, 2007. The authors note: "The construction cost estimates reflect a number of GSA-specific design features and project assumptions; as such, the numbers must be used with caution [and] may not be directly transferable to other project types or building owners" (p. 2).

9. U.S. Green Building Council, "LEED Cost Module Training Workshop," November 2006.

10. This fine turn of phrase derives from Amory Lovins. See, for example, Paul Hawken, Amory Lovins, and Hunter Lovins, *Natural Capitalism* (Boston: Little Brown, 1999), p. 115, for further discussion of this vital principle of integrated design.

11. Gail Lindsey, FAIA, personal communication, March 2007.

12. Rebecca Flora, Green Building Alliance, interview, March 2007.

Chapter 5

1. Fern Siegel, "Future Tense: JWT Spots 2007 Trends," *MediaDailyNews*, December 29, 2006, http://publications.mediapost.com/index.cfm?fuseaction=Articles.san&s=53075&Nid=26151&p=401551, accessed March 21, 2007.

2. *Education Green Building SmartMarket Report,* McGraw-Hill Construction Research & Analytics, 2007, p. 12, available at www.construction.com/greensource/resources/smartmarket.asp.

3. Howard Schultz, chairman of Starbucks, remarks at Starbucks annual meeting, March 20, 2007, as reported in the *Wall Street Journal,* http://online .wsj.com/article/SB117448991525244165.html?mod=index_to_people.

4. This is a far more conservative estimate than that of the USGBC's CEO, Rick Fedrizzi, who announced a goal of 100,000 registered projects by 2010 at the organization's annual conference in November 2006.

5. Jim Haughey, "U.S. Construction Forecast Tables—Based on Put-in-Place Investment and Housing Starts—Issued March 2007," Building Team Forecast, March 5, 2007, www.buildingteamforecast.com/article/CA6421650.html?industryid =44206, accessed March 22, 2007.

6. Richard Florida, *The Rise of the Creative Class: And How It's Transforming Work, Leisure, Community and Everyday Life* (New York: Perseus Books Group, 2002).

7. See, for example, the Natural Marketing Institute web site, www.nmisolutions .com.

8. "What are Energy Star Qualified New Homes?" www.energystar.gov/ index.cfm ?c=new_homes.hm_earn_star, accessed March 30, 2007.

9. "Energy Star Qualified New Homes Market Indices for States," www.energystar .gov/index.cfm?fuseaction=qhmi.showHomesMarketIndex, accessed March 30, 2007.

10. For a PATH (Partnership for Advancing Technology in Housing) evaluation report, see the Toolbase web site, www.toolbase.org/tertiaryT.asp?DocumentID=4120& CATEGORYID=1505.

11. American Institute of Architects, "Architects Call for Fifty Percent Reduction by 2010 of Fossil Fuel Used to Construct and Operate Buildings," press release, December 19, 2005, www.aia.org/press2_template.cfm?pagename=release %5F121905 %5Ffossilfuel.

12. Architecture 2030, "The 2030 Challenge," http://www.architecture2030.com/ open_letter/index.html, accessed June 6, 2007.

13. *Builder Magazine,* May 2007, p. 139, www.builderonline.com.

14. "Energy Star Qualified New Homes Market Indices for States," www.energystar .gov/index.cfm?fuseaction=qhmi.showHomesMarketIndex, accessed March 21, 2007.

15. Jim Broughton, interview, March 2007.

16. "2005 Survey of Green Building Plus Green Building in K-12 and Higher Education," www.turnerconstruction.com/greensurvey 05.pdf, accessed March 6, 2007.

17. Rob Cassidy, "Green Buildings and the Bottom Line," *Building Design+Construction,* November 2006 supplement, p. 8, www.bdcmag.com, accessed March 6, 2007. Reprinted with permission from Building Design+Construction. Copyright 2006 Reed Business Information. All rights reserved.

18. James Goldman, Turner Construction, interview, March 2007.

19. Education Green Building, SmartMarket Report, McGraw-Hill Construction Re-

search & Analytics, 2007, http://www.construction.com/greensource/resources/smartmarket.asp.

20. Jerry Lea, Hines, interview, March 2007.

21. Stephen Kellert and Edward Wilson, eds., *The Biophilia Hypothesis* (Washington, DC: Island Press, 1995).

22. The tax credits and deductions in this act will expire on December 31, 2008, unless extended by Congress.

23. Gail Lindsey, Design Harmony, North Carolina, interview, March 2007.

24. Jason F. McLennan, "The Living Building Challenge," www.cascadiagbc.org/resources/living-buildings/LBC_Two_Pager.pdf, accessed March 21, 2007.

Chapter 6

1. BRE Environmental Assessment Method, www.breeam.org.

2. Nigel Howard, former UK BREEAM staffer, Sydney, Australia, personal communication, February 2007.

3. For an overview of the Japanese approach to rating green buildings, see www.ibec.or.jp/CASBEE/english/index.htm; for the Canadian LEED system and an overview of green buildings in Canada, see www.cagbc.org/building_rating_systems/leed_rating_system.php; for the Indian LEED systems, see www.igbc.in; Brent Morgan, USGBC staff, personal communication regarding licensing of LEED to other countries, March 2007.

4. World Green Building Council, www.worldgbc.org.

5. Kevin Hydes, Stantec Consulting, interview, March 2007.

6. Huston Eubank, World Green Building Council, interview, March 2007.

7. Canada Green Building Council, "Membership Statistics," www.cagbc.org/membership_information/statistics.php, accessed March 18, 2007.

8. Lloyd Atler, "Gulf Islands Park Operations Centre: LEED Platinum," November 8, 2006, www.treehugger.com/files/2006/11/gulf_islands_pa_1.php, accessed April 1, 2007.

9. Thomas Mueller, interview, March 2007.

10. Nils Larsson, Ronald Rovers, Rein Jaaniste, Ove Morck, Ilari Aho, Andrea Moro, Caroline Cheng, Mauritz Glaumann, Marita Wallhagen, and Sonja Persram, "Sustainable Building Policy Initiatives," Canada Mortgage and Housing Corporation, December 2006.

11. I found this out firsthand during a series of meetings with developers in Shanghai in March 2005.

12. Arup, "Collaboration on renewable energy supply to the world's first sustainable city," February 26, 2006, www.arup.com/arup/newsitem.cfm?pageid=8015, accessed March 18, 2007.

13. Peter Head, Arup, presentation at the Green Cities '07 conference, Sydney, Australia, February 13, 2007.

14. Kenneth Langer, interview, March 2007. Further information can be found at www.emsi-green.com.

15. Kenneth Langer and Robert Watson, "Bringing LEED to China," *Environmental Design + Construction*, November 2005.

16. For information on the CII-Sohrabji Godrej Green Business Centre, see www .ciigbc.org/aboutus.asp.

17. Kath Williams, Kath Williams & Associates, interview, March 2007.

18. S. Srinivas, "Green Buildings in India: Lessons Learnt," www.igbc.in/igbc/ mmbase/ attachments/380/Green_Buildings_in_India_-_Lessons_Learnt.pdf, accessed March 18, 2007. See also "Green Buildings in India: Emerging Business Opportunities," no author.

19. Green Cities '07, "Australasian Conference and Expo," www.greencities.org.au.

20. Australia's population is only about 20 million, while that of the United States is about 300 million.

21. Green Building Council Australia, Green Building News: Media Releases, www.gbcaus.org/gbc.asp?sectionid=6, accessed March 18, 2007.

22. Alvento case study, prepared by Z3 sustainable design project consulting firm, Madrid, Spain, www.zeta3.com.

23. Aurelio Ramírez-Zarzosa, founder and president, Spain Green Building Council, interview, March 2007, www.spaingbc.org.

24. Ibid.

Chapter 7

1. Rod Wille, Turner Construction, interview, March 2007.

2. U.S. Census Bureau, www.census.gov/const/www/C30index.html, accessed March 22, 2007.

3. Ibid.

4. USGBC Case Study: Gerding/Edlen Development Company, www.usgbc.org/ ShowFile.aspx?DocumentID=1207, accessed March 23, 2007.

5. Ibid.

6. The Brewery Blocks, www.breweryblocks.com.

7. Scott Lewis, LEED consultant, Brightworks Northwest, personal communication, March 23, 2007.

8. Dennis Wilde, interview, March 2007.

9. USGBC Project Profile: Banner Bank Building, www.usgbc.org/ShowFile.aspx? DocumentID=2057, accessed March 23, 2007.

10. Ibid.

11. Richard Cook, AIA, Cook+Fox Architects, New York City, interview, March 2007.

12. Jerry Lea, Hines, interview, March 2007.

13. Workstage, www.workstage.com.

14. Ibid.

15. Integrated Architecture, www.intarch.com/leed_project_5/index.htm and www .intarch.com/news.htm, accessed June 4, 2007.

16. Vilma Barr, "Green light on PNC's bottom line," Display and Design Ideas. October 1, 2005, www.ddimagazine.com/displayanddesignideas/search/article_dis play.jsp?vnu_content_id=1001307842, accessed March 23, 2007.

17. Steve McLinden, "Making Sustainable Development Profitable," International Council of Shopping Centers, www.icsc.org/srch/sct/sct0207/index.php, accessed March 23, 2007.

18. Timothy Davis, "Visteon Village: How communities can prepare for major economic investment," April 19, 2005, www.umich.edu/~econdev/visteon/index .html, accessed April 1, 2007.

19. U.S. Census Bureau, www.census.gov/const/www/C30index.html, accessed April 1, 2007.

20. "A Green by Any Other Name Would Still Get LEED Silver," Development, Winter 2006, p. 14.

21. U.S. Green Building Council LEED Registered Projects, April 12, 2007, www .usgbc.org/ShowFile.aspx?DocumentID=2313, accessed April 1, 2007.

22. Liberty Property Trust: High-Performance Green Buildings, www.libertyproperty.com/green_buildings.asp?sel=0&id=1, accessed April 1, 2007.

23. Peter S. Longstreth, "Liberty Property Trust's One Crescent Drive Receives LEED Platinum Certification From U.S. Green Building Council," August 22, 2006, www.pidc-pa.org/newsDetail.asp?pid=208, accessed April 1, 2007.

24. Jennifer Dawson, "CalPERS forms 'green' building fund with Houston developer," Sacramento Business Journal, October 13, 2006, http://sacramento.bizjournals .com/sacramento/stories/2006/10/16/story15.html, accessed March 23, 2007.

25. Gary Pivo, "Is There a Future for Socially Responsible Property Investments?" Fall 2005, www.findarticles.com/p/articles/mi_qa3681/is_200510/ai_n15868788, accessed March 23, 2007.

26. "Bank of America Commits $20 Billion to Green Lending," March 6, 2007, http:// blogs.business2.com/greenwombat/2007/03/bank_america_co.html, accessed March 23, 2007.

27. "Citi Targets $50 Billion Over 10 Years to Address Global Climate Change," May 8, 2007, www.citigroup.com/citigroup/press/citigroup.htm, accessed May 30, 2007.

Chapter 8

1. From USGBC unpublished data on LEED registrations and certifications, March 2007, and author's analysis of this data.

2. "Public Works Provides Steady Growth," Engineering News Record, March 26, 2007, p. 25.

3. www.census.gov/const/C30/totsa.pdf, accessed March 30, 2007.

4. Don Horn, U.S. General Services Administration, interview, March 2007.

5. See www.ecotrust.org, and Bettina von Hagen, Erin Kellogg, and Eugénie Frerichs Rebuilt Green: The Natural Capital Center and the Transformative Power of Building (Portland, OR: Ecotrust, 2003).

6. From the author's professional experience.

7. John Boecker, interview, March 2007.

8. USGBC data, from the LEED-NC Technical Review workbook, unpublished, 2006.

9. USGBC LEED Certified Project List, www.usgbc.org/LEED/Project/Certified ProjectList.aspx?CMSPageID=244, accessed March 30, 2007.

10. U.S. Department of Energy, Office of Energy Efficiency and Renewable Energy, www.eere.energy.gov/femp/pdfs/fed_leed_bldgs.pdf, accessed March 30, 2007.

11. David Summers, "Creative Engineering Provides Flexible Control While Saving Energy," August 1, 2006, http://www.glumac.com/section.asp?catid=140&subid=157&pageid=569, accessed March 30, 2007.

12. USGBC LEED Certified Project List: NRDC Santa Monica Office, http://leedcasestudies.usgbc.org/energy.cfm?ProjectID=236, accessed March 30, 2007.

13. Amanda Griscom, "Who's the Greenest of Them All?," in www.grist.org/news/powers/2003/11/25/of, accessed March 30, 2007.

14. "Santa Clarita Transit Maintenance Facility Earns LEED Gold Rating from U.S. Green Building Council," January 3, 2007. http://www.hok.com, accessed June 6, 2007.

15. Mark Murphy, "Santa Clarita Transit Maintenance Facility Earns LEED Gold Rating from U.S. Green Building Council," January 3, 2007, www.fypower.org/pdf/SantaClarita_Facility.pdf, accessed March 30, 2007.

16. Wisconsin Dept. of Natural Resources, "Wisconsin's first "green" state office building opens in Green Bay," June 12, 2006, http://dnr.wi.gov/org/caer/ce/news/rbnews/BreakingNews_Lookup.asp?id=80, accessed April 1, 2007.

Chapter 9

1. "Stalled Momentum," *American School & University,* May 2006, p. 24.

2. U.S. Census Bureau, www.census.gov/const/C30/totsa.pdf, accessed March 30, 2007.

3. U.S. Green Building Council LEED Registered Projects, April 12, 2007, www.usgbc.org/ShowFile.aspx?DocumentID=2313, accessed March 31, 2007.

4. USGBC staff, personal communication, October 2006.

5. *Education Green Building SmartMarket Report,* McGraw-Hill Construction Research & Analytics, 2007, p. 9, available at www.construction.com/greensource/resources/smartmarket.asp.

6. See www.aashe.org. The author is a founding board member.

7. Matthew St. Clair, Sustainability Manager, University of California, interview, March 2007.

8. Judy Walton, Director of Strategic Initiatives, AASHE, interview, March 2007.

9. Robert Roseth, "UW reaches gold standard for energy and environmental design," January 18, 2007, http://uwnews.washington.edu/ni/article.asp?articleID=29606, accessed March 31, 2007.

10. "Trends in Education: The latest and the greatest, both inside and outside the wall, continue to evolve," *College Planning & Management,* January 2006, p. 14, www.peterli.com/archive/cpm/1041.shtm, accessed March 31, 2007.

11. "UC Merced's First Campus Complex Earns 'Gold' Certification," www.ucmerced.edu/news_articles/03132007_uc_merced_s_first.asp, accessed March 31, 2007.

12. Morken Center Fact Sheet, www.plu.edu/~morken/fact-sheet.html, accessed March 31, 2007.

13. Association for the Advancement of Sustainability in Higher Education, www
.aashe.org.

14. Leith Sharp, Harvard University, interview, March 2007.

15. "Green Buildings at Harvard: Harvard Exhibits Its Commitment to 'LEED' by Example," Spring 2007, www.greencampus.harvard.edu/newsletter/archives/2006
/05/green_buildings_1.php, accessed March 31, 2007.

16. Project information furnished by architects Bruner/Cott & Associates, March
2007.

17. Leith Sharp, Harvard University, personal communication, March 2007.

18. Ibid., interview, March 2007.

19. Anne Schopf, Mahlum Architects, interview, March 2007.

20. *Education Green Building SmartMarket Report,* McGraw-Hill Construction Research & Analytics, 2007, p. 9, available at www.construction.com/greensource/
resources/smartmarket.asp.

21. Annual survey data, *American School & University,* April 2006, p. 30.

22. Ibid., p. 17.

23. "Green commercial projects by LPA Architects," August 4, 2006, www.ocregister
.com/ocregister/life/homegarden/article_1234133.php, accessed March 31, 2007.

24. Concrete Masonry Association of California and Nevada: Profiles in Architecture:
Cesar Chavez Elementary School, July 2006, www.cmacn.org/publications/pro-
files/july2006/page2.htm, accessed March 31, 2007.

25. Washington Sustainable Schools: Protocol for High Performance School Facilities.
March 2004, www.k12.wa.us/SchFacilities/pubdocs/FinalProtocol-March2004
.pdf, accessed March 30, 2007.

26. Kathleen O'Brien, O'Brien and Company, Seattle, WA, interview, March 2007.

27. The Collaborative for High Performance Schools, www.chps.net, accessed March
30, 2007.

28. School Districts that are using CHPS Guidelines, www.chps.net/chps_schools/dis-
tricts.htm, accessed March 30, 2007.

29. *Education Green Building SmartMarket Report,* McGraw-Hill Construction Research & Analytics, 2007, p. 9, available at www.construction.com/greensource/
resources/smartmarket.asp.

30. Heschong Mahone Group, Inc, Daylighting and Productivity, Registration Form,
www.h-m-g.com/downloads/Daylighting/day_registration_form.htm, accessed
March 30, 2007.

31. Better Bricks: Ash Creet Intermediate School Case Study, www.betterbricks
.com/LiveFiles/28/6/AshCreek_cs.pdf, accessed March 31, 2007.

32. "Light Fantastic: BOORA Architects proves that green strategies like daylighting
can help kids learn while staying within educators' budgets," http://chatterbox
.typepad.com/portlandarchitecture/files/LightFantastic.doc, accessed March 31,
2007.

33. 2005 Survey of Green Building Plus Green Building in K-12 and Higher Education,
www.turnerconstruction.com/greensurvey05.pdf, accessed March 31, 2007.

34. Gregory Kats, "Greening America's Schools: Costs and Benefits," October 2006, www.cap-e.com/ewebeditpro/items/O59F11233.pdf, accessed March 30, 2007.

Chapter 10

1. U.S. Environmental Protection Agency and U.S. Department of Energy, Energy Star, www.energystar.gov.
2. "'Green' Homeowners Are Happier With Their Homes and Recommending Them; Cost Savings are Top Motivating Factor for Buying Green," March 26, 2007, www.mcgraw-hill.com/releases/construction/20070326.shtml, accessed April 2, 2007.
3. "March 21, 2007 Building Team Forecast by Reed Construction Data," www.build-ingteamforecast.com.
4. Harvey Bernstein, McGraw-Hill Construction, presentation at NAHB National Green Building Conference, St. Louis, Missouri, March 27, 2007. The survey will be available after June 2007 from www.construction.com.
5. Carsten Crossings at Whitney Ranch, www.whitneyranch.net/neighborhood .aspx?nbor=Carsten%20Crossings, accessed April 1, 2007.
6. 2007 EnergyValue Housing Award[sm] Winners, www.nahbrc.org/evha/winners .html, accessed April 1, 2007.
7. Michael Kanellos, "Home builders switch on the 'invisible' solar panels," May 11, 2006, http://news.com.com/Home+builders+switch+on+the+invisible+solar+ panels/2100-11392_3-6070992.html, accessed April 1, 2007.
8. Oikos Green Building Source: Green Building News March 2007. March 14, 2007, http://oikos.com/news/2007/03.html, accessed April 1, 2007.
9. Energy Star Qualified New Homes Market Indices for States, www.energystar .gov/index.cfm?fuseaction=qhmi.showHomesMarketIndex, accessed June 6, 2007.
10. NAHB's Model Green Home Building Guidelines, www.nahb.org/publication_de-tails.aspx?publicationID=1994&sectionID=155 and Green Building Initiative: Bringing Green to the Mainstream, www.thegbi.org/residential, accessed April 1, 2007.
11. NAHB's Model Green Home Building Guidelines, www.nahb.org/publication _details.aspx?publicationID=1994&sectionID=155, accessed April 1, 2007, at page 7.
12. Built Green Colorado: 2005 End of Year Report. January 1, 2006, www.builtgreen .org/about/2005_report.pdf, accessed April 1, 2007.
13. Local and Regional Green Home Building Programs in the U.S., www.usgbc.org/ ShowFile.aspx?DocumentID=2001, accessed April 1, 2007.
14. Build it Green, www.builditgreen.org and Earth Advantage Homes, www.earth-advantage.org.
15. Mosier Creek Homes: Alternative Energy, www.mosiercreek.com/alt-energy .html, accessed April 1, 2007.
16. Peter Erickson, interview, March 2007.

17. John McIlwain, "Sorry Kermit, It's Easy Being Green," *Multifamily Trends* (a supplement to *Urban Land*), July/August 2006, p. 20.

18. Project information furnished by Busby Perkins+Will Architects, March 2007.

19. FXFOWLE Architects, New York City, personal communication, February 2007.

20. Green Communities, www.greencommunitiesonline.org.

21. Green Communities Vision, www.greencommunitiesonline.org/about.asp, accessed April 4, 2007.

22. "March 21, 2007 Building Team Forecast by Reed Construction Data," www.buildingteamforecast.com.

23. Living Homes: Sustainable Mission: Possible, www1.livinghomes.net/about.html, accessed April 1, 2007.

24. 2007 EnergyValue Housing Award Winners, www.nahbrc.org/evha/winners.html, accessed April 1, 2007.

25. Michelle Kaufmann Designs, www.mkd-arc.com/whatwedo/breezehouse/letTheGreenIn.cfm, accessed April 1, 2007.

26. Harvey Bernstein, McGraw-Hill Construction, presentation at NAHB National Green Building Conference, St. Louis, Missouri, March 27, 2007. The survey will be available after June 2007 from www.construction.com.

27. Green Homeowners are More Satisfied—and Motivated by Cost. March 26, 2007, www.nahb.org/news_details.aspx?newsID=4304&print=true, accessed April 2, 2007.

Chapter 11

1. "Understanding the Relationship between Public Health and the Built Environment," a report prepared for the USGBC's LEED-ND core committee by Design, Community and Environment and Lawrence Frank and Company, Inc., May 2006, www.usgbc.org/ShowFile.aspx?DocumentID=1480, accessed March 31, 2007.

2. Ibid., p. 118.

3. Calthorpe Associates, www.calthorpe.com and Duany Plater-Zyberk & Company, www.dpz.com.

4. Congress for the New Urbanism, www.cnu.org and Smart Growth Online, www.smartgrowth.org.

5. Sheila Vertino, National Association of Industrial and Office Properties (www.naiop.org), personal communication, based on a survey commissioned by NAIOP, the International Council of Shopping Centers, the National Multi-Family Housing Council, and the Building Owners and Managers Association, and reported in November 2006.

6. Dockside Green Project Overview, www.docksidegreen.ca/dockside_green/overview/index.php, accessed March 31, 2007.

7. Joe Van Belleghem, personal communication, February 2007.

8. www.docksidegreen.ca/dockside_green/news/index.php, accessed March 31, 2007.

9. Joe Van Belleghem, presentation at Green Cities '07 conference, Sydney, Australia, February 12, 2007.

10. Noisette, Charleston, SC, www.noisettesc.com.
11. Noisette Project Overview, www.noisettesc.com/press_projectover.html, accessed March 31, 2007.
12. Dennis Quick, "A 'green' scene," *Charleston Regional Business Journal*, January 22, 2007, www.noisettesc.com/press_news_article.html?id=69, accessed March 31, 2007.
13. CityCenter—Las Vegas Strip, www.vegasverticals.com/citycenter.html, accessed April 1, 2007.
14. Justin Thomas, "Huge CityCenter Project In Las Vegas Aims To Be Green," January 28, 2007, www.treehugger.com/files/2007/01/the_huge_cityce.php, accessed April 1, 2007.
15. Forest City Enterprises, www.forestcity.net/feature4_practices.html, accessed April 1, 2007.
16. "Melaver Project Receives 2nd LEED Certification," *The Savannah Morning News*, February 22, 2007, www.abercorncommons.com/index.php?option=com_content& task=view&id=20, accessed March 31, 2007.
17. "Shops 600 at Abercorn Common Received LEED Silver Certification," February 25, 2007, www.prleap.com/pr/67257, accessed March 31, 2007.
18. U.S. Green Building Council LEED Registered Projects, www.usgbc.org/Show File.aspx?DocumentID=2313, accessed March 31, 2007.
19. Glenn Hasek, "Hilton Vancouver Washington Among Elite Group of LEED-Certified Hotels," January 14, 2007, www.greenlodgingnews.com/Content.aspx?id=753, accessed March 31, 2007.
20. Melanie LaPointe, "Hotel California," March 1, 2007, www.edcmag.com/Articles/ Feature_Article/BNP_GUID_9-5-2006_A_10000000000000071874,   accessed March 31, 2007.

Chapter 12

1. Robin Guenther, Guenther 5 Architects, New York City, interview, March 2007.
2. Portland Cement Association Case Study: Boulder Community Foothills Hospital, www.cement.org/buildings/buildings_green_boulder.asp, accessed March 27, 2007.
3. GGHC newsletter, January/February 2007, available at www.gghc.org.
4. This number from Robin Guenther, Guenther 5 Architects, New York City, interview, March 2007.
5. Mairi Beautyman, "Three Times LEED at Indiana Psychiatric Hospital," March 19, 2007, www.interiordesign.net/article/CA6425199.html?title=Article, accessed March 27, 2007.
6. Certified projects list, www.usgbc.org, accessed March 27, 2007.
7. Robin Guenther, "Building Green in the Countryside," *Healthcare Design*, November 2004, accessed from www.g5arch.com/portfolio/discovery/, March 27, 2007.
8. Karen P. Shahpoori and James Smith, "Wages in Profit and Nonprofit Hospitals and Universities," Bureau of Labor Statistics, June 29, 2005, www.bls.gov/opub/ cwc/cm20050624aro1p1.htm, accessed March 24, 2007.

9. Robert Cassidy, "14 Steps to Greener Hospitals," *Building Design+Construction*, February 8, 2006, available at www.bdcnetwork.com/article/CA6305831.html, accessed March 27, 2007.

10. Robin Guenther, Guenther 5 Architects, New York City, interview, March 2007.

11. Kim Shinn, TLC Engineering for Architecture, interview, March 2007.

12. Walter Vernon, "Tough Pill for Health Care?," *Building Operating Management*, March 2007, pp. 31–38.

Chapter 13

1. Survey results are at www.gensler.com/news/2006/07-20_workSurvey.html, accessed March 29, 2007.

2. Penny Bonda and Katie Sosnowchick, *Sustainable Commercial Interiors* (New York: Wiley, 2006).

3. Penny Bonda, interview, March 2007.

4. Ibid.

5. Holley Henderson, H2 EcoDesign, Atlanta, interview, March 2007.

6. USGBC unpublished data, personal communication, March 29, 2007.

7. HOK marketing case study, personal communication, March 2007.

8. "InterfaceFLOR Shanghai Receives China's First LEED-CI Gold," December 4, 2006, www.chinacsr.com/2006/12/04/892-interfaceflor-shanghai-receives-chinas-first-leed-ci-gold, accessed April 3, 2007.

Chapter 14

1. The Energy Star for Buildings, www.energystar.gov/index.cfm?c=business.bus_bldgs, accessed March 29, 2007.

2. U.S. Environmental Protection Agency and U.S. Department of Energy, Energy Star, www.energystar.gov, accessed March 29, 2007.

3. Federal Energy Management Program, www1.eere.energy.gov/femp/about/index.html, accessed March 29, 2007.

4. BOOMA: The G.R.E.E.N, www.boma.org/AboutBOMA/TheGREEN, accessed March 30, 2007.

5. BEEP: BOMA Energy Efficiency Program, www.boma.org/TrainingAndEducation/BEEP, accessed March 30, 2007.

6. Federal Tax Credits for Energy Efficiency, www.energystar.gov/index.cfm?c=products.pr_tax_credits, accessed March 30, 2007.

7. "Adobe Wins Platinum Certification Awarded by U.S. Green Building Council," July 3, 2006, www.adobe.com/aboutadobe/pressroom/pressreleases/200607/070306LEED.html, accessed March 29, 2007.

8. USGBC Case Study: Joe Serna Jr. California EPA Headquarters Building, www.usgbc.org/ShowFile.aspx?DocumentID=2058, accessed March 29, 2007.

9. LEED Platinum Certification/Department of Education Building Fact Sheet, Green California, www.green.ca.gov/factsheets/leedebplat0706.htm, accessed March 29, 2007.

10. USGBC Case Study: National Geographic's green headquarters shows off their pioneering spirit,www.usgbc.org/ShowFile.aspx?DocumentID=745, accessed March 29, 2007.

11. USGBC Case Study: JohnsonDiversity, www.usgbc.org/Docs/LEEDdocs/Johnson Diversey%20Narrative%20Case%20Study%20V5.pdf, accessed March 29, 2007.

12. "UCSB Embarks on Sustainability Program for Existing Buildings," December 7, 2006, www.ia.ucsb.edu/pa/display.aspx?pkey=1529, accessed April 1, 2007.

13. Matthew Fleming, Research Director, BOMA, personal communication, January 2007.

Chapter 15

1. "25,000 LEED Professionals and Counting," *Building Design+Construction,* July 2006, p. S5.

2. The American Institute of Architects: Chicago Center for Green Technology, www.aiatopten.org/hpb/energy.cfm?ProjectID=97, accessed April 2, 2007.

3. Giants 300 survey, *Building Design+Construction,* July 2006, p. 61, www.bdcnet work.com/article/CA6354620.html.

4. Sandra Mendler, William Odell, and Mary Ann Lazarus, *The HOK Guide to Sustainable Design,* 2nd ed. (New York: Wiley, 2006).

5. Mary Ann Lazarus, HOK, St. Louis, Missouri, interview, March 2007.

6. Slow Food International. www.slowfood.com, accessed June 6, 2007.

7. "Green Buildings and the Bottom Line," *Environmental Design+Construction,* November 2006, pp. 7–9, www.bdcnetwork.com/article/CA6390371.html?industryid =42784, accessed March 22, 2007. Reprinted with permission from *Building Design+Construction.* Copyright 2006 Reed Business Information. All rights reserved.

8. Giants 300 survey, *Building Design+Construction,* July 2006, p. 62, www.bdcnetwork.com/article/CA6354620.html. Reprinted with permission from *Building Design+Construction.* Copyright 2006 Reed Business Information. All rights reserved.

9. Russell Perry, SmithGroup, Washington, D.C., personal communication, January 2007.

10. David Younger, Lionakis Beaumont, personal communication, March 2007.

11. Much of this language and conceptual structure stems from the work of Bill Reed, AIA, an architect in Boston and an original creator of the LEED system, along with the contributions of Gail Lindsey, FAIA; John Boecker, AIA; Joel Todd; and Nadav Malin. Definitions of these terms are from "7 Levels of Design," created by Gail Lindsey.

12. Bill Reed, "Shifting Our Mental Model—'Sustainability' to Regeneration," presentation at the Rethinking Sustainable Construction 2006 conference, April 2006, available at www.integrativedesign.net.

13. Ben Haggard, Bill Reed, and Pamela Mang, "Regenerative Development," *Revitalization,* January 2006.

14. Mithun, "Lloyd Crossing Sustainable Urban Design Master Plan," www.mithun .com/expertise/LloydSustainableDesignPlan.pdf, accessed March 22, 2007.

Chapter 16

1. Bonneville Environmental Foundation web site, www.b-e-f.org.

2. Michelle Higgins, "Eco-Conscious Travel: How to Keep Flying and Stay Green," *New York Times,* October 15, 2006.

3. For up-to-date information on tax incentives for renewable energy, see www.dsireusa.org.

4. Alexis de Tocqueville, *Democracy in America* (London, New York: Penguin Classics, 2003, 1835 and 1840).

5. "Interface Aims to Extend Efficiency from In-House to At-Home," *Portland Daily Journal of Commerce,* February 20, 2007, p. 1.

6. "Bank of America Commits $20 Billion to Green Lending," March 6, 2007, http://blogs.business2.com/greenwombat/2007/03/bank_america_co.html, accessed March 23, 2007.

7. Yudelson Associates, www.greenbuildconsult.com.

8. City of Portland, Oregon: Office of Sustainable Development, www.green-rated.org. For the history of the organization, see www.portlandonline.com/ osd/index.cfm?c=42248&a=126515, accessed March 22, 2007.

9. Brainy Quote, www.brainyquote.com/quotes/quotes/m/margaretme100502 .html, accessed March 22, 2007.

10. MuniNetGuide: Babylon, New York, www.muninetguide.com/states/new_york/ municipality/Babylon.php, accessed March 22, 2007.

11. USGBC, LEED Initiatives in Governments and Schools, April 1, 2007, www .usgbc.org/ShowFile.aspx?DocumentID=691, accessed March 22, 2007.

12. Cliff Feigenbaum, GreenMoney Interviews: Amy Domini, www.greenmoneyjour nal.com/article.mpl?newsletterid=36&articleid=451, accessed March 22, 2007.

13. Joel Makower, Ron Pernick, and Clint Wilder, "Clean Energy Trends 2007," Clean Edge Venture Network, available at www.cleanedge.com/reports/Trends2007 .pdf, accessed March 22, 2007.

Index

About the Author

Jerry Yudelson is one of the country's leading authorities on green development and marketing green buildings, with five books on these subjects. He has been actively involved in the green building industry and in the green building movement since 1999. Prior to that, he spent his career developing new technologies and providing services in the areas of renewable energy, environmental remediation, and environmental planning. As a consultant, Jerry worked with state government, utilities, local governments, Fortune 500 companies, small businesses, architecture and engineering firms, and product manufacturers.

He holds an MBA with highest honors from the University of Oregon and has taught fifty MBA courses on topics such as marketing, business planning, organizational development, and public relations. A registered professional engineer in Oregon, he holds degrees in civil and environmental engineering from the California Institute of Technology and Harvard University, respectively. He has been a management consultant to more than seventy-five CEOs of various-sized firms and a marketing consultant to more than one hundred companies.

Currently, as principal at Yudelson Associates, a green building consultancy based in Tucson, Arizona, he works with developers, design teams, and product manufacturers seeking to make their projects and products as green as possible. His work on design projects involves early-stage consultation, eco-charrette facilitation, and LEED expertise and coaching for design teams. He works with development teams to create effective marketing programs for large-scale green projects, and with manufacturers and private-equity firms to provide due diligence on product marketing and investment opportunities.

He is a frequent speaker and lecturer on green building topics, keynoting regional, national, and international conferences and conducting workshops for building industry professionals on marketing green building services and developing green projects.

Since 2001, Jerry has trained more than 3,000 building industry professionals in the LEED rating system. Since 2004, he has chaired the USGBC's annual Greenbuild conference, the largest green building conference in the world.

Jerry also served on the national committees charged with producing the LEED for Core and Shell (LEED-CS) rating system and the next version of the LEED for New Construction (LEED-NC) system.

In 2004, the Northwest Energy Efficiency Alliance named him the Green Building Advocate of the Year, and *Sustainable Industries Journal* named him

Jerry Yudelson, PE, MS,
MBA, LEED AP.

one of the top twenty-five leaders of the green building industry in the Pacific
Northwest. In 2006, the U.S. General Services Administration named him to
its national roster of Peer Professionals who advise its Design Excellence program for major federal facilities.

He serves on the editorial boards of a national trade journal, *Environmental Design & Construction,* and *The Marketer,* the monthly publication of the
Society for Marketing Professional Services. He is senior editor of the web site
www.igreenbuild.com.

Jerry and his wife, Jessica, and their Scottish terrier, Madhu, live on the
edge of the Sonoran Desert in Tucson, Arizona.